Florian Faion

Tracking Extended Objects in Noisy Point Clouds with Application in Telepresence Systems

Karlsruhe Series on Intelligent Sensor-Actuator-Systems

Volume 19

ISAS | Karlsruhe Institute of Technology
Intelligent Sensor-Actuator-Systems Laboratory

Edited by Prof. Dr.-Ing. Uwe D. Hanebeck

Tracking Extended Objects in Noisy Point Clouds with Application in Telepresence Systems

by
Florian Faion

KIT Scientific Publishing

Dissertation, Karlsruher Institut für Technologie (KIT)
Fakultät für Informatik, 2015

Impressum

KIT Scientific Publishing

Karlsruher Institut für Technologie (KIT)
KIT Scientific Publishing
Straße am Forum 2
D-76131 Karlsruhe

KIT Scientific Publishing is a registered trademark of Karlsruhe Institute of Technology. Reprint using the book cover is not allowed.

www.ksp.kit.edu

Print on Demand 2016

ISSN 1867-3813
ISBN 978-3-7315-0517-4
DOI 10.5445/KSP/1000054248

Tracking Extended Objects in Noisy Point Clouds with Application in Telepresence Systems

zur Erlangung des akademischen Grades eines

Doktors der Ingenieurwissenschaften

von der Fakultät für Informatik
des Karlsruher Instituts für Technologie (KIT)

genehmigte

Dissertation

von

Florian Faion

aus Freiburg im Breisgau

Tag der mündlichen Prüfung:	18.12.2015
Erster Gutachter:	Prof. Dr.-Ing. Uwe D. Hanebeck
Zweiter Gutachter:	Priv.-Doz. Dr. Wolfgang Koch

Acknowledgment

This thesis is the result of my research at the Intelligent Sensor-Actuator-Systems lab (ISAS) at the Karlsruhe Institute of Technology (KIT). Though only my name appears on the cover, many people have contributed to its production in various ways, and I owe my gratitude to all those people who have made this dissertation possible.

First, I would like to thank my advisor Uwe D. Hanebeck for giving me the opportunity to perform this research at the ISAS, for his patience and continuous support, and for his guidance to help me recover whenever my steps faltered. Furthermore, I am very grateful to Wolfgang Koch for co-advising, and sharing his knowledge with me.

I am indebted to my current and former colleagues at the ISAS, who always supported me with their companionship and knowledge: Antonia Pérez Arias, Evgeniya Ballmann, Marcus Baum, Frederik Beutler, Christof Chlebek, Maxim Dolgov, Patrick Dunau, Henning Eberhardt, Jörg Fischer, Simon Friedberger, Igor Gilitschenski, Achim Hekler, Vesa Klumpp, Peter Krauthausen, Gerhard Kurz, Daniel Lyons, Benjamin Noack, Ferdinand Packi, Florian Pfaff, Marc Reinhardt, Patrick Ruoff, Jannik Steinbring, and Antonio Zea. This dissertation has greatly benefited from their input and feedback. Especially, I enjoyed our excessive discussions about research, the world, or everything else, while drinking coffee in the kitchen.

I want to thank Marcus Baum for providing me the first glance into the world of research and letting me in on the field of extended object tracking. Another big thank you goes to my mates and friends Sebastian Brechtel, Christian Hirsch, Sebastian Kobbe, Sebastian Wirkert, Andreas Geiger, and Tilmann Kopp. I will not forget our Wednesday lunches, discussions, and revelry. Special thanks go to my office mates Antonio Zea and Jannik Steinbring with whom I went through thick and thin — their friendship and support made a crucial contribution to this thesis. In addition, I really enjoyed the time we spent together eating Wurstsalat, maintaining the garden in our office room, and throwing little colorful plastic balls at each other. I am also thankful to the technical and administrative ISAS staff who always supported me by, e.g., building last-minute constructions for my experiments, maintaining the Holodeck, or giving me advice in technical/administrative questions.

My family and friends receive my deepest gratitude for sharing joy and sorrow with me, and for always staying by my side. In particular my parents Dorothee and Hermann, as well as my sisters, together with their respective families, have always been an important anchor for me.

Finally, I would like to thank my beloved wife Jasmin for her patience and understanding all the times I had urgent research to do on weekends or at night. Her love, encouragement, and unconditioned support all along the way allowed me to bring this thesis to a happy end.

Thank you!

Karlsruhe, January 2016 Florian Faion

Contents

Notation

General Notation

x	Scalar (lowercase)
$\underline{x}$	Vector (underlined, lowercase)
$\mathbf{A}$	Matrix (bold, uppercase)
$\mathbf{A}^T$	Transposed matrix
$\mathbf{A}^{-1}$	Inverse matrix
$\mathbf{I}$	Identity matrix
$\mathbb{N}$	Natural numbers
$\mathbb{R}$	Real numbers
$\underline{x}_k$	Time index k

Functions and Operators

$p(\underline{x})$	Probability distribution
$p(\underline{y}\|\underline{x})$	Conditional probability distribution
$\mathcal{N}(\underline{\mu}, \mathbf{C})$	Gaussian distribution with mean $\underline{\mu}$ and covariance matrix $\mathbf{C}$
$\mathcal{N}(\underline{x}; \underline{\mu}, \mathbf{C})$	Gaussian distribution $\mathcal{N}(\underline{\mu}, \mathbf{C})$ evaluated at $\underline{x}$
$\delta(\cdot)$	Dirac-δ distribution
$\|\cdot\|$	Euclidean distance
$\lfloor \cdot \rfloor$	Floor function
$\mathbf{J}$	Jacobian matrix

Glossary

EIV	Errors-In-Variables
ICP	Iterative Closest Point
PCA	Principal Component Analysis
PGM	Probabilistic Graphical Model
RMSE	Root Mean Squared Error
GAM	Greedy Association Model
KAM	Known Association Model
PIM	Partial Information Model
RHM	Random Hypersurface Model
SDM	Spatial Distribution Model
EKF	Extended Kalman Filter
PGF	Progressive Gaussian Filter
S^2KF	Smart Sampling Kalman Filter
UKF	Unscented Kalman Filter

Kurzfassung

Telepräsenzsysteme erlauben es Benutzern, mittels Tracking und Videobrillen virtuelle oder entfernte Zielumgebungen zu besuchen und dort intuitiv durch Umherlaufen und Umherschauen zu navigieren. Entsprechende Systeme sind inzwischen ausgereift genug, dass sie Einzug in den Entertainmentmarkt gehalten haben. Um das Gefühl der Immersion weiter zu steigern, muss den Benutzern zusätzlich ermöglicht werden, mit der Zielumgebung intuitiv zu interagieren, indem sie vorhandene Objekte, wie beispielsweise Möbel, Haushaltsgegenstände, Pointer oder Stifte aus der Benutzerumgebung verwenden. Dazu muss das Telepräsenzsystem die Form und Lage von beliebigen sich bewegenden Objekten in einem etwa Wohnzimmer großen Bereich erfassen und verfolgen können.

Im Rahmen dieser Arbeit wird ein entsprechendes Trackingverfahren, basierend auf Tiefenkameras, entwickelt und evaluiert. Im Gegensatz zu herkömmlichen Kameras messen Tiefenkameras für jedes Pixel nicht nur einen Farbwert, sondern zusätzlich auch dessen 3D Position im Raum. Tiefenkameras haben seit 2010, mit Erscheinen der ersten Microsoft Kinect, stark an Popularität zugenommen. Allerdings reicht ein einzelner Sensor in der Regel nicht aus, um einen ganzen Raum zu erfassen. Aus diesem Grund muss das gewünschte Verfahren auch Sensornetzwerke unterstützen.

Die in dieser Arbeit betrachtete Trackingaufgabe ist besonders schwierig, da das Sensorrauschen verhindert, dass die gemessenen Punkte eindeutig zu ihren Messquellen auf dem zu verfolgenden Objekt zugeordnet werden können (Herausforderung 1). Dieses Problem der Datenassoziation wird noch dadurch verschärft, dass die Objektform selbst a priori unbekannt ist (Herausforderung 2) und dass durch Verdeckungen und Sensorartefakte zu jedem Zeitpunkt nur Teile des Objekts sichtbar sind (Herausforderung 3). Stand der Forschung in diesen Situationen ist es, die Objektform zu schätzen, indem die kleinsten Abstände zwischen Messungen und Objektoberfläche minimiert werden. Dieser Ansatz ist jedoch nachweislich nicht erwartungswerttreu und liefert für hohes Sensorrauschen keine zufriedenstellenden Schätzergebnisse.

Der Hauptbeitrag dieser Arbeit ist ein Trackingalgorithmus zur kontinuierlichen Schätzung der Form und Lage von beliebigen ausgedehnten Objekten. Als Besonderheit liefert dieser selbst bei starkem Sensorrauschen noch ein erwartungswerttreues Schätzergebnis. Der vorgeschlagene Ansatz bietet neue Lösungen für jede der drei oben genannten Herausforderungen und leistet einen signifikanten Beitrag zum Stand der Technik bezüglich Robustheit und Genauigkeit des Schätzers. Im Folgenden werden die Kernideen skizziert.

Zunächst wird ein neues probabilistiches Modell für ausgedehnte Objekte hergeleitet, das im Gegensatz zu den Standardmodellen nur den verwertbaren Anteil der in den Messungen enthaltenen Information verwendet. Für dieses „Partial Information Model“ wird dazu für jede Messung zunächst bestimmt, „wie gut“ sie zu einem gegebenen Objekt passt und „von wo“ auf der Objektoberfläche sie stammt. Indem der Schätzer nur den „wie gut“-Anteil der Messung verwendet und den unbekannten Teil, woher sie stammt, ignoriert, benötigt er keine explizite Assoziations-Heuristik mehr und ist trotzdem erwartungswerttreu. Darüber hinaus kann das vorgeschlagene Partial Information Model unmittelbar mit anisotropem Sensorrauschen umgehen und lässt sich immer noch mit einem herkömmlichen nichtlinearen Kalmanfilter schätzen.

Im zweiten Schritt wird ein flexibles probabilistisches Modell für 3D Objekte entwickelt, deren Oberfläche durch die Transformation einer planaren Kurve konstruiert werden kann. So kann beispielsweise ein Zylinder durch die Extrusion eines Kreises konstruiert werden. Das entwickelte Modell ist in der Lage, auch komplizierte Formen mit einer dennoch niedrigen Anzahl an Parametern zu repräsentieren. Im vorgeschlagenen

Modell wird die Wahrscheinlichkeit der Transformationen explizit modelliert, aber die Assoziation von Messungen zu ihren Messquellen auf der Kurve durch die Verwendung des Partial Information Models vermieden. Dabei erbt der Schätzer die Erwartungswerttreue des Partial Information Models.

Als dritter Beitrag werden für die vorgeschlagenen Modelle Erweiterungen entwickelt, die den Schätzer robuster gegenüber Verdeckungen und fehlenden Messungen machen. Dazu wird gezeigt, dass die gemessenen Punktwolken unter bestimmten Bedingungen in einen Bruchteil des ursprünglichen Raums gefaltet (gespiegelt) werden können, der durch die Objektsymmetrie bestimmt wird. Durch diese Faltung lassen sich vereinfachte probabilistische Modelle herleiten, die nur noch in dem entsprechenden Bruchteil des Raums definiert werden müssen. Der Schätzer erreicht dadurch sowohl eine reduzierte Rechenkomplexität als auch eine höhere Robustheit gegenüber fehlenden Messungen.

Abschließend wird der vorgeschlagene Trackingalgorithmus in Experimenten mit realen Sensordaten evaluiert. Dazu wird ein Sensornetzwerk, bestehend aus vier Kinect Sensoren, installiert und ein probabilistisches Sensormodell hergeleitet, um die Unsicherheit der gemessenen Punktwolken in Form anisotroper Gaussverteilungen zu bewerten. Als Experimente betrachten wir zunächst die Längen- und Lageschätzung eines sich bewegenden Lichtschwerts und anschließend die Form- und Lageschätzung einer geworfenen quaderförmigen Box, ohne allerdings zu wissen, dass es sich um eine Box handelt. Die Experimente zeigen, dass der in der Arbeit vorgeschlagene Ansatz den aktuellen Stand der Forschung hinsichtlich der Robustheit und Genauigkeit signifikant verbessert.

Abstract

Telepresence systems have recently matured enough to enter the home entertainment market. These systems transport users virtually to distant or imaginary places, allowing them to naturally interact, look around, and walk in the virtual world through body tracking and head mounted displays. However, for true immersion, the user must be enabled to interact with the virtual world by using existing physical objects from the user environment, such as furniture, household items, and interaction tools such as pointers and pens. This technological shift raises the need for a mechanism to track the pose and shape of arbitrary moving objects in the usually room-sized user environment.

In this thesis, we aim at developing an appropriate tracking algorithm for arbitrarily shaped objects based on depth cameras. In contrast to classical cameras, depth cameras do not only measure a color for each pixel but also 3D information about the object geometry. These sensors have become popular since 2010, when Microsoft introduced the first version of the Kinect. However, as the user environment generally cannot be covered by a single sensor, the desired algorithm should also work with sensor networks.

The considered tracking task is challenging, as (Challenge 1) sensor noise prevents a correct association of points in the measured cloud to their originating sources on the object, (Challenge 2) the object shape itself is unknown a priori which aggravates the data association problem, and (Challenge 3) due to occlusion effects, only parts of the object are visible at a given time. State-of-the-art tracking algorithms usually apply distance minimization between the point cloud and the object surface, but these techniques introduce a bias in the estimated parameters in the presence of noise.

The main contribution of this thesis is a general approach to track the pose and shape parameters of arbitrary objects that is unbiased even for high sensor noise. This approach provides a new solution to each of the above challenges and marks a significant advance to the state of the art in terms of robustness and estimation accuracy. In the following, we outline the basic ideas.

First, we propose a new probabilistic model for extended objects that uses only the valuable part of the information encoded in the measurements. Specifically, we propose to decouple the measurement information into "how well" the measurements fit the object and "where" on the boundary they correspond to. Ignoring the unknown "where"-information lets us derive an unbiased estimator that does not rely on an explicit association heuristic and naturally incorporates even anisotropic sensor noise characteristics, which is typical for depth cameras. Still, the model can be used in a standard nonlinear Kalman filter.

In a second step, we develop a flexible probabilistic model for 3D objects whose shape can be constructed by transforming a plane curve, such as a circle, which can be used to construct a cylinder. This "Partial Information Model" is capable of flexibly representing complex shapes by keeping the number of parameters manageable. By assuming a probability for each transformed curve and ignoring the unknown information of "where" on the curve a measurement is related to, the resulting estimator inherits the unbiasedness of the Partial Information Model and its capability of dealing with anisotropic noise.

Third, we develop extensions for the proposed models in order to make the estimator more robust against occlusions and missing measurements. Specifically, we see that, under specific conditions, the measurements can be folded (mirrored) into a small fraction of the original domain according to the object symmetry. This allows for designing a simplified probabilistic model that only operates in this reduced domain. The resulting estimator has reduced computational complexity and increased robustness against missing measurements.

Finally, the proposed tracking algorithm is evaluated in real tracking experiments. For this purpose, we set up a multi-Kinect network and derive a probabilistic sensor model to rate the measurement quality of Kinect point clouds by anisotropic Gaussian distributions. For the experiments we first consider length and pose tracking of a moving lightsaber, and then look at tracking the shape and the pose of a box in free fall without actually knowing that it is a box. In particular, our approach manages to find the box shape in less than a second, despite of its fast motion and rotation. In sum, the experiments confirm our theoretical results and demonstrate the practical suitability of our approach.

CHAPTER 1

Introduction

Contents

1.1 Scope

Telepresence systems [1], such as the one shown in Figure 1.1, transport users virtually to distant or imaginary places, allowing them to naturally interact, look around, and walk long distances in a virtual world. This is implemented by presenting the user multi-modal sensory impressions, such as audio and video, from this target environment, as if they were there in person, while in reality they remain in a local room called the user environment. An essential task to keep immersion, i.e., to convincingly maintain the illusion of being in the different place, is to ensure proper ways of input and interaction. On the one hand, it is necessary to track the user's movements in the usually room-sized user environment. On the other hand, the user must be enabled to interact with the target environment by using physical objects from the user environment, such as furniture, household items, and interaction tools such as pointers, pens, or toy lightsabers.

Considered Task Developing an immersive telepresence system raises the need for a mechanism to track the pose, shape, and motion of arbitrary physical objects in the user environment. An affordable implementation can be realized using depth cameras, which yield not only color but also 3D information about the object geometry. These sensors have become popular since 2010, when Microsoft introduced the first version of the Kinect [2]. As the user environment generally cannot be covered by a single sensor, multiple sensors can be combined into a sensor network. Figure 1.2 shows point cloud data for the lightsaber example. The desired tracking algorithm should derive an estimate of the lightsaber's pose, shape, and motion based on this noisy data. However, right at the start, the algorithm has neither information about the values of the required parameters, nor the knowledge that the object is a lightsaber. In consequence, all information is to be extracted from the noisy point clouds.

Thesis Goal In this thesis, we aim at developing an algorithm for tracking arbitrary objects with a priori unknown shapes using a network of consumer 3D cameras, such as the Microsoft Kinect.

Figure 1.1.: Telepresence system.

Figure 1.2.: Example for the considered tracking task. The lightsaber must be tracked based on the noisy point cloud data, which is captured by the depth camera.

Related Topics and Applications The considered tracking task is known as *extended object tracking* [3] and falls right in between the fields of *object tracking* [4] and *shape reconstruction* [5, 6], having some overlap with both. The main difference between these related fields is that object tracking generally focuses on estimating the pose and motion parameters of objects with known or negligible shape, while shape reconstruction generally considers estimating the shape of static objects or scenes. Against this background, extended object tracking can be seen as connecting link.

From a practical point of view, estimating object parameters based on point cloud data has applications in many fields [7] including robotics [8], autonomous driving [9], innovative control for entertainment devices [10], telepresence applications [11], industrial production lines [12], architecture [13], healthcare [14], to name only a few. Depending on the application, a variety of sensor classes is used to produce the point clouds, including laser scanners, time-of-flight cameras, structured-light cameras, stereo cameras, and radar systems. All of these sensors produce 3D point measurements, where each point encodes geometric information about the object's surface and, depending on the sensor, its color. In particular, any given sensor produces measurements with different degrees of quality which is reflected by the number of measurements per scan, as well as the degree of uncertainty introduced by sensor noise. In Figure 1.3, typical sensors are classified according to their measurement quality and typical application.

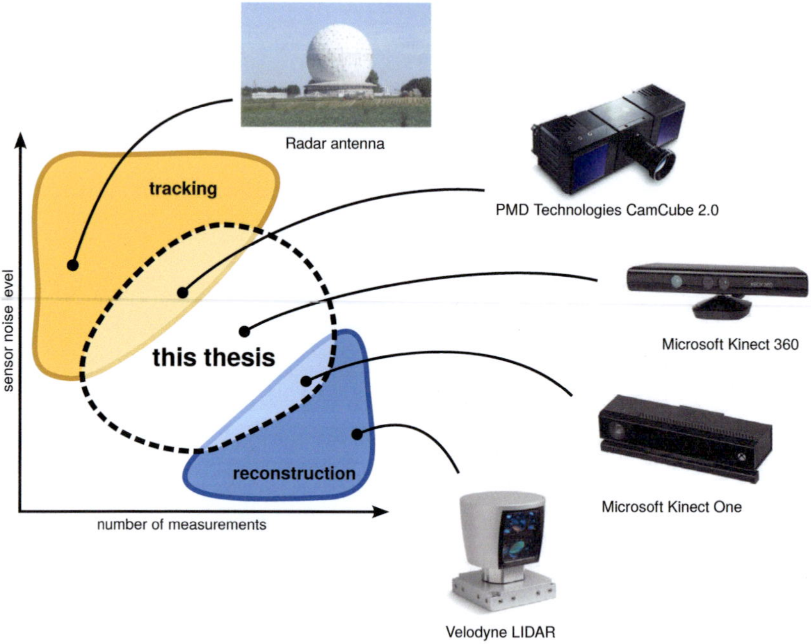

Figure 1.3.: Characterization of point cloud measurements and sensors. Radar by Gunther (Own work) GFDL, CC-BY-SA-3.0, via Wikimedia Commons, Kinect v1 and Kinect v2 by Evan-Amos (Own work) [Public domain], via Wikimedia Commons.

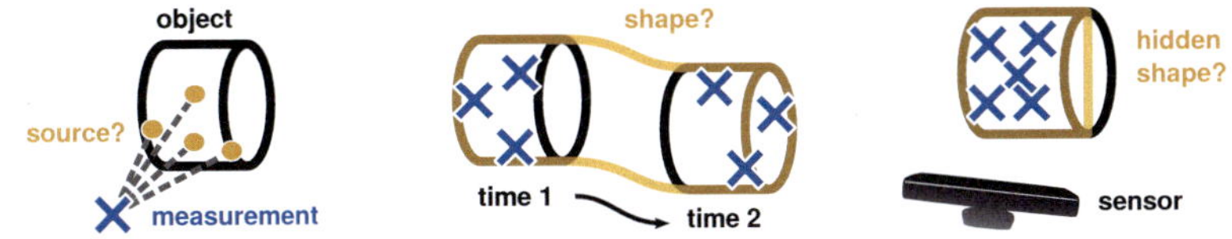

(a) Measurement association.   (b) Unknown shape.   (c) Missing measurements.

Figure 1.4.: Challenges that occur in the considered tracking task.

1.2 Challenges

In the considered tracking task, three major challenges can be highlighted, sorted in the order they will be discussed in this thesis.

Challenge 1: Measurement Association In order to find accurate estimates, the tracking algorithm needs to assess how well a point cloud and an object boundary fit together. However, when it comes to data obtained by real sensors, we have to deal with sensor-specific noise which yields varying measurement quality depending on factors such as distance, angle, surface material, and external influences. In particular, this noise may have anisotropic characteristics, meaning that the measurement quality of a point is not equal in all directions. For example, a depth camera typically can measure laterally more accurate than in its depth direction [15, 16]. Due to this sensor uncertainty, it is usually impossible to know from which source on an object a specific measurement occurred, and, in consequence, how well it fits to the object. In Figure 1.4a, this issue is illustrated for an example measurement (blue), and its potential measurement sources (yellow). State-of-the-art tracking approaches usually apply distance minimization between point cloud and object surface [17] which implicitly associates the points to their closest sources on the shape. Unfortunately, this simple heuristic does not account for the sensor noise and, even worse, introduces a bias in the estimated parameters in the presence of noise [18].

Challenge 2: Unknown Shape The problem of measurement association becomes even more challenging when we take into account that, on the one hand, the object shape itself is unknown, and, on the other hand, it actually is in continuous motion. How could we infer the shape of an object, when we know neither its motion, nor how to associate measurements to its boundary? An illustrative example is shown in Figure 1.4b, where the algorithm must distinguish whether the object has moved from one measured point cloud to the next (black), or the measurements just originate from another, previously unknown part of the object (yellow). As a consequence of this uncertainty, pose, shape and motion become inherently connected and must be estimated simultaneously by the tracking algorithm. Moreover, as the object shape will not always be visible as a whole, the estimated information must be aggregated and updated during run-time. In doing so, (i) the underlying geometric model must be flexible enough to adapt to a wide spectrum of shapes, and (ii) the estimator must explicitly take into account the involved uncertainty and correlation between shape, pose, and motion. We want to emphasize that this challenge does not occur in most related work on tracking, as in these cases a previously learned model [19] of the desired object is typically used.

Challenge 3: Missing Measurements In addition to the random sensor noise that can be described by a probabilistic sensor model, there are other unpredictable effects such as occlusion or sensor artifacts which cause parts of the object to become invisible for a long period. For example, the object in Figure 1.4c is observed by a sensor that can only observe one side of the object. In consequence, as long as the object does not move, the back of the object will never be measured, causing an ambiguity where the yellow estimate is valid as well. State-of-the-art approaches usually implement a physical energy mechanism [20] in order to extrapolate the boundary, which, however, involves the definition of problematic coefficients and, in addition, negatively affects the observed parts as well. In these situations, the desired algorithm should compensate for the missing measurements by making more reasonable assumptions about the unobserved parts. This feature is very important in practice, as permanent occlusions occur almost always in real-world scenarios.

1.3 Contributions and Outline

As the main contribution of this thesis, we develop a general approach to track the pose and shape parameters of extended objects. This approach provides a new solution to each of the above challenges which mark significant contributions to the state of the art. In the following, we outline the basic ideas of these solutions.

Solution to Challenge 1: Partial Information Model In Chapter 2, we propose the *Partial Information Model*, which is a new probabilistic model for extended objects that avoids an explicit association of measurements to the boundary. For this purpose, we propose to separate the measurement information in two parts, one which describes "where" on the boundary the measurement corresponds to, and another which describes "how well" it fits to the object. Ignoring the unknown "where"-information lets us derive an estimator that does not rely on explicit association heuristics. In contrast to traditional estimators that minimize some sort of distance between the point cloud and the object boundary, the new model yields an unbiased estimator that can even incorporate anisotropic sensor noise characteristics common to depth cameras. Furthermore, the simplicity of the proposed model allows for an implementation even with standard nonlinear Kalman filters.

Solution to Challenge 2: 3D Random Hypersurface Model In Chapter 3, we develop a flexible probabilistic model for 3D objects whose surface can be constructed by transforming a plane curve such as a cylinder by extruding a circle. This *3D Random Hypersurface Model* is capable of flexibly representing relatively complex shapes while keeping the number of parameters manageable. Specifically, we consider translation, rotation and scaling operations for surface construction. By assuming a probability for each transformed curve and ignoring the unknown information of "where" on the curve a measurement corresponds to, the model can be seen as combination of the traditional Spatial Distribution Model (which assumes a probability for each measurement source) and the Partial Information Model. In addition, we show that the resulting estimator based on the 3DRHM inherits the unbiasedness of the Partial Information Model.

Solution to Challenge 3: Exploiting Shape Symmetry In Chapter 4, we develop an extension for the proposed models in order to make the estimator more robust against occlusions and missing measurements. For this purpose, we incorporate assumptions about symmetry in the object geometry by exploiting the fact that, under specific conditions, the estimator will find exactly the same estimates when the measurements are folded into a small fraction of the original domain according to the object symmetry. This allows us to design simplified probabilistic models that inherently exploit the object symmetry by only operating in the folded domain. The resulting estimator has an increased robustness against missing measurements and, in addition, a reduced computational complexity. We demonstrate that, even in the case of simple objects such as a line segment, which only have one reflectional symmetry, estimation can be significantly improved.

Experimental Evaluation in a Multi-Kinect Network Finally, in Chapter 5, the proposed tracking algorithm is evaluated in real tracking experiments. We set up a sensor network based on four Microsoft Kinect cameras of the second generation and derive a probabilistic sensor model that rates the measurement quality of the point clouds. The experiments show that our approach allows for estimating shape details even for objects observed while in free fall. In doing so, the real-data experiments validate the previous simulations, making our approach a significant contribution beyond the state of the art in terms of robustness and estimation accuracy.

1.4 Related Work

Let us briefly summarize related work on estimation approaches that fall in the range between reconstruction and tracking. More specific discussions on relevant literature are given at the corresponding paragraphs in the thesis.

Focus on Reconstruction Approaches with focus on reconstruction of a static (non-moving) object or scene can be roughly divided in whether they describe shapes using a *non-parametric* model, or a *parametric* model.

- **Non-parametric Model** Occupancy grids [21], point clouds [22], or polygon meshes [23] can be used for representing the scene geometry. Occupancy grids partition the Cartesian space into small binary [24] or probabilistic [25] cells which encode how likely they intersect with the scene geometry. For example the popular Kinect-Fusion algorithm [26] and its extension for larger scenes [27] use occupancy grids. Point-based shape representations are less memory consuming, as they store the scene geometry in the form of a set of geometric locations. In addition to the pure location, higher level information [28] such as colors or surface normals [29] can be stored for each point. As the Kinect-like depth sensors immediately extract point measurements from the scene, point clouds recently gained more and more popularity. This popularity resulted in a powerful community-driven toolbox called the Point Cloud Library (PCL) [30], which aggregates several related algorithms for segmentation, registration, and surface reconstruction. Surface reconstruction, in turn, often refers to basis functions [31] or polygonal meshes [32], where the latter forms the third popular non-parametric representation of scene geometry. In the last decades, several probabilistic algorithms for detailed mesh reconstruction have been developed, ranging from maximum likelihood [33] to full

Bayesian approaches [34]. Other techniques, which are often used in the context of scene reconstruction are *random sample consensus* (RANSAC) [35] and the *iterative closest points* (ICP) algorithm [17].

- **Parametric Model** A parametric model relates a set of parameters to a surface that, in turn, describes the object or scene geometry. Often, either geometric primitives [36] or splines [37] are used as model. Popular geometric primitives include planes [38], cylinders [39], ellipsoids [40], cones [41], and bounding boxes [42]. For the spline-based shape reconstruction, energy functionals in the fashion of active contours [20] are often incorporated, in order to ensure surface properties such as smoothness. Other geometric models, which are similar to the one proposed in this thesis, are constructed by transforming a base shape [43], such as the case of a cylinder constructed by translating a circle. Techniques for estimating the parameters of these models include those mentioned for the non-parametric models, as well as the *Hough transformation* [44], which is often applied together with *mean shift* [45] or RANSAC.

Focus on Tracking Approaches with focus on tracking typically do not attempt to estimate the shape of the target object. Instead, they assume the object to have a negligible extent or a known shape.

- **Tracking Point Objects** Modeling objects as a point is reasonable in situations where the sensor resolution is too low to distinguish different measurement sources on the object surface, e.g., for radar applications in Figure 1.3. Hence, related approaches often focus on estimating the position and motion parameters of the object [4]. The majority of approaches employ instances of Bayesian recursive estimators such as (nonlinear) Kalman filters or particle filters [46]. Accurately predicting the object motion is an important topic in tracking algorithms and has resulted in several canonical motion models [47], which will also be used in this thesis. In order to allow the estimator to adapt to sudden motion changes, multiple motion hypotheses can be incorporated [48] as well. Another line of related research is concerned with simultaneously tracking multiple point objects [49]. These approaches are often based on a form of *probability hypothesis density* (PHD) filter [50] and are related to the approach in this thesis in the sense that they also have to deal with the data association problem.

- **Tracking Objects with Known Shape** Approaches for tracking the pose of known objects based on previously learned templates or geometric models is another related topic. Recently, the number of object libraries has dramatically increased, as listed in the PCL [30], with varying scope such as furniture [51] or kitchens [52]. For estimating the pose parameters either instances of ICP or Bayesian estimators are used. Another major topic of interest has been tracking the human body [53]. Of note are works tracking the pose [54, 55], some of them with stochastic models [56, 57]. Others focus on individual body parts such as hands [58].

Simultaneous Reconstruction and Tracking Finally, there are approaches which simultaneously perform *reconstruction and tracking* tasks. We can roughly distinguish between approaches where a moving object wants to localize itself in an a priori unknown environment, and approaches where the pose and shape of a dynamic extended object is to be estimated.

- **Simultaneous Localization and Mapping (SLAM)** Essentially, most approaches from the "focus on reconstruction" paragraph somehow perform an instance of SLAM [59], as they have to align multiple point cloud measurements of a moving sensor [60]. In this context, the scene geometry (e.g., a building [61]) can be interpreted as a priori unknown landmarks.

- **Extended Object Tracking** In contrast to the "tracking objects with known shape" approaches, the object shape is a priori unknown and is to be estimated online, while the object potentially is in continuous motion. While there are several approaches using non-parametric models [62, 9], the majority of approaches (including this thesis) use parametric models. Well-established techniques include

Random Hypersurface Models [63], Spatial Distribution Models [64], and Random Matrices [65], all of which will be discussed later in this thesis. However, up to date, these models are mostly used in applications where a region in 2D is to be tracked based on few measurements per scan. Furthermore, in 3D, shape and pose of objects has been simultaneously estimated for medical applications using splines [66, 67]. Other approaches use simpler geometric approximations, such as bounding boxes [68]. A rather different approach formulates the moving object as a shape in 4D [69].

CHAPTER 2

Unbiased Extended Object Tracking

Contents

The goal in this chapter is to develop a Bayesian framework for tracking extended objects based on noisy point measurements from their boundary. In contrast to classical target tracking, where objects are assumed to be points with no extent, the shape and size of an extended object is not negligible as the sensor obtains measurements from all over the boundary. Specifically, we will see that the major task when developing a tracking algorithm boils down to specifying a *likelihood* that rates how well the measured points fit to a given boundary. This task immediately leads to the question

how to associate the noisy points to the object boundary?

However, finding an answer to this question is non-trivial as it is typically unknown from "where" on the boundary the measurements originate. This is due to the fact that (i) measurements are subject to sensor noise and (ii) the object shape itself is only uncertainly known. This association problem refers to Challenge 1 from Section 1.2. Typically, there are two major approaches to solve the association problem in the context of extended object tracking and shape fitting. First, *Spatial Distribution Models* [70] incorporate a probability distribution that specifies for each location on the boundary how likely it is measured by the sensor. Second, *Greedy Association Models* [159] greedily associate each measurement to a specific location on the boundary, for example to the one that is closest to the measurement. However, both approaches have drawbacks. The former is computationally expensive and requires detailed knowledge of the measurement principle. The latter is biased in the presence of noise. Indeed, there are debiasing techniques available for the greedy approach but, typically, they do not account for anisotropic sensor noise. We found that *partial likelihood* [71], a statistical concept from related errors-in-variables (EIV) problems [72], can be employed to design a *Partial Information Model* for extended objects that compensates for both drawbacks.

Contribution Our main contribution in this chapter is the *Partial Information Model* (PIM), which is a new probabilistic model for extended objects that specifies how likely a given object boundary has *produced* point measurements. The main characteristics of the PIM is that it uses only the *valuable* part of the available information that is encoded in the measurements. In particular, we propose to decouple the measurement information into "how well" they fit to the object boundary and "where" on the boundary they correspond to. Ignoring the second type of measurement information lets us derive an estimator that

- does not rely on a probability distribution for measurement sources over the boundary,
- is unbiased according to [73] even for high sensor noise,
- can naturally deal with anisotropic noise characteristics,

- and can be implemented using common recursive Bayesian estimation techniques such as a nonlinear Kalman filter.

For the implementation of the PIM, we make a second contribution in this chapter. That is, for evaluating the likelihood of the PIM, it is necessary to propagate the moments of a random variable through a nonlinear function. To achieve a low computational complexity, we propose to approximate the first two moments of the propagated variable using deterministic sampling. This approach can be shown to produce results that are very close to the ground-truth for a fair number of samples.

Remark 2.1. *The PIM is published in [157] and the discussion on de-biasing techniques is based on our studies in [159].*

2.1 Recursive Bayesian Object Tracking

In this section, we introduce the general concept of recursive Bayesian estimation [46] which forms the basis of the tracking algorithm. The object to be estimated can be modeled as a *dynamic system* that obeys the Markov property and whose actual *state* is described by a D-dimensional vector $\underline{x} \in \mathbb{R}^D$. Typically, the parameters in the state vector encode information related to position, orientation, shape, and its dynamics, e.g., velocity and acceleration. Assume, at an initial time step $k-1$, uncertain knowledge about these state parameters $\underline{x}$ is given in the form of a probability density $p(\underline{x}_{k-1})$. Then, at the next time step k, the sensor network observes $n_k \in \mathbb{N}_0$ noisy measurements $\underline{y}_{k,1}, \dots, \underline{y}_{k,n_k}$ of the object. Assuming the sensor noise to be mutually independent for all measurements, the corresponding *Probabilistic Graphical Model* [74] yields Figure 2.1. In this model, $\underline{y}_{k,1}, \dots, \underline{y}_{k,n_k}$ are observable variables, while $\underline{x}_{k-1}, \underline{x}_k$ are latent variables that are not directly accessible. The task of the tracking algorithm is (i) to predict the object parameters over time and (ii) to update the parameters according to the measurements.

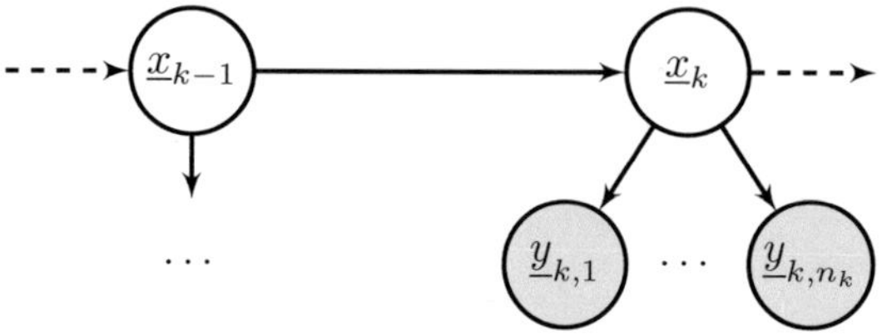

Figure 2.1.: Probabilistic Graphical Model for dynamic state estimation.

Time Update Step The *time update step* determines how a distribution $p(\underline{x}_{k-1})$ that is known at a time $k-1$, will have evolved at the time k. Under the assumption that the object behavior can be described as a Markov process, the time update can be calculated by means of the Chapman–Kolmogorov equation [75]

$$p(\underline{x}_k^p) := \int_{\mathbb{R}^D} p(\underline{x}_k^p | \underline{x}_{k-1}) \cdot p(\underline{x}_{k-1}) \, \mathrm{d}\underline{x}_{k-1} \; ,$$

where $p(\underline{x}_k^p)$ denotes the distribution of the predicted state, and $p(\underline{x}_k^p | \underline{x}_{k-1})$ is called the *transition probability*, which is specified by the *dynamic model.* Related to object tracking there are classical dynamic models for the pose that will be used in this thesis [47], including a *constant velocity model* for the object position and a *constant turn rate model* for its orientation. For the shape of an object we typically cannot assume any systematic behavior, except from staying as it is. Thus, for the shape parameters, we will always use a *random walk model* which accounts for unpredictable minor changes.

Measurement Update Step Knowledge about the object that is encoded in the measurements $\underline{y}_{k,1}, \ldots, \underline{y}_{k,n_k}$ can be incorporated into a given distribution $p(\underline{x}_k^p)$ according to Bayes' rule

$$\begin{aligned} p(\underline{x}_k^p | \underline{y}_{k,1}, \ldots, \underline{y}_{k,n_k}) &= \frac{p(\underline{y}_{k,1}, \ldots, \underline{y}_{k,n_k} | \underline{x}_k^p) \cdot p(\underline{x}_k^p)}{p(\underline{y}_{k,1}, \ldots, \underline{y}_{k,n_k})} \\ &\propto p(\underline{y}_{k,1}, \ldots, \underline{y}_{k,n_k} | \underline{x}_k^p) \cdot p(\underline{x}_k^p) \; . \end{aligned} \tag{2.1}$$

The *likelihood* $p(\underline{y}_{k,1}, \ldots, \underline{y}_{k,n_k} | \underline{x}_k^p)$ rates how well the object parameters fit to the measurements with respect to their measurement noise. The term $p(\underline{y}_{k,1}, \ldots, \underline{y}_{k,n_k})$ is considered as a normalization constant. In order to close the recursion, the updated distribution is considered to be the new prior $p(\underline{x}_k) := p(\underline{x}_k^p | \underline{y}_{k,1}, \ldots, \underline{y}_{k,n_k})$.

Preliminaries In this thesis, we are mainly interested in the measurement update step, specifically in the task of deriving likelihoods for extended objects. Thus, most of the time, we consider a single time step, which lets us drop the time index k in $\underline{y}_n := \underline{y}_{k,n}$ and, when it is clear from the context, we also write $\underline{x} := \underline{x}_k^p$ as an abbreviation for the predicted state. In addition, the independence of the measurement noise lets us factorize the likelihood as

$$p(\underline{y}_1, \ldots, \underline{y}_n | \underline{x}) = \prod_{i=1}^{n} p(\underline{y}_i | \underline{x}) \ .$$

This marks an important simplification as it allows us to consider each measurement $\underline{y}_i$ individually. For readability, we will drop the measurement index i whenever possible.

Incorporating the sensor noise in the form of the d-dimensional random variable $\underline{v} \sim p(\underline{v})$, the likelihood for a single measurement $\underline{y}$ can be written as

$$p(\underline{y} | \underline{x}) = \int_{\mathbb{R}^d} p(\underline{y} | \underline{x}, \underline{v}) \cdot p(\underline{v}) \, \mathrm{d}\underline{v} \ . \qquad (2.2)$$

The term $p(\underline{y} | \underline{x}, \underline{v})$ encodes the relation between state $\underline{x}$, measurement $\underline{y}$, and noise $\underline{v}$, and can be conveniently expressed by means of a typically nonlinear measurement function

$$\underline{y} = h(\underline{x}, \underline{v}) \ . \qquad (2.3)$$

Note that likelihood (2.2) and measurement function (2.3) are closely related through the Dirac-δ distribution $p(\underline{y} | \underline{x}, \underline{v}) = \delta\big(\underline{y} - h(\underline{x}, \underline{v})\big)$.

When approaching to derive the Bayes update in (2.1), there are closed-form formulas available for special cases, e.g., the Kalman filter [76] for $h(\underline{x}, \underline{v}) = H\underline{x} + \underline{v}$ being linear, $p(\underline{v})$ being additive Gaussian, and $p(\underline{x})$ being Gaussian as well. However, when it comes to more general problems such as extended object tracking, measurement functions are no longer linear and/or the probability distributions are no longer Gaussian. Then, only approximations of the Bayes update can be derived. In Appendix A, we briefly summarize two widely-used approximation techniques.

2.2 Modeling Extended Objects

The measurement update step in recursive Bayesian estimation requires specifying a likelihood $p(\underline{y}_1, \ldots, \underline{y}_n|\underline{x})$ that rates how well the measurements $\underline{y}_1, \ldots, \underline{y}_n$ fit to an object boundary that is parametrized by the state vector $\underline{x}$. In this section, we derive a prototype of this likelihood for the case that the sensor measures the object boundary as a set of points, affected by additive, zero-mean, and mutually independent Gaussian sensor noise. In doing so, we explicitly model the probability of measurements originating from a given object and discuss the association problem, which was referred to as Challenge 1. Subsequently, we deal with variations of the prototype likelihood in order to solve the association problem.

Introductory Example The considered estimation task can be seen as an instance of errors-in-variables (EIV) problems [157]. To show this relation, let us start our considerations with the familiar example of fitting a line to noisy data. Assume we want to estimate slope and intercept parameters (both encoded in the vector $\underline{x}$) of a linear constraint from noisy points $\underline{y}$. In classical regression, as illustrated in Figure 2.2a, the abscissa can be measured exactly, while the ordinate is subject to noise. As can be seen, for a given instance of slope and intercept parameters, the originating source $\underline{z}$ (black circle) of a measurement $\underline{y}$ (blue cross) can be uniquely determined. The likelihood then simply would be evaluating the Gaussian (shaded blue line) centered on the source in the measurement. In doing so, the estimator adjusts the parameters, so that the error

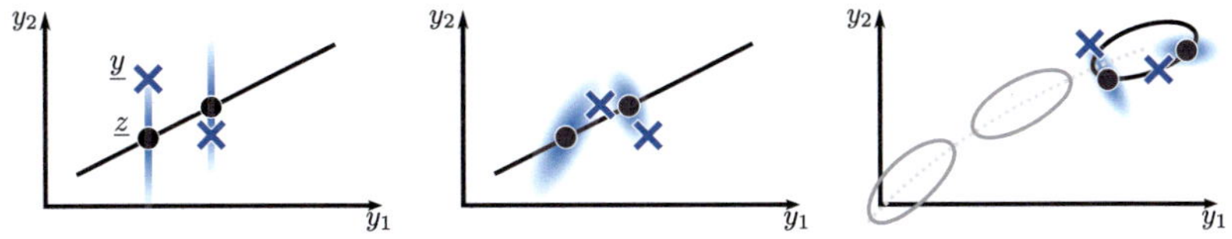

(a) Classical regression. **(b)** EIV regression. **(c)** Ext. object tracking.

Figure 2.2.: In classical regression (a), each measurement $\underline{y}$ can be exactly associated to its originating source $\underline{z}$, where in EIV regression (b), this is not possible. Extended object tracking can be seen as a dynamic, nonlinear EIV regression task (c).

between line and measurements along the ordinate is minimized. Note that in this estimation task, the measurements are correctly associated to their generating sources $\underline{z}$ on the line. In contrast, in an EIV regression task, all dimensions of $\underline{y}$ are subject to noise, as illustrated in Figure 2.2b. This makes the association of a measurement to its source on the line an ambiguous task.

Extended object tracking, as considered in this thesis, is closely related to the EIV regression. That is, essentially we want to estimate the time-variant parameters of an object boundary based on measurements that are subject to sensor noise in all dimensions. Figure 2.2c illustrates this scenario for a moving ellipse. In consequence, we have to make assumptions on the measurement source $\underline{z}$ for each $\underline{y}$ in order to design an estimator. To make things worse, each additional measurement introduces another unknown measurement source which, in turn, requires an additional assumption. In literature, this association problem is referred to as the *Neyman-Scott problem* [77] and $\underline{z}$ is called a *nuisance parameter* [73].

Formal Problem Statement We want to derive a likelihood function $p(\underline{y}_1, \ldots, \underline{y}_n | \underline{x})$ for extended objects. For this purpose, we have to specify the relationship between state and measurements. In this thesis, we consider the following model. Each measurement $\underline{y}_i$ is assumed to be a noisy observation of a true value $\underline{z}_i$, denoted as measurement source, which is distorted by additive noise according to

$$\underline{y}_i = \underline{z}_i + \underline{v}_i \; . \tag{2.4}$$

The noise terms are assumed to be mutually independent and Gaussian distributed according to $\underline{v}_i \sim \mathcal{N}(\underline{0}, \mathbf{C}_{v_i})$ with known, but not necessarily identical, covariance matrices. The measurement source $\underline{z}_i$ lies on the object boundary and fulfills the implicit and typically nonlinear relationship

$$g(\underline{x}, \underline{z}_i) = 0 \; . \tag{2.5}$$

For convenience, we will write $g_x(\underline{z}_i) := g(\underline{x}, \underline{z}_i)$. Note that, due to the noise, the measurements themselves generally do not fulfill the constraint and, thus, measurements $\underline{y}_1, \dots, \underline{y}_n$ and state $\underline{x}$ are only related via the unknown measurement sources. In consequence, designing the likelihood $p(\underline{y}_1, \dots, \underline{y}_n | \underline{x})$ requires incorporating the measurement sources through (2.4) and (2.5). The important role of the measurement sources becomes even clearer, when we approach to define a measurement function $\underline{y}_i = h(\underline{x}, \underline{v}_i)$ for extended objects. Without modeling the source, it is not straightforward to specify it at all.

2.2.1 Probabilistic Graphical Model

For a more intuitive treatment, we encode the dependencies between all involved variables visually using a Probabilistic Graphical Model [74], as shown in Figure 2.3. This graphical model details the relationship between state $\underline{x}$ and measurements $\underline{y}$ from Figure 2.1.

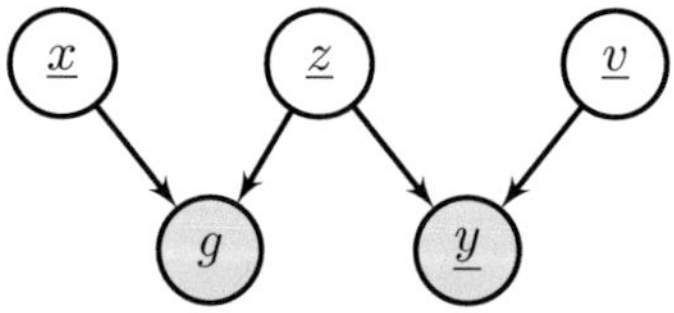

Figure 2.3.: Probabilistic Graphical Model for errors-in-variables.

That is, $\underline{y}$ and g are observable variables while $\underline{x}$, $\underline{z}$, and $\underline{v}$ are latent variables which are not directly accessible. Specifically, g represents the constant *pseudo-measurement* 0, which arises from the relationship $g_x(\underline{z}) = 0$ in (2.5). From the dependency structure that is indicated by the directed edges between the variables in Figure 2.3, we obtain the joint probability distribution

$$p(\underline{x}, \underline{z}, \underline{v}, g, \underline{y}) = p(\underline{x}) \cdot p(\underline{z}) \cdot p(\underline{v}) \cdot p(g|\underline{x}, \underline{z}) \cdot p(\underline{y}|\underline{z}, \underline{v}) \ . \tag{2.6}$$

From this joint distribution, we can derive a likelihood for $\underline{y}$ by marginalizing out $\underline{z}, \underline{v}$ and dividing by $p(\underline{x}, g) = p(g|\underline{x}) \cdot p(\underline{x})$, in the form of

$$\begin{aligned} p(\underline{y}|\underline{x}, g) &= \int_{\mathbb{R}^d} \int_{\mathbb{R}^d} \frac{p(\underline{x}, \underline{z}, \underline{v}, g, \underline{y})}{p(g|\underline{x}) \cdot p(\underline{x})} \, \mathrm{d}\underline{v} \, \mathrm{d}\underline{z} \\ &\overset{(2.6)}{=} \int_{\mathbb{R}^d} \underbrace{\int_{\mathbb{R}^d} p(\underline{y}|\underline{z}, \underline{v}) \cdot p(\underline{v}) \, \mathrm{d}\underline{v}}_{p(\underline{y}|\underline{z})} \cdot \underbrace{\frac{p(g|\underline{x}, \underline{z}) \cdot p(\underline{z})}{p(g|\underline{x})}}_{p(\underline{z}|\underline{x}, g)} \, \mathrm{d}\underline{z} \\ &= \int_{\mathbb{R}^d} p(\underline{y}|\underline{z}) \cdot p(\underline{z}|\underline{x}, g) \, \mathrm{d}\underline{z} \ . \end{aligned} \tag{2.7}$$

We refer to the components $p(\underline{y}|\underline{z})$ and $p(\underline{z}|\underline{x}, g)$ as *sensor model* and *source model*, where both are visualized in Figure 2.4. In the following, we briefly discuss both models and show how they can be derived.

Sensor Model The sensor model $p(\underline{y}|\underline{z})$, as illustrated in Figure 2.4a, describes the distribution of measurements $\underline{y}$, given that it is known that $\underline{z}$ is the source. According to the additive noise model from (2.4), it is immediately given as the Gaussian

$$p(\underline{y}|\underline{z}) = \mathcal{N}(\underline{y}; \underline{z}, \mathbf{C}_v) \ .$$

Note that, once the source $\underline{z}$ is known, the measurement is conditionally independent of the state. In Chapter 5, we derive a sensor model to assess the covariance matrix $\mathbf{C}_v$ for real data, measured by a Microsoft Kinect. This model then is used in the real data experiments.

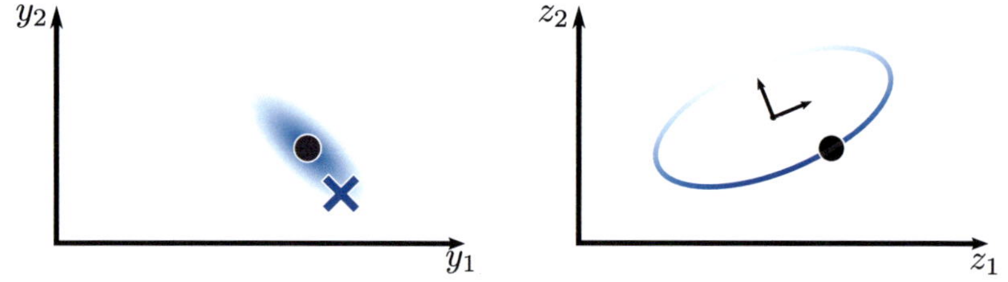

(a) Sensor Model. **(b)** Source Model.

Figure 2.4.: Illustration of source model (a) and sensor model (b).

Source Model The source model $p(\underline{z}|\underline{x}, g)$ describes how likely a point $\underline{z}$, which fulfills the constraint $g_x(\underline{z}) = 0$ for a given state $\underline{x}$ (i.e., it lies on the object boundary), will be a measurement source. For an elliptical object, this probability distribution could look as in Figure 2.4b. In order to calculate $p(\underline{z}|\underline{x}, g)$, we have to condition the probability distribution $p(\underline{z})$ on the boundary of the object. In particular, $p(\underline{z})$ is the overall probability that a point $\underline{z}$ in the domain will be measured by the sensor (e.g., uniformly), and the object boundary is a curve or a surface, depending on the considered object. Then, in order to evaluate $p(\underline{z}|\underline{x}, g)$, we have to find a suitable parametrization of the boundary.

2.2.2 Object Parametrization

For the boundary parametrization, we can use a vector $\underline{s} \in S \subseteq \mathbb{R}^2$ that specifies each point on a surface, or a scalar $s \in S \subseteq \mathbb{R}$ that specifies each point on a curve. Then, the parametrization is given by a bijective function $\phi_x : S \to \mathbb{R}^d$ that maps parameters s to their corresponding Cartesian coordinates $\underline{z}$ as visualized in Figure 2.5 for a curve in 2D. Within this thesis, we refer to ϕ_x as the *boundary function* of the object.

Before we proceed with formally substituting $\underline{z}$ by $\phi_x(s)$ in the probabilistic model, let us study the parametrization for several examples. As already mentioned, we can essentially distinguish two cases of modeling an object boundary, where the first one is a parametric curve and the second one is a parametric surface. However, this distinction is more difficile than it might seem, as both curve and surface can be embedded into the 2D and 3D domain, e.g., consider a 1D line segment in 3D space or a 2D circular surface in 2D space.

Parametric Curves A parametric curve can be characterized by a 1-dimensional parametrization of $s \in S$ and can be used to model objects in 2D and 3D. The special case of a line segment can be even embedded into 1D.

Example 2.1 (Line Segment). *A highly relevant shape in extended object tracking is a line segment whose shape can be characterized by its length* $2 \cdot r$*, yielding a state vector* $\underline{x} = [r]$*. Assuming the segment to be centered on the origin, it can be embedded in a 1D domain by*

$$\phi_x(s) = s \cdot r \ ,$$

where $s \in S = [-1, 1]$ *implements a linear shift from one end* $-r$ *of the segment, to the other end* r*. A line segment can also be embedded into 2D and 3D space by adding dimensions to the function* $\phi_x(s)$ *in the form of* $\phi_x(s) = [s \cdot r, 0]^{\mathrm{T}}$ *and* $\phi_x(s) = [s \cdot r, 0, 0]^{\mathrm{T}}$*, respectively.* □

Despite their simple character, line segments are an important type of shape and form the basis for the 3D shapes that we construct in Chapter 3. There, a detailed discussion on line segments, including the derivation of a likelihood, is given in Section 3.3.

Example 2.2 (Ellipse). *An axis-aligned ellipse with axes* a *and* b *that is centered on the origin can be characterized by the state vector* $\underline{x} = [a, b]^{\mathrm{T}}$*. Then, we can iterate through all points on the boundary by the boundary function*

$$\phi_x(s) = \begin{bmatrix} a \cdot \cos(s) \\ b \cdot \sin(s) \end{bmatrix} \ ,$$

where s *can be interpreted as an angle in* $S = [0, 2\pi)$*. Note that ellipses contain the important special case of circles for* $a = b$*. An ellipse can be embedded into 3D space according to* $\phi_x(s) = [a \cdot \cos(s), b \cdot \sin(s), 0]^{\mathrm{T}}$*, meaning that it would lie in a plane.* □

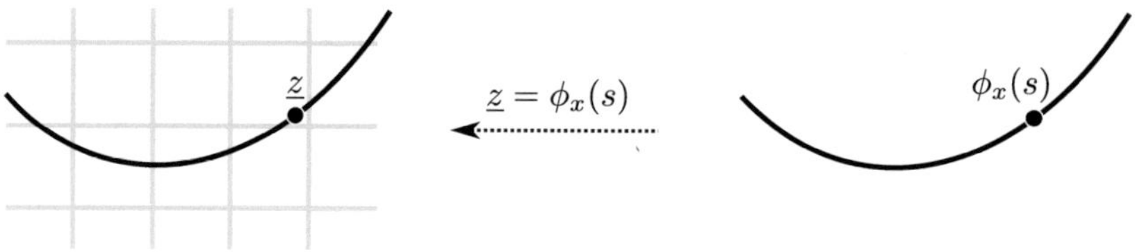

Figure 2.5.: Sketch of the Cartesian (left) and the constraint parametrization (right). The object boundary is drawn as a black curve.

Parametric Surfaces A parametric surface can be characterized by a 2-dimensional parametrization of $\underline{s} = [s_1, s_2]^{\mathrm{T}} \in S$ and can be used to model objects in 3D. In addition, the special case of planar regions can be also embedded into 2D.

Example 2.3 (Ellipsoid). *An axis-aligned ellipsoid with the axes a, b, c that is centered on the origin can be characterized by the state vector $\underline{x} = [a, b, c]^{\mathrm{T}}$. Then, we can iterate through all points on the boundary by*

$$\phi_x(\underline{s}) = \begin{bmatrix} a \cdot \sin(s_1) \cdot \cos(s_2) \\ b \cdot \sin(s_1) \cdot \sin(s_2) \\ c \cdot \cos(s_1) \end{bmatrix} ,$$

where s_1, s_2 can be interpreted as angles $s_1 \in [0, \pi]$ and $s_2 \in [0, 2\pi)$ respectively. Note that ellipsoids, just as the ellipse from Example 2.2, contain the important special case of spheres for $a = b = c$. □

Objects in this Thesis According to the principal goal of this thesis, we are mainly interested in modeling parametric surfaces. Despite of this focus, for the following considerations, we proceed with deriving a likelihood for parametric curves in 2D for two reasons. First, using a scalar parameter s simplifies formulas and can be extended to surfaces in a straight-forward fashion. Second, in Chapter 3, we develop a model for surfaces in 3D based on transformed planar curves, which requires a model for curves.

Incorporating the Object Pose All above examples have specified the objects in their respective object coordinate systems, i.e., axis-aligned, and centered on the origin. However, measurements are generally given in a world coordinate system, which differs from the object coordinate system. In order to add pose information to an object, its state $\underline{x}$ must include rotation and translation parameters that refer to a rotation matrix $\mathbf{R}$ and a translation vector $\underline{c}$, respectively. Then, a point $\underline{y}^W$ and covariance $\mathbf{C}^W$ in world coordinates can be transformed into a point $\underline{y}$ and covariance $\mathbf{C}$ into the object coordinate system (and vice versa) by

$$\begin{aligned} \underline{y}^W &= \mathbf{R}\underline{y} + \underline{c} \,, & \underline{y} &= \mathbf{R}^{\mathrm{T}}\underline{y}^W - \mathbf{R}^{\mathrm{T}}\underline{c} \,, \\ \mathbf{C}^W &= \mathbf{R}\mathbf{C}\mathbf{R}^{\mathrm{T}} \,, & \mathbf{C} &= \mathbf{R}^{\mathrm{T}}\mathbf{C}^W\mathbf{R} \,. \end{aligned} \tag{2.8}$$

2.2.3 Prototype Likelihood for Extended Objects

Let us now proceed with substituting $\underline{z}$ by $\phi_x(s)$ in (2.7) for a parametric curve in 2D space. This substitution has to be applied carefully to $p(\underline{z})$ as it also requires changing the differential $\mathrm{d}\underline{z}$ to $|\phi_x'(s)|\mathrm{d}s$, which follows from the fundamental theorem of calculus. With $p(\underline{z}) = f_z(\underline{z})$ being the probability distribution of $\underline{z}$, we can plug in $\phi_x(s)$ and write

$$f_z(\underline{z})\ \mathrm{d}\underline{z} = f_z(\phi_x(s)) \cdot |\phi_x'(s)|\ \mathrm{d}s \,.$$

Then, by expressing (2.7) in terms of $\phi_x(s)$, we obtain

$$p(\underline{y}|\underline{x}, g) = \int_S \underbrace{\mathcal{N}(\underline{y}; \phi_x(s), \mathbf{C}_v)}_{\text{sensor model}} \cdot \underbrace{\frac{f_z(\phi_x(s))}{\int_S f_z(\phi_x(s)) \cdot \phi_x'(s)\mathrm{d}s} \cdot |\phi_x'(s)|}_{\text{source model}}\ \mathrm{d}s \,. \tag{2.9}$$

It can be seen from this intermediate result that (i) the integration range could be reduced from $\mathbb{R}^2$ to S, and (ii) the dependency on g was resolved. Figure 2.6b illustrates the probabilistic graphical model at this intermediate step.

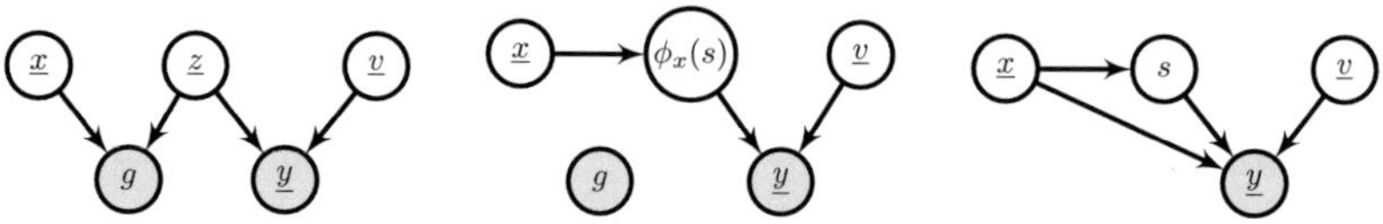

(a) Original model. (b) Intermediate model. (c) Final model.

Figure 2.6.: Probabilistic Graphical Models, showing the process of directly relating the state $\underline{x}$ to the measurement $\underline{y}$.

Finally, by expressing the probabilistic model with respect to s instead of $\phi_x(s)$ and removing the obsolete g from the equation, we can rewrite (2.9) to the well-known likelihood prototype for extended objects

$$p(\underline{y}|\underline{x}) = \int_S \underbrace{\mathcal{N}(\underline{y}; \phi_x(s), \mathbf{C}_v)}_{p(\underline{y}|\underline{x},s)} \cdot p(s|\underline{x}) \, \mathrm{d}s \; . \tag{2.10}$$

Its probabilistic graphical model is shown in Figure 2.6c. Note that in terms of measurement functions, the prototype likelihood (2.10) translates to

$$\begin{aligned} \underline{y} &= h(\underline{x}, \underline{v}, s) \\ &= \phi_x(s) + \underline{v} \; , \end{aligned} \tag{2.11}$$

and incorporates the parameter s. At this point, in order to evaluate the likelihood (or the measurement function), we are left with the task of specifying the probability distribution $p(s|\underline{x})$, which is an instance of the association problem with s being the unknown *nuisance parameter*.

2.3 Traditional Models

In the following, we discuss three existing approaches to address the association problem for extended object tracking. In particular, we consider a model, where the association is assumed to be known, the Spatial Distribution Model (SDM), and finally a model, where the association is greedily approximated. We chose this order of explanation according to the amount of heuristic assumptions that are required, starting with the most demanding one.

2.3.1 Known Association Model (KAM)

In selected cases, e.g., when unique markers are attached to the object [67], we can exactly solve the association problem and yield a "Known Association Model" (KAM). For this model, it is assumed that the parameter s^* of the true generating source $\phi_x(s^*)$ is known for each measurement $\underline{y}$. Then, $p(s|\underline{x})$ simplifies to a Dirac δ-distribution according to

$$p(s|\underline{x}) = \delta(s - s^*) \ .$$

This distribution exclusively supports the true source, and the likelihood (2.10) can be simplified to

$$\begin{aligned} p(\underline{y}|\underline{x}) &= \int_S \mathcal{N}(\underline{y}; \phi_x(s^*), \mathbf{C}_v) \cdot \delta(s - s^*) \, \mathrm{d}s \\ &= \mathcal{N}(\underline{y}; \phi_x(s^*), \mathbf{C}_v) \end{aligned} \tag{2.12}$$

by applying the sifting property. The corresponding measurement function is given by

$$\begin{aligned} \underline{y} &= h(\underline{x}, \underline{v}, s^*) \\ &= \phi_x(s^*) + \underline{v} \ , \end{aligned}$$

where s^* acts as a deterministic model parameter. Besides its practical relevance for specific tracking tasks (unique markers), we will use it as a benchmark model in synthetic evaluations as it perfectly solves the association problem.

2.3.2 Spatial Distribution Model (SDM)

When the true measurement sources are not known exactly, a straightforward way to deal with the association problem is to assign a probability to each point on the object boundary that specifies how likely it is that it will be the measurement source. This popular model is known as the Spatial Distribution Model (SDM) [70] and probabilistically solves the association problem. It is widely-used in extended object tracking [64, 78, 149] but requires that the distribution $p(s|\underline{x})$ is known a priori. Then, likelihood and measurement function are directly given by (2.10) and (2.11), respectively. In statistics, (2.10) is denoted as an *integrated likelihood*, and the nuisance parameter s is said to be integrated out [79]. In practice, $p(s|\underline{x})$ is generally unknown and often approximated by a uniform distribution over the boundary [64], or, in the form of a Gaussian distribution in the popular *Random Matrices* approach [80]. Recent approaches [81, 82] also incorporate heuristics based on the sensor to object geometry. For example, when the sensor observes only one side of the object, $p(s|\underline{x})$ can be assumed as a uniform distribution over the visible part. When incorporating the correct distribution, it was empirically shown in [70] that the SDM yields an unbiased estimator.

However, there are three major issues that are responsible for the fact that SDMs are only applied to rather simple estimation problems yet. First, it is non-trivial to obtain $p(s|\underline{x})$ as it has to be extracted from (2.9) and wrong assumptions about it generally cause biased estimates [159, 157]. Second, using SDMs for complex objects is computationally demanding as evaluating the likelihood (2.10) typically requires numerically solving the involved integral(s) — one for a curve or two for a surface. This is

(a) Greedy Association. **(b)** PGM for the GAM.

Figure 2.7.: Visual explanation of the Greedy Association Model. (a) illustrates the association heuristic and (b) shows the resulting Probabilistic Graphical Model. The mutual dependency between s and $\underline{y}$ causes a cycle in the model, which is indicated by the dashed arrow.

especially inconvenient in particle filters, as they evaluate the likelihood for each particle and measurement. Finally, using SDMs in nonlinear Kalman filters typically yields a poor estimation quality as s acts as a non-additive noise variable in (2.11) and typically is not Gaussian.

2.3.3 Greedy Association Model (GAM)

Another widely-used model, which we will denote as the Greedy Association Model (GAM), does not require any prior knowledge about $p(s|\underline{x})$ at all. Instead, the association problem is solved greedily by finding the specific source on the boundary that fits *best* to a given measurement $\underline{y}$, e.g., its maximum likelihood estimate. In doing so, the estimator will minimize some sort of distance [159]. Formally, approximating $s^* \in S$ of the true generating source $\phi_x(s^*)$ by its maximum likelihood estimate can be calculated according to

$$s^* \approx \pi_x(\underline{y}) := \arg\max_{s \in S} \mathcal{N}(\underline{y}; \phi_x(s), \mathbf{C}_v) \ . \tag{2.13}$$

Then, the function $\pi_x(\underline{y})$ refers to the most likely source $\phi_x(\pi_x(\underline{y}))$ on the boundary for a measurement $\underline{y}$, as shown in Figure 2.7a. Based on (2.13), we can set up $p(s|\underline{x})$ similarly to the KAM as the Dirac δ-distribution

$$p(s|\underline{x}, \underline{y}) = \delta(s - \pi_x(\underline{y})) \ , \tag{2.14}$$

except for the difference that it now additionally depends on the measurement $\underline{y}$. Intuitively, this distribution exclusively supports the greedily selected source $\phi_x(\pi_x(\underline{y}))$, and by plugging (2.14) into the likelihood prototype (2.10), it can be simplified to

$$\begin{aligned} p(\underline{y}|\underline{x}, \underline{y}) &= \int_S \mathcal{N}(\underline{y}; \phi_x(s), \mathbf{C}_v) \cdot \delta\left(s - \pi_x(\underline{y})\right) \,\mathrm{d}\underline{s} \\ &= \mathcal{N}(\underline{y}; \phi_x(\pi_x(\underline{y})), \mathbf{C}_v) \,. \end{aligned} \tag{2.15}$$

However, this expression is not well-defined in the sense that it has a cyclic dependency between measurement and its originating source. This issue is illustrated in Figure 2.7b, and in order to additionally emphasize it, we intentionally abuse the notation $p(\underline{y}|\underline{x}, \underline{y})$. In statistics, (2.15) is denoted as a *profile likelihood*, and the nuisance parameter s is said to be profiled out [83]. The corresponding measurement function is given by

$$\begin{aligned} \underline{y} &= h(\underline{x}, \underline{y}, \underline{v}) \\ &= \phi_x(\pi_x(\underline{y})) + \underline{v} \end{aligned} \tag{2.16}$$

and also contains the cyclic dependency, as $\underline{y}$ appears on both sides of the equation. Thus, $\underline{y}$ simultaneously acts as a measurement and model parameter.

One major advantage of GAMs over SDMs is that, typically, they are easier to calculate, as they replace the integration by some kind of projection. In addition, they do not require explicitly modeling a prior distribution for s and are more robust to unpredictable occlusions. However, these advantages come with the problematic issue that GAMs are not well-defined in a mathematical sense. As a consequence, estimators based on GAMs are generally biased for nonlinear boundaries in the presence of noise, even for an infinite number of measurements [18]. Nevertheless, it is worth mentioning that, despite of their mathematical issues, GAMs mark the prototype for the popular geometric fitting approach. In the following, we show this relationship.

Relationship to Geometric Fitting Consider the task of fitting the parameters $\underline{x}$ of a boundary $\phi_x(s)$ based on noisy measurements $\underline{y}_i$ with identical, isotropic noise covariance matrices $\mathbf{C}_{v_i} = \sigma^2 \cdot \mathbf{I}$. For this special case, the greedy source estimate $\phi_x(\pi_x(\underline{y}_i))$ coincides with the point on the constraint that is closest to $\underline{y}_i$ in terms of the Euclidean distance. When applying the substitution $\underline{e}_i := \underline{y}_i - \phi_x(\pi_x(\underline{y}_i))$ in the likelihood (2.15), it can be rearranged to

$$\begin{aligned} \mathcal{N}(\underline{e}_i; \underline{0}, \sigma^2 \cdot \mathbf{I}) &= c \cdot \exp\left(-\frac{1}{2} \cdot \underline{e}_i^{\mathrm{T}} \frac{1}{\sigma^2} \cdot \mathbf{I}\, \underline{e}_i\right) \\ &= c \cdot \exp\left(-\frac{1}{2\sigma^2} \|\underline{e}_i\|^2\right) , \end{aligned} \tag{2.17}$$

where c is a normalization constant and $\|\underline{e}_i\|^2$ is the squared Euclidean distance between measurement and boundary, i.e, the squared error. A maximum likelihood estimator would try to minimize $\|\underline{e}_i\|^2$ and, in doing so, would find the least-squares estimate

$$\begin{aligned} \underline{x}_{\mathrm{ML}} &= \arg\max_{\underline{x}} \prod_{i=1}^{n} c \cdot \exp\left(-\frac{1}{2\sigma^2} \|\underline{y}_i - \phi_x(\pi_x(\underline{y}_i))\|^2\right) \\ &= \arg\min_{\underline{x}} \sum_{i=1}^{n} \|\underline{y}_i - \phi_x(\pi_x(\underline{y}_i))\|^2 . \end{aligned} \tag{2.18}$$

□

Origin of Bias in GAMs Effort [84, 85, 72, 86, 87, 88, 18, 89] has been made to understand the bias of GAMs. A visual explanation [159] of its origin is given in Figure 2.8. The true boundary in each figure is marked in black, a selected source is drawn as a black dot, and isotropic uncertainty around it is schematically indicated by the filled circle. Probability mass for expected measurements $y = \phi_x(s) + \underline{v}$ from this source is schematically colored in blue (inside the object) and gray (outside the object). The estimated boundary that minimizes the least-squares of the Euclidean distance error in (2.18) is schematically depicted as dashed, red line. This can be thought of, roughly speaking, finding the boundary that balances probability mass on the left and the right side. For the line shape, this estimate coincides with the true shape and, in consequence, the algorithm will find the true parameters. However, for the curve and corner shape, the estimates will not coincide with the true shape. This is due to the fact that the there is more probability mass for points on one side of the boundary. In consequence, the algorithm will find biased parameters, as it assumes a balanced ratio. Thus, bias is a local phenomenon whose effect depends on the local curve within the magnitude of the measurement noise, as indicated in Figure 2.8c.

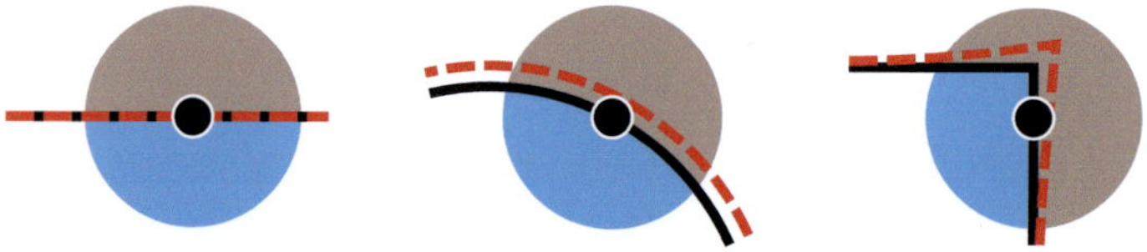

(a) No bias. **(b)** Curvature bias. **(c)** Corner bias.

Figure 2.8.: Origin of parameter bias in curve fitting.

In literature, there are approaches to model this ratio and to re-engineer the likelihood in order to reduce its effect [90, 18, 159]. Some of these approaches are related to the new model, which we will develop in the following section.

2.4 Partial Information Model (PIM)

In this section, we propose a new, mathematically sound model for extended objects based on the statistical concept of *partial likelihood* [91, 71]. As the major advantage over SDMs and GAMs, this model will yield an unbiased estimator while neither requiring probabilistic assumptions about the measurement sources, nor requiring artificial re-engineering of a model that is not well-defined. The key idea consists of a re-parametrization of the measurements that decouples their encoded information into "how well" they fit to the object boundary and "where" on the boundary they correspond to. From this new parametrization,

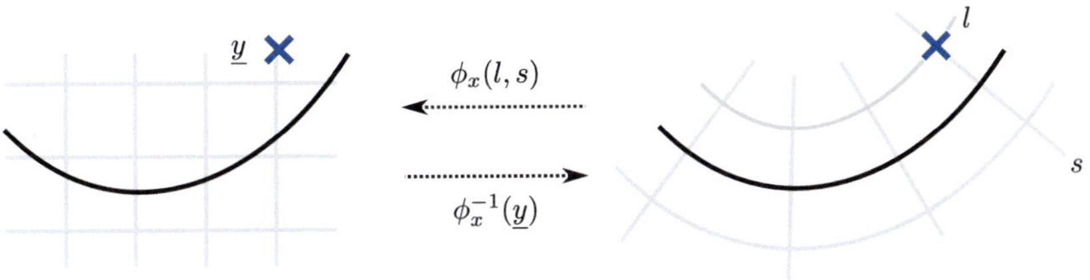

Figure 2.9.: Sketch of the Cartesian (left) and the constraint-induced parametrization (right). The object boundary is drawn as a black curve.

we just exploit the *valuable* "how well" information for the measurement update, and ignore the unknown "where" component. As only a part of the measurement information will be used, we denote the model as the *Partial Information Model* (PIM).

2.4.1 Key Idea

Let us now explain the key idea in more detail by considering a curve in 2D. For the traditional models in Section 2.3, we parametrized the potential sources $\underline{z}$ on the boundary by $s \in S \subseteq \mathbb{R}$ in the form of $\phi_x(s) = \underline{z}$. Now, we want to apply a similar parametrization to the measurements $\underline{y}$, as visualized in Figure 2.9. For this purpose, we need to extend the previous parametrization, as the measurements occur in the full 2D domain but $\phi_x(s)$ only describes points that lie on the curve. Nevertheless, we want to keep s as one dimension of the parametrization in order to expresses "where" on the boundary a measurement corresponds to. In addition, we introduce another parameter $l \in L \subseteq \mathbb{R}$ that refers to "how well" $\underline{y}$ fits to the boundary. Let us define that $l = 0$ denotes that a measurement fits perfectly, i.e., it lies on the boundary, and increasing negative/positive values l indicate that measurements increasingly differ to the one/other side of the boundary. Using this convention, l and s together allow for representing measurements in the full domain by re-defining the boundary function ϕ_x in the form of $\phi_x(l_y, s_y) = \underline{y}$. Note that this re-defined boundary function generalizes its previous definition as $\phi_x(0, s) = \phi_x(s)$ holds, and still parametrizes the boundary for $s \in S$.

While it is clear that the true value of the measured l_y is $l = 0$, designing the likelihood $p(l_y, s_y|\underline{x})$ is actually difficult, as we do not know the true originating value s of the measured value s_y. Hence, the key idea of our approach is using only the l_y-information of a measurement in the likelihood while ignoring on the problematic s_y-information. Mathematically, this refers to the statistical concept of partial likelihood, which is an approximation of the full likelihood according to

$$\begin{aligned} p(l_y, s_y|\underline{x}) &= p(l_y|\underline{x}) \cdot p(s_y|\underline{x}) \\ &\approx p(l_y|\underline{x}) \ , \end{aligned} \tag{2.19}$$

and requires that l_y and s_y are mutually independent. Then, by dropping $p(s_y|\underline{x})$, we ignore the association of measurements to their sources and, in consequence, do not need a heuristic for s anymore. Of course, we have to trade this ignorance for the amount of measurement information that was encoded in s_y. The effect of this trade-off will be discussed in Section 2.6.3. Our tasks are now (i) finding a constraint-induced parametrization $\phi_x(l_y, s_y)$ for measurements $\underline{y}$, such that l_y and s_y become mutually independent, and (ii) deriving the partial likelihood $p(l_y|\underline{x})$.

2.4.2 Constraint-induced Parametrization

For the definition of the l- and s-axes, we do not need to start from scratch. We already know that the s-axis must lie in the object boundary as, for $l = 0$, the s-component lets us iterate through the boundary via $\phi_x(0, s)$.

Thus, we have to specify the l-axis in such a way that the measurement noise is independent in l_y and s_y. According to the measurement function in (2.11), measurements $\underline{y}$ of a source $\phi_x(0, s)$ occur according to

$$\underline{y} = \phi_x(0, s) + \underline{v} \ , \tag{2.20}$$

as illustrated in Figure 2.10a. When expressing these measurements in terms of $\phi_x(l_y, s_y) = \underline{y}$, the generative model can be rewritten to

$$\begin{bmatrix} l_y \\ s_y \end{bmatrix} = \begin{bmatrix} 0 \\ s \end{bmatrix} + \begin{bmatrix} l_v \\ s_v \end{bmatrix} \ , \tag{2.21}$$

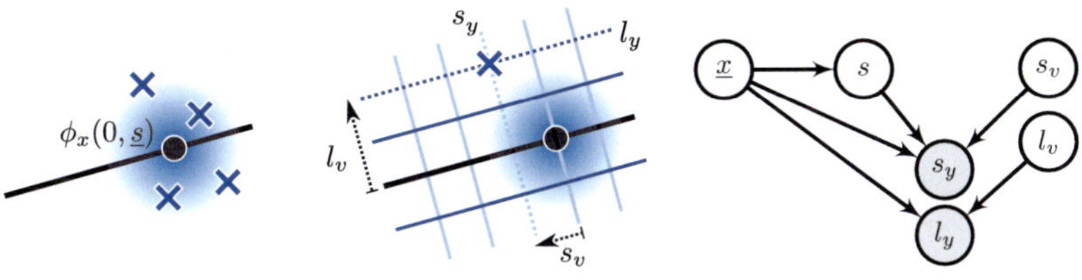

(a) Generative model. **(b)** Uncorrelated l and s. **(c)** Prob. Graphical Model.

Figure 2.10.: Ideal case, where the constraint-induced parametrization makes the l_y and s_y dimensions (gray grid) independent.

where the measurement noise $\underline{v}$ is also represented in terms of l_v and s_v. Figure 2.10b visually explains these notations. From this illustration, it can be seen that l_v and s_v will be independent if (and only if) the l- and s-axes coincide with the *principal components* of the Gaussian measurement covariance matrix $\mathbf{C}_v$. As the principal components of a Gaussian are always orthogonal to each other, we can conclude that the l-axis must lie orthogonal to the s-axis, i.e, to the object boundary. However, when considering anisotropic noise and/or nonlinear boundaries, it becomes clear that these orthogonal lines will not always coincide with the principal components of the Gaussian. Before we look at this general case, let us study the ideal case of a linear boundary and isotropic noise that is illustrated in Figure 2.10b, where independence can be achieved.

The Ideal Case We consider a linear boundary and isotropic Gaussian noise $\underline{v}$ with covariance matrix $\mathbf{C}_v = \sigma^2 \cdot \mathbf{I}$. The variances of l_v and s_v are both σ^2, due to the isotropic characteristic of the noise and the fact that the ls-coordinate system is a rotated version of the Cartesian coordinate system. For this reason, measurements $\underline{y}$ that originate from a source $\phi_x(0, s)$ according to (2.21) are independent in their l_y and s_y component. Thus, we can write the prototype likelihood from (2.10) in terms of l and s according to

$$p(l_y, s_y|\underline{x}) = \int_S \mathcal{N}\left(\begin{bmatrix} l_y \\ s_y \end{bmatrix}; \begin{bmatrix} 0 \\ s \end{bmatrix}, \begin{bmatrix} \sigma^2 & 0 \\ 0 & \sigma^2 \end{bmatrix}\right) \cdot p(s|\underline{x}) \, \mathrm{d}s$$

$$= \underbrace{\mathcal{N}(l_y; 0, \sigma^2)}_{p(l_y|\underline{x})} \cdot \underbrace{\int_S \mathcal{N}(s_y - s; 0, \sigma^2) \cdot p(s|\underline{x}) \, \mathrm{d}s}_{p(s_y|\underline{x})} \ .$$

The corresponding probabilistic graphical model for this example is illustrated in Figure 2.10c.

Note that all information about the unknown s is isolated in the term $p(s_y|\underline{x})$ and, thus, when deriving the partial likelihood $p(l_y|\underline{x})$, we do not need to explicitly model $p(s|\underline{x})$ anymore. As an important observation, note that the ls-coordinate system can be constructed using the signed Euclidean distance of points to the boundary. Specifically, for all points $\underline{y} = \phi_x(l_y, s_y)$, their closest point on the boundary in terms of the Euclidean distance is given by $\phi_x(0, s_y)$. From this observation, we can formally define the concepts "how well" and "where" as

- **"How well:"** all points on a level l_y have the same signed Euclidean distance to the boundary.
- **"Where:"** all points on a level s_y have the same closest point $\phi_x(0, s_y)$ on the boundary.

As a remark, the maximum likelihood estimator for the partial likelihood in this example corresponds to the *orthogonal least squares* estimator as it will minimize the squared Euclidean error between measurements and line, analogously to (2.17).

The General Case While for the linear constraint and isotropic noise, perfect independence could be achieved, for a nonlinear constraint (and/or anisotropic noise), we find ourselves in a dilemma. On the one hand, the s-axis in the boundary dictates the l-axis to lie orthogonal, as indicated in Figure 2.11a. On the other hand, the noise will only be independent if the

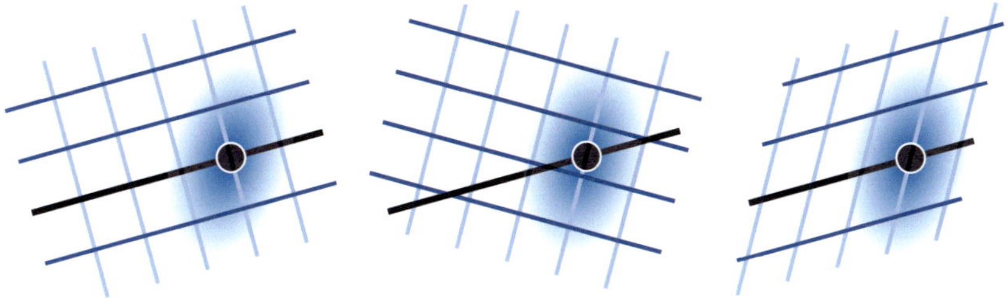

(a) Constraint-induced **(b)** Noise-induced **(c)** Compromise

Figure 2.11.: Competing design properties for the ls-parametrization.

axes coincide with the *principal components* of the Gaussian measurement covariance matrix as shown in Figure 2.11b. However, these noise-induced axes no longer have a meaningful interpretation in terms of "how well" and "where" measurements correspond to the boundary.

As a compromise, we propose to sacrifice orthogonality of the ls-coordinate system, in order to come up with the parametrization in Figure 2.11c, which retains the meaning of the axes for the Mahalanobis distance with respect to the noise covariance. That is, s_y specifies the closest point $\phi_x(0, s_y)$ on the boundary by

$$s_y = \pi_x(\underline{y}) := \arg\min_{s \in S} \left(\underline{y} - \phi_x(0, s)\right)^{\mathrm{T}} \mathbf{C}_v^{-1} \left(\underline{y} - \phi_x(0, s)\right) , \quad (2.22)$$

and l_y specifies the signed distance of $\underline{y}$ to this point by

$$l_y = g_x(\underline{y}) := \pm \left((\underline{y} - \phi_x(0, s_y))^{\mathrm{T}} \mathbf{C}_v^{-1} (\underline{y} - \phi_x(0, s_y)) \right)^{\frac{1}{2}} , \quad (2.23)$$

where the sign indicates on which side of the constraint the measurement lies. We intentionally re-use the symbols π_x and g_x here in order to emphasize that the former exactly corresponds to the projection of measurements to the boundary from (2.13) and the latter is a specific implementation of the boundary constraint from (2.5). Note that the sign for l_y naturally comes into play as the l-axis is 0 on its intersection with the constraint. Based on (2.22) and (2.23) we can finally define the desired parametrization according to

$$\begin{bmatrix} l_y \\ s_y \end{bmatrix} = \phi_x^{-1}(\underline{y}) := \begin{bmatrix} g_x(\underline{y}) \\ \pi_x(\underline{y}) \end{bmatrix} . \tag{2.24}$$

Note that this parametrization includes the ideal case that was discussed before, as the Mahalanobis distance corresponds to the Euclidean distance for an isotropic noise covariance matrix $\mathbf{C}_v$. Figure 2.12 illustrates the ls-coordinate system for several examples where the measurement covariances $\mathbf{C}_v$ are indicated as shaded blue ellipses/circles. The levels for more complex objects can generally not be obtain in closed-form, as evaluating $\phi_x(l_y, s_y)$ usually involves a nonlinear optimization for s_y in (2.22). Fortunately, in practice, we will only have to evaluate ϕ_x at a few points. Nevertheless, for the special case of a circular boundary, we can find closed-form solutions for s_y and l_y.

Example 2.4 (Circle). *We consider a circle that is centered on the origin with radius* $\underline{x} = [r]$. *For measurements* $\underline{y}$ *of the circular boundary, let us assume isotropic measurement noise. From this follows the* ls*-parametrization in Figure 2.12a, which is closely related to polar coordinates with* $\pi_x(\underline{y}) = \text{atan2}(y_2, y_1)$ *being the angular coordinate, and* $g_x(\underline{y}) = \|\underline{y}\| - r$ *being the radial coordinate. Then,* $\phi_x(l_y, s_y)$ *can be specified by*

$$\phi_x(l_y, s_y) = (r + l_y) \cdot \begin{bmatrix} \cos(s_y) \\ \sin(s_y) \end{bmatrix} . \tag{2.25}$$

□

Due to the skewness of the ls-coordinate system and potential nonlinearities in the boundary, l_v and s_v may be still slightly correlated. In consequence, the partial likelihood for extended objects will generally rather look like $p(l_y|\underline{x}, s_y)$ instead of $p(l_y|\underline{x})$ (2.19) as

$$\begin{aligned} p(l_y, s_y|\underline{x}) &= p(l_y|\underline{x}, s_y) \cdot p(s_y|\underline{x}) \\ &\approx p(l_y|\underline{x}, s_y) . \end{aligned}$$

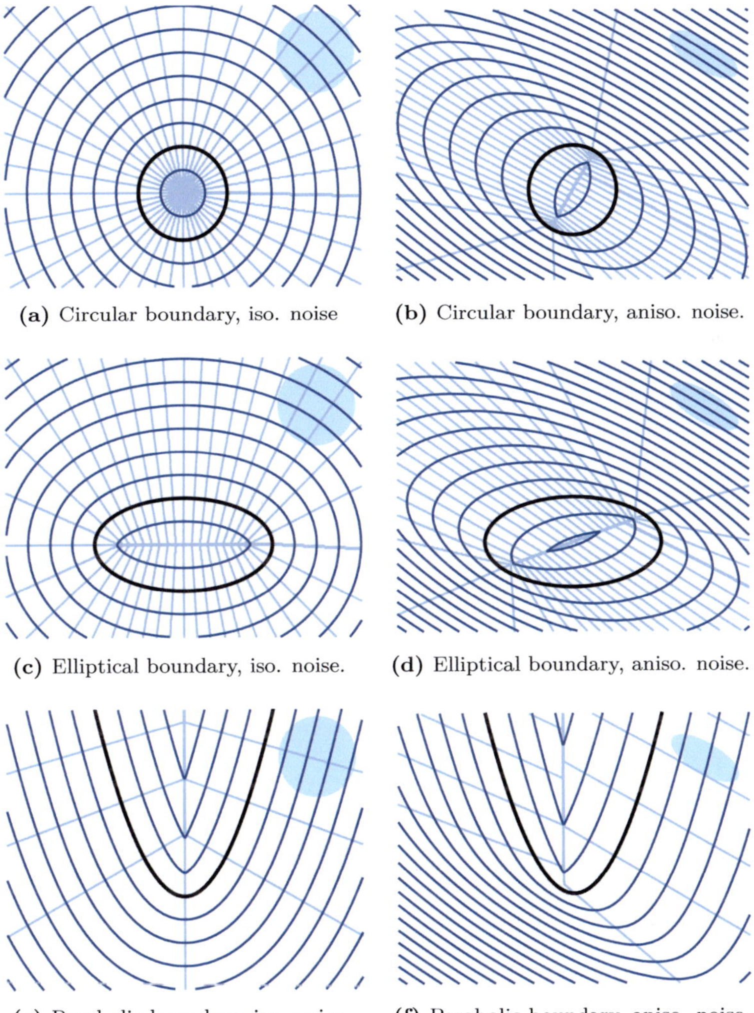

(a) Circular boundary, iso. noise

(b) Circular boundary, aniso. noise.

(c) Elliptical boundary, iso. noise.

(d) Elliptical boundary, aniso. noise.

(e) Parabolic boundary, iso. noise.

(f) Parabolic boundary, aniso. noise.

Figure 2.12.: Examples of the ls-parametrization.

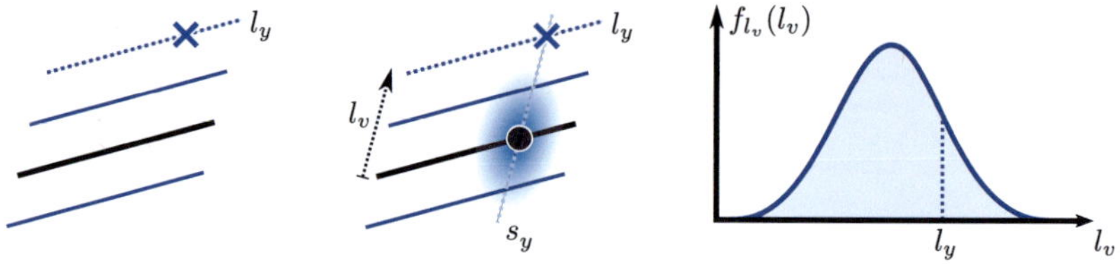

(a) Measurement. **(b)** Original noise. **(c)** Partial noise.

Figure 2.13.: The partial likelihood is obtained by evaluating the partial noise in l_y.

2.4.3 Partial Likelihood

Prepared with the constrained-induced parametrization of measurements $\underline{y} = \phi_x(l_y, s_y)$ from (2.24), we can now derive the partial likelihood $p(l_y|\underline{x}, s_y)$. The following considerations are visually explained in Figure 2.13. As can be seen from Figure 2.13a, we only want to consider l_y as measurement information of $\underline{y}$, while taking s_y as a given parameter. Then, a given s_y-value immediately refers to the source $\phi_x(0, s_y)$ which in turn refers to the generative model in Figure 2.13b. Incorporating the known relationship $l_y = 0 + l_v$ as known from (2.21), we can express the partial likelihood in terms of

$$\begin{aligned} p(l_y|\underline{x}, s_y) &= \int_L p(l_y|\underline{x}, s_y, l_v) \cdot p(l_v|\underline{x}, s_y)\, \mathrm{d}l_v \\ &= \int_L \delta\left(l_y - (0 + l_v)\right) \cdot f_{l_v}(l_v)\, \mathrm{d}l_v \\ &= f_{l_v}(l_y)\ , \end{aligned}$$

where $p(l_v|\underline{x}, s_y) = f_{l_v}(l_v)$ is the distribution of the noise variable l_v. In consequence, the partial likelihood essentially is the distribution $f_{l_v}(l_v)$ that describes the l-value of the sensor noise, evaluated in l_y. This distribution is schematically shown in Figure 2.13c and will be referred to as *partial noise*.

Partial Noise As the next step, we have to derive the distribution of the partial noise $p(l_v|\underline{x}, s_y)$. Conceptually, it can be extracted from the distribution of the original sensor noise $p(\underline{v})$. This requires (i) expressing the variable $\underline{v}$ in terms of l_v and s_v, (ii) deriving their joint distribution $p(l_v, s_v|\underline{x}, s_y)$, and (iii) marginalizing out the s_v-component

$$p(l_v|\underline{x}, s_y) = \int_S p(l_v, s_v|\underline{x}, s_y)\, \mathrm{d}s_v \; . \tag{2.26}$$

Let us start with expressing $p(\underline{v})$ in terms of l_v and s_v. Given the state $\underline{x}$ and the s_y-value of $\underline{y}$, hypothetical measurements $\tilde{\underline{y}}$ from the source $\phi_x(0, s_y)$ occur according to the additive noise model in (2.20) as $\tilde{\underline{y}} = \phi_x(0, s_y) + \underline{v}$ (see Figure 2.13b). We use the tilde symbol in order to distinguish the hypothetical measurements from the original one $\underline{y}$. By solving this generative model for the noise $\underline{v}$ and applying the ls-parametrization to $\tilde{\underline{y}}$, we obtain

$$\begin{aligned} \underline{v} &= \tilde{\underline{y}} - \phi_x(0, s_y) \\ &= \phi_x(\tilde{l}_y, \tilde{s}_y) - \phi_x(0, s_y) \\ &= \phi_x(0 + l_v, s_y + s_v) - \phi_x(0, s_y) \; . \end{aligned} \tag{2.27}$$

Based on this relationship, we can apply a change of variables to the distribution $p(\underline{v})$, which is actually known to be the zero-mean Gaussian $\mathcal{N}(\underline{v}; 0, \mathbf{C}_v)$. The general formula for changing variables of a probability distribution follows from the fundamental theorem of calculus according to

$$\begin{aligned} & p(l_v, s_v|\underline{x}, s_y) \\ &= p(\underline{v}) \cdot \left| \det\left(\mathbf{J}_{\underline{v}}(l_v, s_v)\right) \right| \\ &= \mathcal{N}\left(\underline{v}; \underline{0}, \mathbf{C}_v\right) \cdot \left| \det\left(\mathbf{J}_{\underline{v}}(l_v, s_v)\right) \right| \\ &= \mathcal{N}\left(\phi_x(0 + l_v, s_y + s_v) - \phi_x(0, s_y); \underline{0}, \mathbf{C}_v\right) \cdot \left| \det\left(\mathbf{J}_{\underline{v}}(l_v, s_v)\right) \right| \end{aligned} \tag{2.28}$$

and incorporates the determinant of the Jacobian matrix

$$\mathbf{J}_{\underline{v}}(l_v, s_v) = \begin{bmatrix} \dfrac{\partial \underline{v}}{\partial l_v} & \dfrac{\partial \underline{v}}{\partial s_v} \end{bmatrix} \; . \tag{2.29}$$

Note that (2.28) is nothing else but the distribution of the measurement noise $p(\underline{v})$ expressed in ls-coordinates, where the differential expression (2.29) accounts for the skewness of the coordinate system. Then, by marginalizing s_v out of $p(l_v, s_v|\underline{x}, s_y)$ according to (2.26) we obtain the distribution of the partial noise as

$$\begin{aligned} p(l_v|\underline{x}, s_y) &= \int_S \mathcal{N}\left(\phi_x(l_v, s_y + s_v); \phi_x(0, s_y), \mathbf{C}_v\right) \cdot \left|\det\left(\mathbf{J}_{\underline{v}}(l_v, s_v)\right)\right| \, \mathrm{d}s_v \\ &= f_{l_v}(l_v) \, . \end{aligned} \tag{2.30}$$

Main Result Finally, by plugging l_y into the distribution $f_{l_v}(l_v)$ of the partial noise (2.30), we arrive at the partial likelihood, which marks the main result of this chapter. Its definition is given as follows.

Definition 2.1 (Patial Likelihood for Extended Objects)**.** *For a given state $\underline{x}$ and a measurement $\underline{y} = \phi_x(l_y, s_y)$ that is parametrized in terms of its Mahalanobis distance to the object boundary according to* (2.24) *(with respect to the noise covariance matrix $\mathbf{C}_v$), the partial likelihood for l_y is given by*

$$\begin{aligned} p(l_y|\underline{x}, s_y) &= f_{l_v}(l_y) \qquad (2.31) \\ &= \int_S \mathcal{N}\left(\phi_x(l_y, s_y + s_v); \phi_x(0, s_y), \mathbf{C}_v\right) \cdot \left|\det\left(\mathbf{J}_{\underline{v}}(l_y, s_v)\right)\right| \, \mathrm{d}s_v \, . \end{aligned}$$

□

The partial likelihood has an intuitive geometric interpretation. Essentially, it is the integral of a Gaussian (centered on the most likely source $\phi_x(0, s_y)$) over all potential measurements that fit equally well (i.e., l_y) to the given boundary. In order to illustrate this idea, let us look at a circle.

Example 2.5 (Partial Likelihood for a Circle). *We consider a circle that is centered on the origin with radius* $\underline{x} = [r]$ *and assume the sensor noise to be isotropic with* $\mathbf{C}_v = \sigma^2 \cdot \mathbf{I}$. *In order to derive the partial likelihood* (2.31), *we need the function* $\phi_x(l_y, s_y)$ *that specifies the ls-coordinate system. For the circle, we can use* (2.25) *from Example 2.4. Using this formula, the determinant of the Jacobian* $\mathbf{J}_\phi(l_y, s_y)$ *evaluates to*

$$\begin{aligned}\det\left(\mathbf{J}_\phi(l_y, s_v)\right) &= \det\left(\begin{bmatrix}\cos(s_y + s_v) & -(r + l_y)\cdot\sin(s_y + s_v)\\ \sin(s_y + s_v) & (r + l_y)\cdot\cos(s_y + s_v)\end{bmatrix}\right)\\ &= r + l_y \ ,\end{aligned}$$

and the partial likelihood evaluates to

$$\begin{aligned}&p(l_y|\underline{x}, s_y) \\ &= \int_0^{2\pi} \mathcal{N}\left((r + l_y)\cdot\begin{bmatrix}\cos(s_y + s_v)\\ \sin(s_y + s_v)\end{bmatrix}; r\cdot\begin{bmatrix}\cos(s_y)\\ \sin(s_y)\end{bmatrix}, \mathbf{C}_v\right)\cdot(r + l_y)\,\mathrm{d}s_v \ .\end{aligned} \tag{2.32}$$

Note that all potential measurements with l_y *lie on a circle with radius* $r + l_y$. *Thus, the partial likelihood requires integrating over this circle. As the skewness of the ls-coordinate system is constant for each location on the circle (for isotropic noise), the partial likelihood is independent of the specific instance* s_y, *which allows us to set* $s_y = 0$ *and obtain* $p(l_y|\underline{x})$. □

Measurement Equation The underlying generative model that yields the partial likelihood from (2.31) can be obtained from the relationship $l_y = 0 + l_v$. We can rearrange this equation to a measurement equation in classical notation in the form of

$$\begin{aligned}0 &= h(\underline{x}, \underline{v}, \underline{y})\\ &= g_x(\underline{y}) - g_x(\phi_x(0, \pi_x(\underline{y})) + \underline{v}) \ ,\end{aligned} \tag{2.33}$$

by substituting $l_y = g_x(\underline{y})$ and $l_v = g_x(\phi_x(0, \pi_x(\underline{y})) + \underline{v})$, where the latter can be obtained from (2.27). In this measurement equation, $\underline{x}$ is the state, $\underline{v}$ is non-additive Gaussian noise, $\underline{y}$ acts as a model parameter, and 0 is a *pseudo-measurement*.

Relationship to the Greedy Association Model Conceptually, the PIM from (2.33) is related to the GAM $\underline{y} = \phi_x(0, \pi_x(\underline{y})) + \underline{v}$ from (2.16) in the sense that it can be obtain by first taking $g_x(\,\cdot\,)$ on both sides and then rearranging it. However, the GAM derives the likelihood of a measurement producing itself (roughly speaking), the PIM derives the likelihood of one dimension of the measurement (s_y) producing another dimension (l_y).

2.5 Implementation

Generally, analytic solutions to the integral in (2.31) cannot be found, not even for the circle and the case of isotropic noise (2.32). This raises the need for approximation techniques. In this section, we show how to implement an estimator based on approximations of the new Partial Information Model (PIM). For this purpose, we first derive a measurement equation with additive Gaussian noise as an approximation for (2.33). Then, for its evaluation, we propose a sampling-based approach and, for special cases, a closed-form approach.

2.5.1 Measurement Equation with Additive Gaussian Noise

Let us start with approximating the measurement equation from (2.33) by a simpler one with additive noise. For this purpose, we can interpret $l_v = g_x(\phi_x(0, \pi_x(\underline{y})) + \underline{v})$ as a distinct noise variable which lets us rewrite the original measurement equation to

$$\begin{aligned} 0 &= h(\underline{x}, l_v, \underline{y}) \\ &= g_x(\underline{y}) - l_v \; . \end{aligned} \tag{2.34}$$

In this measurement equation, $\underline{x}$ is the state, l_v is an additive, but not necessarily Gaussian noise variable, $\underline{y}$ acts as a model parameter, and 0 is a *pseudo-measurement*. For practical purposes, it is convenient to use moment matching in order to approximate the distribution of l_v as a Gaussian distribution $f_{l_v}(l_v) \approx \mathcal{N}(\mathrm{E}\{l_v)\}\,, \mathrm{Var}\{l_v\})$. Mathematically, this requires propagating the moments of the random variable $\underline{v}$

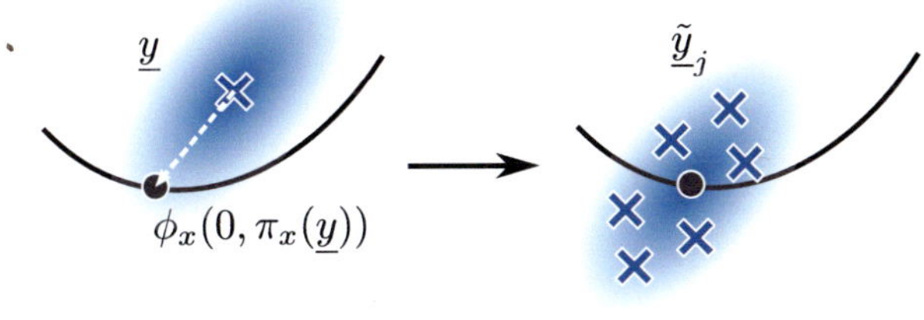

Figure 2.14.: Sampling-based approximation of the partial noise.

through $l_v = g_x(\phi_x(0, \pi_x(\underline{y})) + \underline{v})$. Then, the measurement equation (2.34) immediately refers to the likelihood

$$\begin{aligned} p(l_y|\underline{x}, s_y) &= f_{l_v}(l_y) \\ &\approx \mathcal{N}\left(l_y; \mathrm{E}\{l_v\}, \mathrm{Var}\{l_v\}\right) \\ &= \mathcal{N}\left(g_x(\underline{y}); \mathrm{E}\{l_v\}, \mathrm{Var}\{l_v\}\right) \ , \end{aligned} \tag{2.35}$$

which, thus, can be seen as approximation of the partial likelihood from (2.31). Next, we propose two approaches to derive the moments $\mathrm{E}\{l_v\}$ and $\mathrm{Var}\{l_v\}$.

2.5.2 Sampling-based Moment Matching

A well-known approach to propagate moments of a random variable $\underline{v}$ through a nonlinear function $l_v = g_x(\phi_x(0, \pi_x(\underline{y})) + \underline{v})$ is based on samples, which are drawn randomly or deterministically [92, 93] from the original distribution $p(\underline{v})$. We can adapt this idea to calculate the mean $\mathrm{E}\{l_v\}$ and the variance $\mathrm{Var}\{l_v\}$ of l_v based on J samples of $p(\underline{v})$. This approach boils down to

1. calculate $\pi_x(\underline{y})$ using (2.13) (see Figure 2.14 left),
2. draw J samples $\{\underline{v}_1, \ldots, \underline{v}_J\}$ from $\mathcal{N}(\underline{v}; \underline{0}, \mathbf{C}_v)$,

3. simulate J measurements $\underline{\tilde{y}}_j = \phi_x(0, \pi_x(\underline{y})) + \underline{v}_j$ (see Figure 2.14 right), and

4. calculate sample moments according to

$$\mathrm{E}\{l_v\} \approx \frac{1}{J}\sum_{j=1}^{J} g_x(\underline{\tilde{y}}_j) , \tag{2.36}$$

$$\mathrm{Var}\{l_v\} \approx \frac{1}{J}\sum_{j=1}^{J} \left(g_x(\underline{\tilde{y}}_j)^2 - \mathrm{E}\{l_v\}^2 \right) .$$

It is important to note that this sampling-based approach can easily be also applied to anisotropic noise with covariance matrices $\mathbf{C}_v$. We recommend drawing the noise samples deterministically (e.g., by using [92]) as this allows keeping the numbers of samples low and, in addition, ensures reproducible results.

2.5.3 Closed-Form Moment Matching

For the special case of the Euclidean distance and a boundary with existing derivatives, there is a closed-form solution available for $\mathrm{E}\{l_v\}$ and $\mathrm{Var}\{l_v\}$. This solution goes back to [94] and was used by Okatani [18], in order to re-engineer a biased GAM-likelihood. That is, for a given source $\phi_x(s)$ on the boundary, the signed Euclidean distance of its expected measurements to the curve is approximately Gaussian distributed, where the moments of the Gaussian depend on the local *mean curvature* $\kappa_x(s)$ of the boundary and the extent σ_v^2 of the noise. Generally, the mean curvature is the arithmetic average of the *principal curvatures* [95]. For the case of a 1D curve in 2D space, the mean curvature is given by

$$\kappa_x(s) = \frac{\phi_x^{(1)'}(s) \cdot \phi_x^{(2)''}(s) - \phi_x^{(1)''}(s) \cdot \phi_x^{(2)'}}{\left(\phi_x^{(1)'}(s)^2 + \phi_x^{(2)''}(s)^2 \right)^{\frac{3}{2}}} , \tag{2.37}$$

where $\phi_x^{(1)}(s)$, $\phi_x^{(2)}(s)$ are abbreviations for the first and second components of $\phi_x(0, s)$, and the terms $(\cdot)'$ and $(\cdot)''$ represent the first and second derivatives of these scalar components with respect to s. Generalizations to higher dimensions are discussed in [95, 96].

Based on the mean curvature, the closed-form approximation for constraints in a d-dimensional space can be boiled down to

1. calculate $s_y = \pi_x(\underline{y})$ using (2.13) (see Figure 2.15 left)
2. calculate mean curvature $\kappa_x(s_y)$ at $\phi_x(0, s_y)$ using (2.37) (see Figure 2.15 right)
3. calculate moments according to

$$\mathrm{E}\{l_v\} = \sigma_v^2 \left(\frac{1}{2} \cdot (d-1) \cdot \kappa_x(s_y)\right) , \tag{2.38}$$

$$\mathrm{Var}\{l_v\} = \sigma_v^2 \left(1 - \sigma_v^2 \left(\frac{1}{2} \cdot (d-1) \cdot \kappa_x(s_y)\right)^2\right)^2 ,$$

where d is the dimension of the measurements.

In 2D for $d = 2$, approximating the constraint locally by its mean curvature allows for a very intuitive geometric interpretation, based on the fact that the curvature κ actually is the absolute reciprocal radius of the osculating circle $r = 1/|\kappa|$. In consequence, the constraint is locally approximated by its *osculating circle* as indicated in the right part of Figure 2.15. Note that the sign of the curvature in (2.38) is important, as it distinguishes concave from convex parts of the constraint.

2.5.4 Deriving the Measurement Update

Finally, for deriving the measurement update step using the new Partial Information Model, we can either use a nonlinear Kalman filter update, or a Particle Filter update, both of which are introduced in Appendix A.

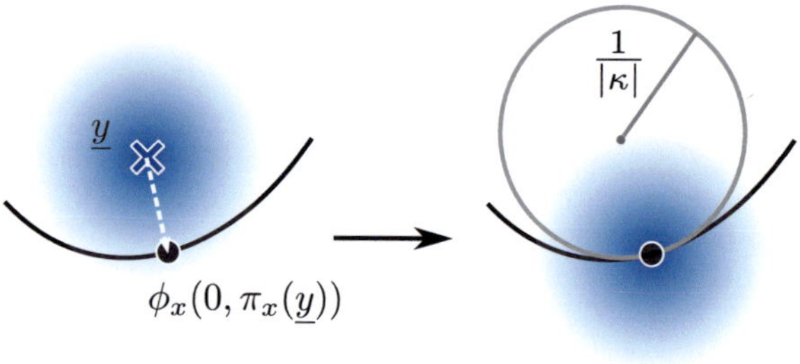

Figure 2.15.: Analytic approximation of the partial noise using the local mean curvature κ of the constraint.

Nonlinear Kalman Filter Update For the nonlinear Kalman filter update according to Algorithm A.1, the joint distribution of measurement and state has to be calculated using the PIM measurement equation. In contrast to the generic measurement function $\underline{y} = h(\underline{x}, \underline{v})$ from (2.3), the proposed PIM measurement equation $0 = h(\underline{x}, l_v, \underline{y})$ from (2.34) slightly differs in the sense that it produces pseudo measurements 0 rather than the original measurement $\underline{y}$. Nevertheless, the classical measurement update can be derived by simply assuming 0 to be the measurement and $\underline{y}$ to be a parameter.

Particle Filter Update For the particle filter update according to Algorithm A.2, we have to evaluate the likelihood for a set of instances of the state $\underline{x}$. For using the PIM, we can simply substitute the generic likelihood function $p(\underline{y}|\underline{x})$ by the partial likelihood $p(l_y|\underline{x}, s_y)$ from (2.35).

2.6 Evaluation

Let us now study the new model and its estimation quality. For this purpose, we (i) show that the PIM theoretically yields an unbiased estimator, (ii) investigate the quality of its Gaussian approximation, and (iii) evaluate its performance in two recursive ellipse estimation experiments against the state of the art.

2.6.1 Unbiasedness

We start with a theoretical analysis of potential estimation bias in PIMs. Godambe and Thompson [73] defined that an *estimating equation*, i.e., an implicit measurement equation $h^*(\underline{x}, \underline{y}) = 0$, is unbiased if

$$\mathrm{E}\big\{h^*(\underline{x}, \underline{y})\big\} = 0 \tag{2.39}$$

holds for the true parameters $\underline{x}$. That is, if we had an infinite number of measurements $\underline{y}$, the estimating equation would be fulfilled in average. This definition was motivated by the fact that the likelihood $\mathcal{N}(h^*(\underline{x}, \underline{y}); 0, \sigma^2)$ then has a maximum for the true parameters which, in consequence, ensures that a maximum likelihood estimator theoretically can converge to the true parameters. In addition, they found that an originally biased estimating equation $h(\underline{x}, \underline{y}) = 0$, which includes a nuisance parameter s, can be modified in order to make it unbiased in the sense of (2.39). For this purpose, let $\phi_x(s)$ with $s \in S$ denote all points, which fulfill the original estimating equation $h(\underline{x}, \phi(s)) = 0$. Then, in order to obtain an unbiased estimating equation, they propose to subtract the expected value $\mathrm{E}\{h(\underline{x}, \phi_x(s) + \underline{v}\}$ from the original measurement equation in the form of $h^*(\underline{x}, \underline{y}) = h(\underline{x}, \underline{y}) - \mathrm{E}\{h(\underline{x}, \phi_x(s) + \underline{v}\}$ with respect to the noise variable $\underline{v}$. For this derivation, the unknown nuisance parameter s is to be substituted by its maximum likelihood estimate.

Following this approach, the PIM measurement equation (2.33) can be interpreted as an unbiased estimating equation

$$h^*(\underline{x}, \underline{y}) = g_x(\underline{y}) - \mathrm{E}\big\{g_x(\phi_x(\pi_x(\underline{y})) + \underline{v})\big\} \ , \tag{2.40}$$

where the nuisance parameter s has been set to its maximum likelihood estimate $\pi_x(\underline{y})$. In consequence, The PIM is theoretically unbiased according to (2.39).

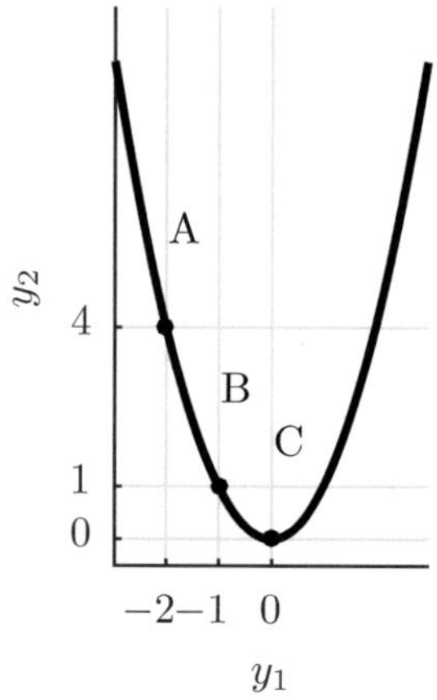

Figure 2.16.: Considered parabola. Three locations A = $(-2, 4)$, B = $(-1, 1)$, and C = $(0, 0)$ are used for evaluation.

Unbiasedness of PIMs with other ls-coordinate systems From the unbiasedness condition in (2.39), we can conclude a general statement about ls-coordinate systems in a PIM. That is, as long as the s_y-component is chosen to referring to the most likely source on the boundary, we can choose any other constraint function $g_x(\underline{y})$ and still obtain an unbiased estimating equation (2.40).

2.6.2 Approximation Quality of the Partial Noise

In Section 2.5, we presented two approaches to approximate the partial noise $p(l_v|\underline{x}, s_y)$ for the PIM by a Gaussian distribution $\mathcal{N}(\mathrm{E}\{l_v\}, \mathrm{Var}\{l_v\})$. We considered sampling-based and closed-form moment matching of the propagated sensor noise variable $\underline{v} \sim \mathcal{N}(\underline{0}, \mathbf{C}_v)$. In this section, we empirically compare both techniques against the true moments. We decided for a parabola to be the test shape as it has a varying curvature along the curve. Evaluating different curvatures is important, as we can conclude from [18] that the moments of the partial noise essentially depend on (i) the local curvature of the boundary and (ii) the level of the noise. By considering different parts of the parabola, we can compare the moments for different local curvatures and different levels of noise. In order to allow a fair comparison, we focus on isotropic noise as the closed-form approach cannot deal with anisotropic noise.

Modeling a Parabola A parabola is a polynomial of degree two that can be described by three parameters $\underline{x} = [a, b, c]^{\mathrm{T}}$ and has a boundary function

$$\phi_x(s) = \begin{bmatrix} s \\ a \cdot s^2 + b \cdot s + c \end{bmatrix} , \tag{2.41}$$

where $s \in \mathbb{R}$. We consider the task of approximating the moments $\mathrm{E}\{l_v\}$, $\mathrm{Var}\{l_v\}$ of the partial noise. For the sampling-based moment matching, it is required to simulate J measurements $\underline{\tilde{y}}$ of $\phi_x(s)$ and then find their most likely points on the parabola. This calculation can be performed by solving

$$s_y = \arg\min_{s \in \mathbb{R}} \|\underline{\tilde{y}} - \phi_x(s)\| ,$$

which refers to finding the minimum root of the derivative $\|\underline{\tilde{y}} - \phi_x(s)\|'$ with respect to s. As the expression simplifies to a polynomial of degree three, all roots can be calculated analytically. For the closed-form approach [18], the parabola boundary is to be approximated by its osculating circle at $\phi_x(s)$. For this purpose, we need the formula for the parabola curvature $\kappa(s)$, which can be evaluated by plugging (2.41) into (2.37) according to

$$\kappa(s) = \frac{2a}{((2as + b)^2 + 1)^{\frac{3}{2}}} .$$

Experiment For the empirical comparison, the parabola in Figure 2.16 with $\underline{x} = [1, 0, 0]^{\mathrm{T}}$ is used. We focus on three locations A, B, and C, with increasing local curvature. The ground truth moments of the partial noise for noise levels from $\sigma^2 = 0.01$ to $\sigma^2 = 0.75$ are calculated using sampling-based moment matching (2.36) with 10^7 random samples. Against this ground truth we compare three approaches.

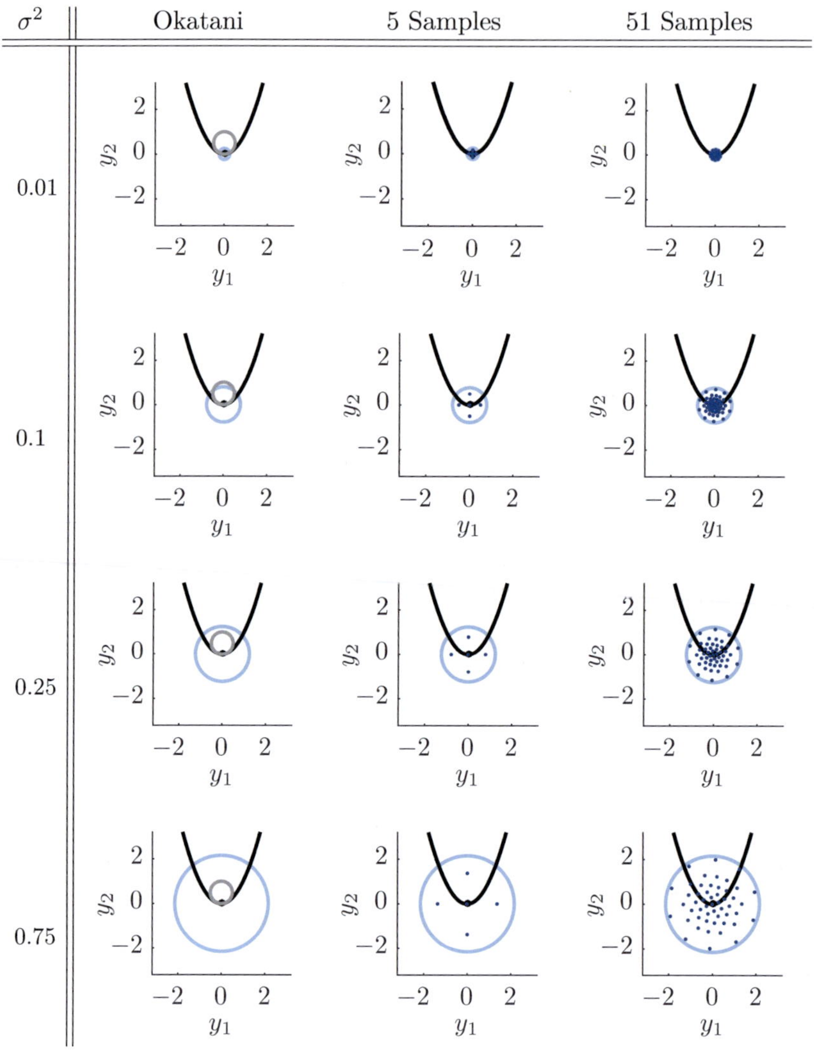

Figure 2.17.: Approximating the moments of the partial noise for a parabola at position $\mathrm{C} = (0, 0)$ and isotropic noise with variance σ^2. Each column shows one technique. Within each column, the cells illustrate different noise levels. The 3σ-bounds are drawn as light blue circles.

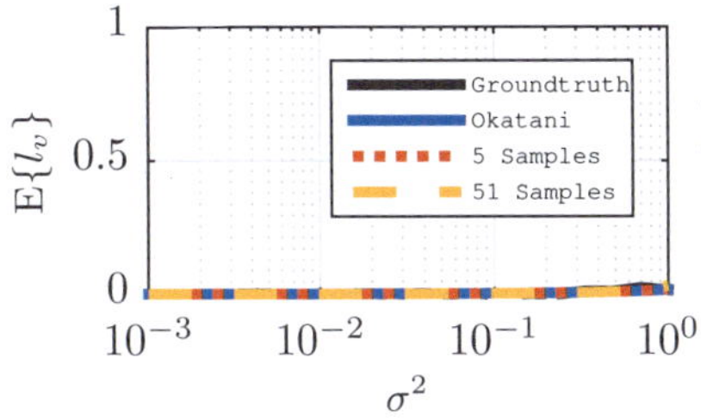

(a) Mean at location A.

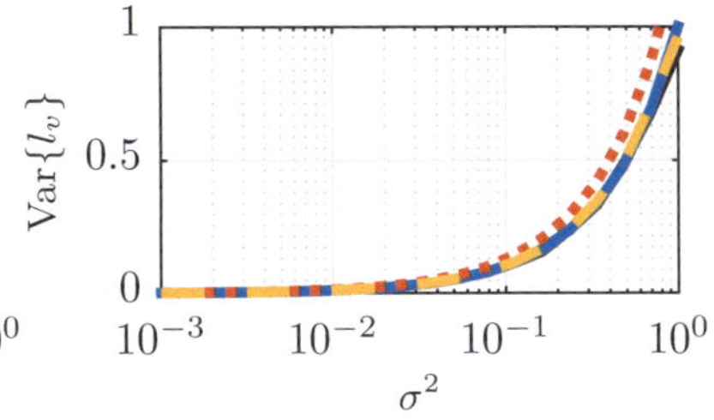

(b) Variance at location A.

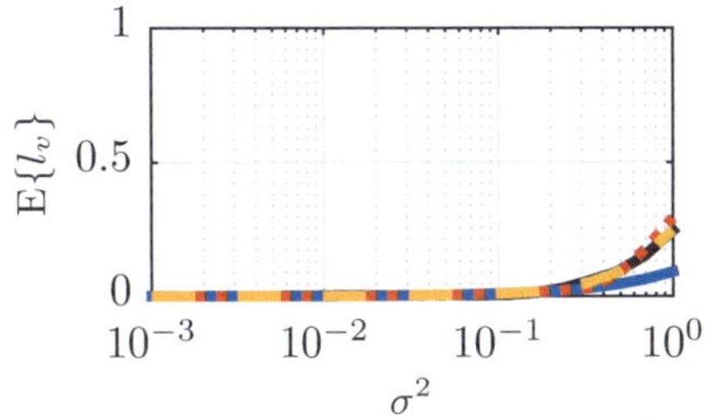

(c) Mean at location B.

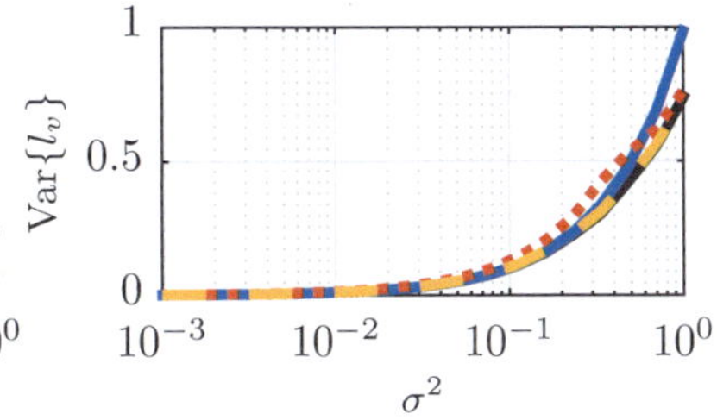

(d) Variance at location B.

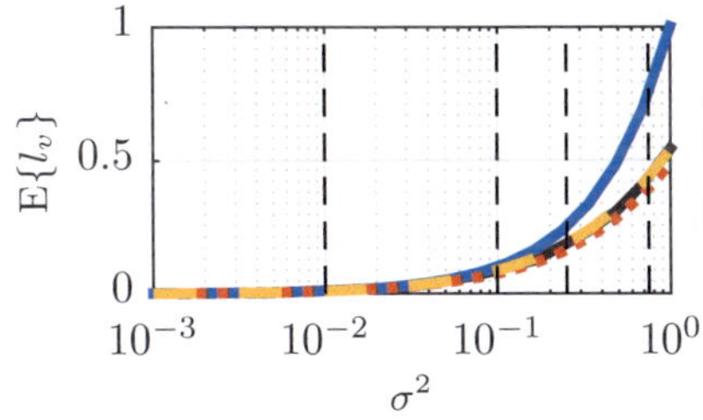

(e) Mean at location C.

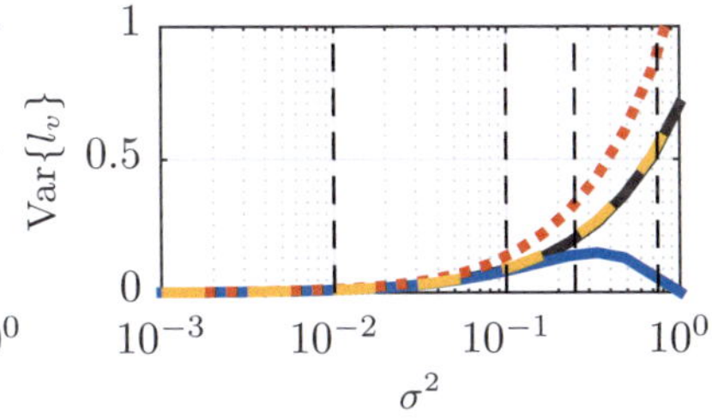

(f) Variance at location C.

Figure 2.18.: Moments of the partial noise of the parabola at the different locations A, B, and C.

- **Okatani:** closed-form moment matching using (2.38),
- **5 Samples:** sampling-based moment matching using (2.36) and the deterministic sampling technique known from the unscented Kalman filter [92], and
- **51 Samples:** sampling-based moment matching using (2.36) and the deterministic sampling technique proposed in [93].

Results Figure 2.17 illustrates intermediate steps for the different approaches at location C.

In each image, the 3σ-bounds of the actual sensor noise are drawn as a blue circle. These circles encompass 99.7% of the probability mass and can be interpreted as the region of interest where the curvature of the boundary affects the moments of the partial noise. In the left column, the 3σ-bounds are drawn against the osculating circle (gray) that approximates the parabola boundary in "Okatani". The second and third column show the simulated measurements $\underline{\tilde{y}}$ for the "5 Samples" and "51 Samples" approach, respectively. As can be seen from the figure, the approximation of the parabola boundary by its osculating circle in "Okatani" is only valid for small regions of interest, i.e., for low noise levels. In contrast, the sampling-based approaches always consider the entire boundary. In consequence, we expect the sampling-based moment matching to yield more accurate results than the closed-form approach with increasing noise.

Figure 2.18 visualizes the numerical results of the comparison. In the first column, the graphs show the mean $\mathrm{E}\{l_v\}$ at each location for the different noise levels and the second column shows the variances $\mathrm{Var}\{l_v\}$. For location C, the dashed black lines in Figure 2.18 refer to the noise levels that are considered in Figure 2.17. The mean determines the average signed distance from measurements of $\phi_x(s)$ to the curve. At location A, the parabola is approximately linear and results in a mean of value 0 for all considered noise levels, as the probability mass divided equally on both sides of the curve [159]. As can be seen in Figure 2.18a, all approaches approximately coincide with the ground truth. This also holds for the closed-form approach, as the osculating circle at location A has a large radius about 35 and approximates the linear part of the curve quite well. At location B and C, the curvature becomes increasingly large and causes a biased ratio of probability mass which results in increasing values for the mean.

While all approaches perform very similar for low noise, the sampling-based approaches are more accurate than "Okatani" for high noise. This result is as we expected due to the invalid circular approximation of the parabola curve. The closed-form moment matching (2.38) is even subject to a singularity where the variance for specific combinations of noise level and curvature yields 0 values. This issue can be seen in Figure 2.18f. The comparison of the sampling-based approaches lets us conclude that the mean $\mathrm{E}\{l_v\}$ can be approximated accurately in both approaches, while the variance $\mathrm{Var}\{l_v\}$ can only be accurately approximated by the "51 Samples" approach.

2.6.3 Estimation Quality of the Partial Information Model

In this section, we evaluate the PIM in the common task of tracking a moving ellipse. Specifically, we conducted two Monte Carlo experiments, one without and one with occlusion.

Experiment We consider recursively estimating an ellipse with size $[a, b]^{\mathrm{T}} = [2, 1]^{\mathrm{T}}$ that moves along the U-shaped track in Figure 2.19. While it is moving, a simulated sensor performs 250 point cloud measurements, where each of contains 10 noisy points. For some selected locations, exemplary measurements are drawn as black dots in Figure 2.19. In the first experiment, the measurement sources are uniformly drawn from the full ellipse boundary and distorted by anisotropic Gaussian noise with $\mathbf{C}_v = 2 \cdot \mathrm{diag}(10^{-1}, 10^{-2})$ (see Figure 2.19a). In the second experiment, we simulate a permanent occlusion of the ellipse front and draw sources only from the visible fraction (see Figure 2.19b). For the evaluation, we consider the traditional models from Section 2.3, as well as the proposed Partial Information Model.

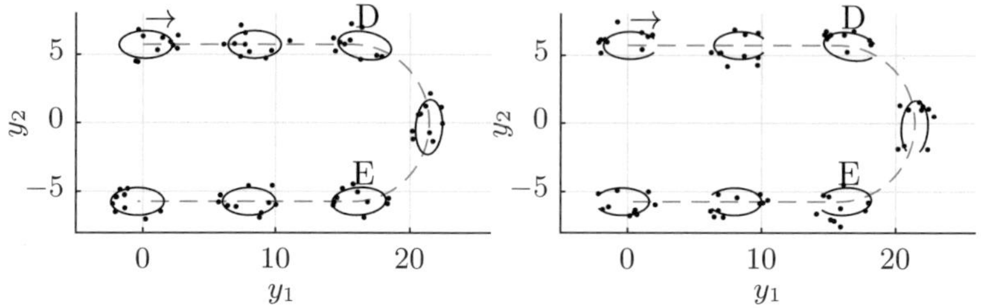

(a) Without occlusion. **(b)** With occlusion.

Figure 2.19.: Ellipse tracking experiments. In (a), measurements originate from the whole ellipse. In (b), only a part of the ellipse is measured. The labels "D" and "E" mark motion changes.

- **Known Association Model:** For reference, we set up the KAM from (2.12) and provide it with the true source index s^* for each measurement. Due to the perfect association of the KAM, it can be seen as a benchmark for the other models.
- **Spatial Distribution Model:** We also consider an SDM (2.10), where $p(s|\underline{x})$ is modeled by a uniform distribution over the full ellipse boundary. This uniform distribution is indeed true for the experiment without occlusion, but not for the one with occlusion. The integral is numerically evaluated, using a polygon approximation [159] for the ellipse with 72 vertices.
- **Greedy Association Model:** As a representative for the distance-minimizing approaches, we set up a GAM according to (2.15). For finding the most likely sources on the ellipse, we again approximate the ellipse by a polygon.
- **Partial Information Model:** For the proposed PIM (2.35), we use the sampling-based moment-matching technique from Section 2.5.2 with 5 samples [92] for calculating mean $\mathrm{E}\{l_v\}$, and variance $\mathrm{Var}\{l_v\}$ of the partial noise. Again, we use a polygon approximation of the ellipse for finding the most likely sources.

In order to allow for a fair comparison of these models, we want to use the same filter for all models. Actually, we would prefer using a simple nonlinear Kalman filter such as the EKF or UKF. However, due to the high complexity of the SDM, these filters are not suitable. In consequence, we decide for a *Progressive Gaussian Filter* (PGF) [97], which is a nonlinear Gaussian filter with a particle-based measurement update. Between the measurement update steps, we add prediction steps using a *constant velocity model* for the position [47], and a *constant turn rate model* for the orientation [47]. The process covariance matrix is set to a diagonal matrix $10^{-6} \cdot \mathbf{I}$ for position, angle and axes, and $10^{-5} \cdot \mathbf{I}$ for velocity and turn rate, in order to adapt to motion changes. The initial ellipse state $\underline{x}$ for the estimators is set to an ellipse that is obtained from a set of initial measurements. Specifically, the center is set to the mean of the initial measurements, and the angle and ellipse axes a, b are set according to the principal components of their covariance. The initial covariance is set to a diagonal matrix $10^{-1} \cdot \mathbf{I}$. The following results are obtained from 1000 runs of each experiment.

Results Figure 2.20 and Figure 2.21 visualize the intermediate results for both experiments. In (a-d), the average estimated ellipses are drawn against the black ground truth ellipses and in (e-g), the RMSEs for selected parameters are shown. As can be seen, the KAM approach obtains unbiased average estimates for both experiments, as the blue ellipses perfectly cover the black ground truth. This unbiasedness is also true for the PIM approach, as the red ellipses perfectly cover the true ones, too. In contrast, the SDM approach finds the true ellipse in the experiment without occlusion, yet in the presence of occlusion it produces biased estimates. This can be seen in Figure 2.21d, where the purple ellipses do not cover the black ground truth. This systematic error for position and semi-major axis also affects the RMSE for position and extent in Figure 2.21f and Figure 2.21g. The GAM approach is even worse than the SDM, as it is subject to bias for both experiments. The average ellipses are representative, as their standard deviation through all runs and parameters is in a magnitude of 10^{-2}. In order to illustrate what that means, several estimates for the last time step 250 are drawn together in Figure 2.22 and Figure 2.23.

These behaviors have an intuitive interpretation: The SDM bias boils down to the correct (without occlusion) and incorrect (with occlusion) assumptions about $p(s|\underline{x})$, and the GAM bias is a result of its corrupt likelihood (see Section 2.3.3). As our approach neither requires assumptions on $p(s|\underline{x})$, nor builds upon a corrupt probabilistic model, it is not affected by these systematic errors.

However, the proposed PIM-based estimator has a slightly slower convergence compared to the SDM approach. We suspect this issue to be the price of ignoring the source distribution. In numerical terms, where the SDM approach finds the true ellipse right after 10 update steps, our approach takes approximately 25 updates until convergence. Even though this drawback should be of minor importance in practice, it must be kept in mind when designing the initialization procedure.

2.7 Conclusions from Chapter 2

In this chapter, we have developed a new probabilistic model for extended object tracking that can be used in situations when (i) there is no knowledge about the distribution of the measurement sources and (ii) in the presence of high (potentially anisotropic) sensor noise. Under these conditions, traditional models, such as the Spatial Distribution Model and the Greedy Association Model are likely to be biased.

The key idea of the new Partial Information Model essentially is to remove the association heuristics from the general probabilistic model. For this purpose, we transform the coordinate system of the measurement domain in a way that one axis lies in the object boundary, and place the remaining one such that the correlation of the sensor noise is minimal to those in the boundary. The axis in the boundary then specifies "where" on the object a measurement corresponds to and the remaining axis determines "how well" it fits to the boundary. Usually, designing a probabilistic model for the “where”-component requires knowledge of the originating source of a measurement. However, by expressing the measurements in this transformed coordinate system, a partial likelihood can be derived for the “how well”-component exclusively that does not require modeling the originating source.

The resulting estimator based on this model was shown to be theoretically unbiased and to outperform state-of-the-art models in a simulated tracking experiment. Specifically, we considered the common task of recursively estimating the parameters of a moving ellipse based on sequentially arriving measurements with anisotropic Gaussian noise characteristics and unexpected occlusions.

In the considered tracking experiment, we observed that our approach converges to the true ellipse boundary, regardless of whether measurements originate only from a part of the ellipse boundary or whether they were affected by high anisotropic noise. The common approaches that (i) use a spatial distribution or (ii) minimize a distance to the boundary were either biased when applied to a non-uniform source distribution or biased in the case of high noise. In numerical terms, the systematic error in the estimated parameters could be reduced by a full order of magnitude compared to both traditional approaches.

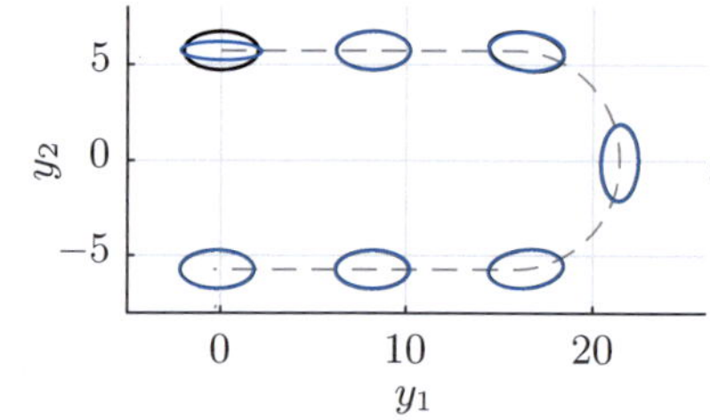

(a) Known Association Model (KAM).

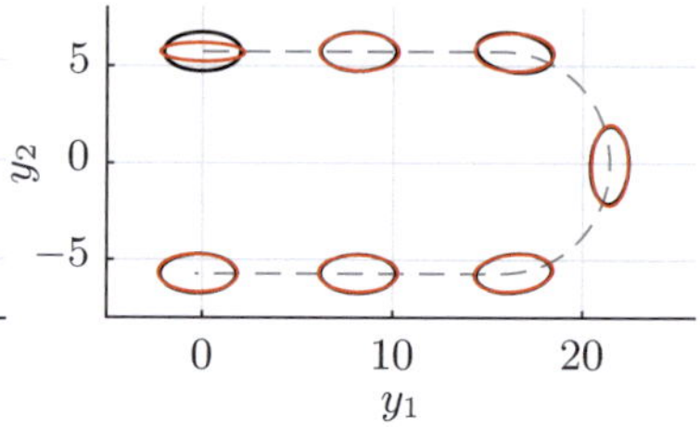

(b) Partial Information Model (PIM).

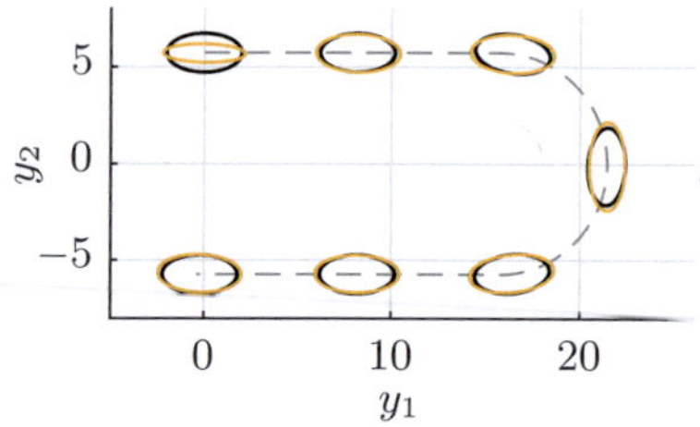

(c) Greedy Association Model (GAM).

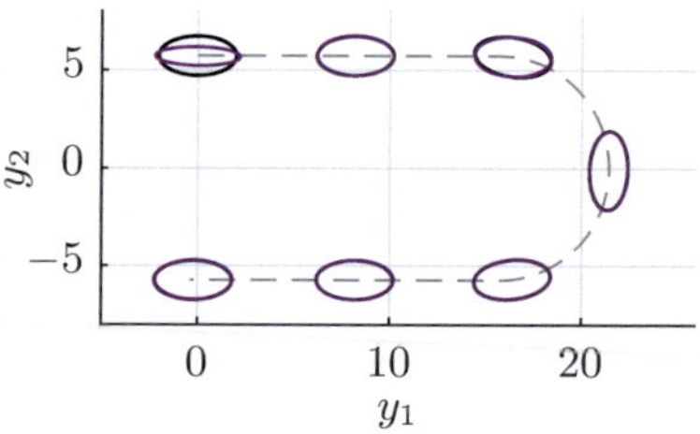

(d) Spatial Distribution Model (SDM).

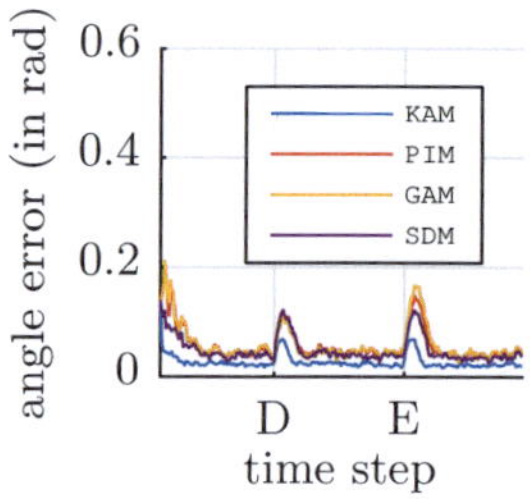

(e) Orientation.

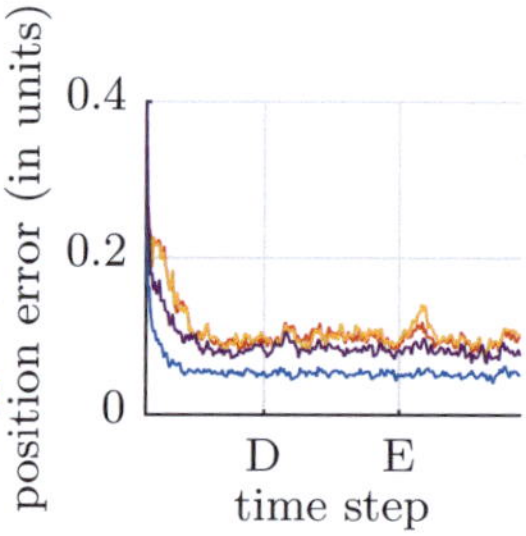

(f) Position.

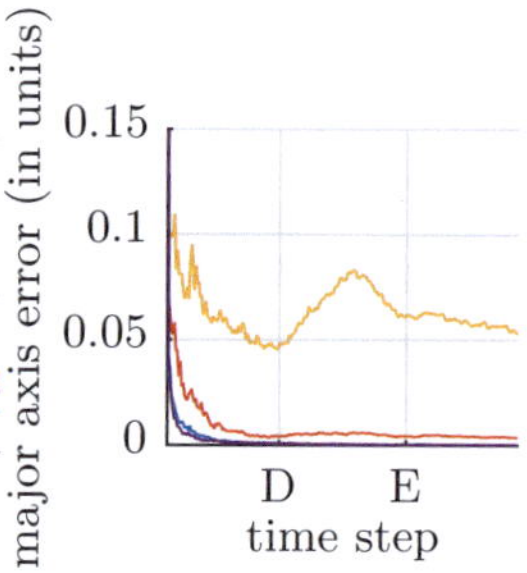

(g) Extent.

Figure 2.20.: Results of the experiment without occlusion.

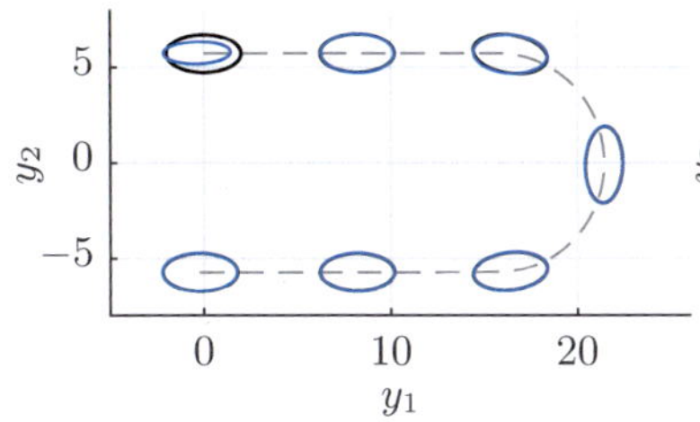

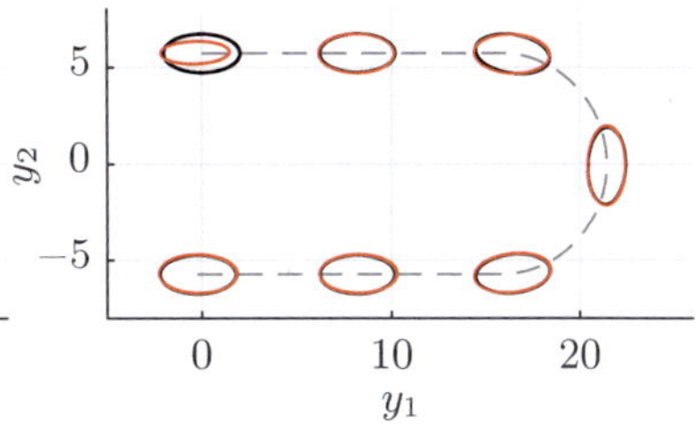

(a) Known Association Model (KAM). **(b)** Partial Information Model (PIM).

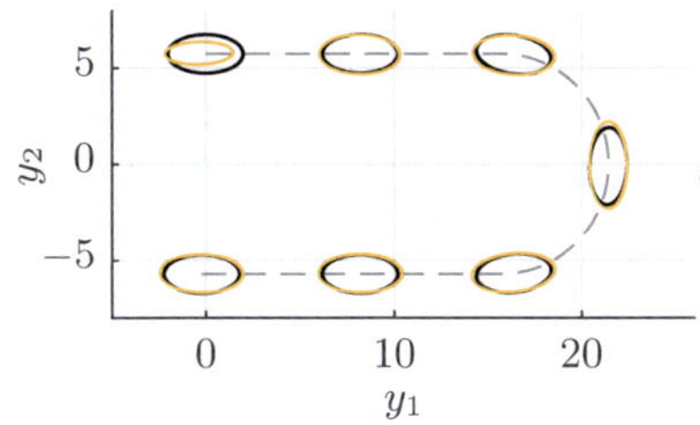

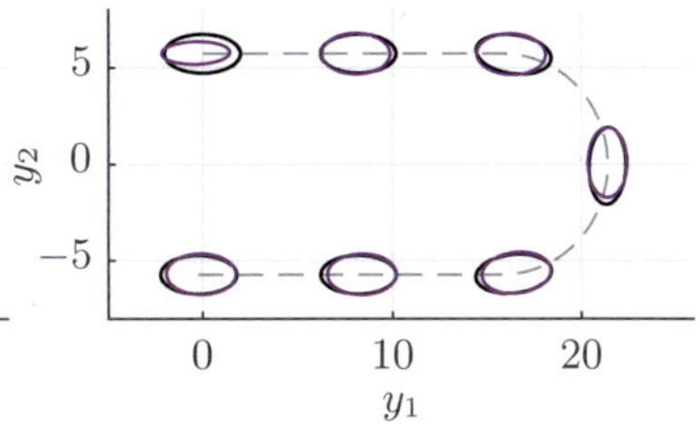

(c) Greedy Association Model (GAM). **(d)** Spatial Distribution Model (SDM).

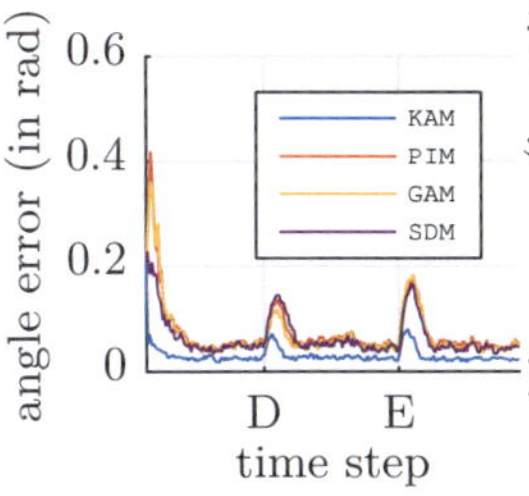

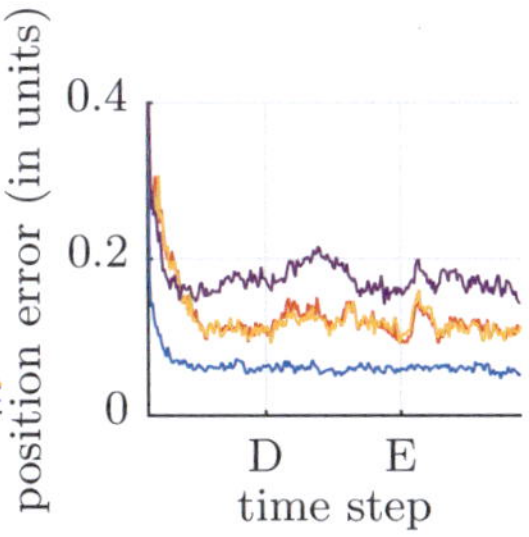

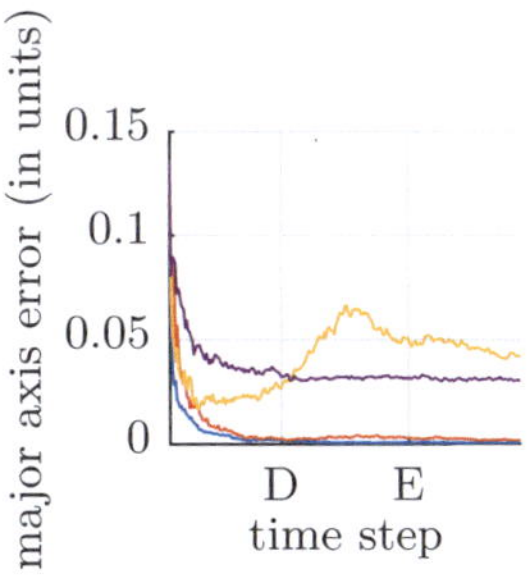

(e) Orientation. **(f)** Position. **(g)** Extent.

Figure 2.21.: Results of the experiment with occlusion.

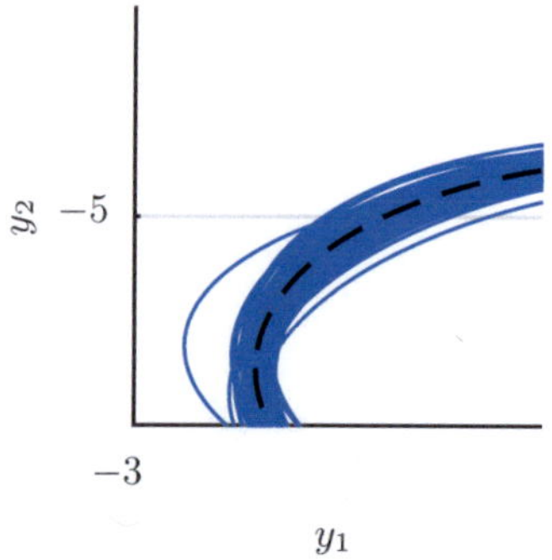

(a) KAM.

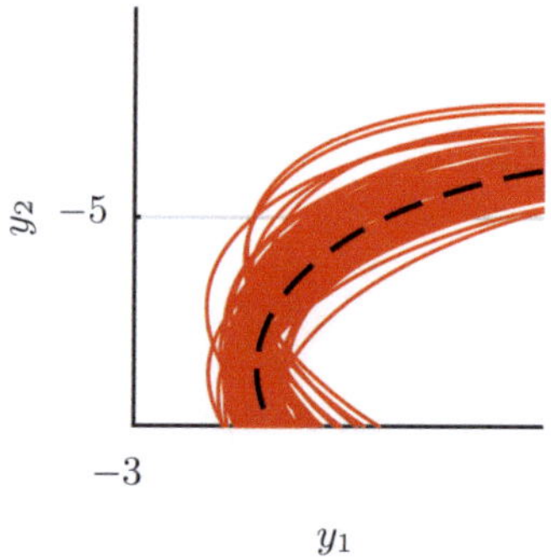

(b) PIM.

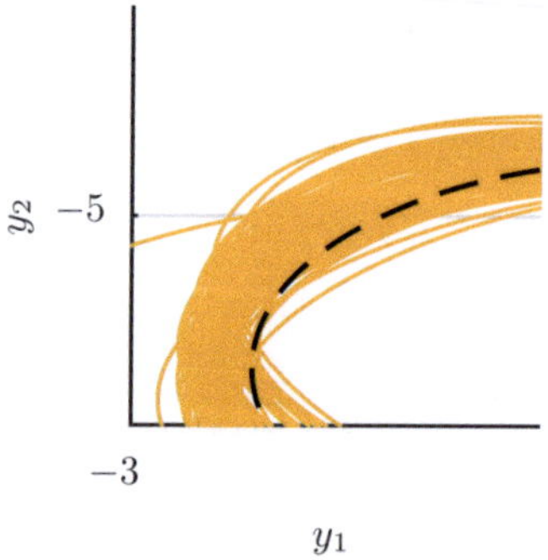

(c) GAM.

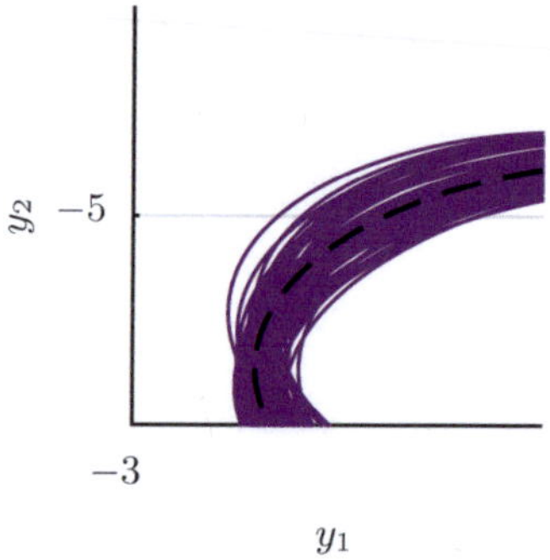

(d) SDM.

Figure 2.22.: Estimates at time step 250 for the experiment without occlusion.

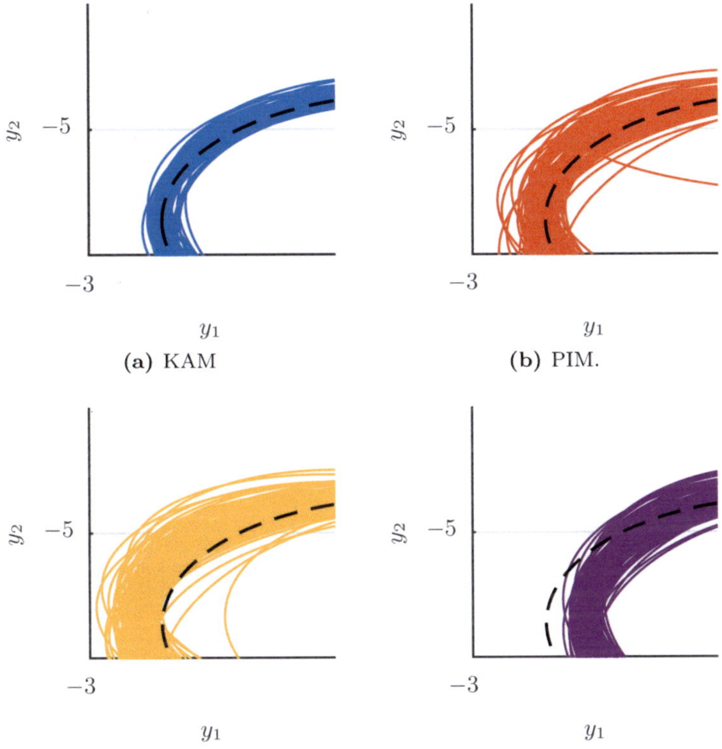

(a) KAM

(b) PIM.

(c) GAM.

(d) SDM.

Figure 2.23.: Estimates at time step 250 for the experiment with occlusion.

CHAPTER 3

Modeling 3D Extended Objects by Transforming Plane Curves

Contents

In this chapter, we develop a tracking algorithm for objects in 3D based on the theoretical insights from the previous chapter. In contrast to situations, where the object shape is known in advance and only its pose is to be estimated, we look at situations where the shape initially is unknown as well (Challenge 2). Then, the question is

how to model arbitrary shapes in 3D?

As the primary requirement, the desired model should be capable of representing a wide spectrum of geometries in order to adapt to various objects. In addition, it must be flexible enough to scale the shape detail from rough to fine in order to adapt to a different amount of measurement information. Thus, the goals in this chapter are (i) to specify a flexible model that relates a manageable number of parameters to potentially complex surfaces in 3D and (ii) to develop a tracking algorithm for this model.

In literature, there are roughly two lines of research to this task. On the one side, *non-parametric* models can represent detailed shapes by occupancy grids [26], point clouds [9], or polygon meshes [23]. However, varying the shape complexity requires non-trivial refinement and coarsening operations. On the other side, *parametric* models typically use only a small number of parameters, as they focus on simple shapes such as ellipsoids [40] or bounding boxes [42]. In this thesis, we follow the parametric approach, but, in contrast to related approaches, we consider more general 3D objects. For this purpose, we propose to construct surfaces by *transforming* plane curves. In particular, using a combination of translation, rotation, and scaling operations allows for constructing complex shapes, such as the ones shown in Figure 3.1. However, developing a probabilistic model for these shapes is challenging, as it may have issues such as bias or unobservable parameters. Even the proposed Partial Information Model from Section 2.4 may yield an estimator that is not capable of finding values for specific parameters, e.g., the length of an object.

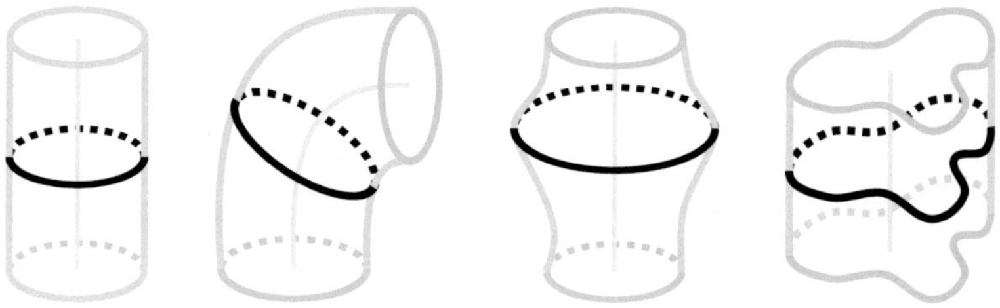

(a) Translation. **(b)** Translation and rotation. **(c)** Translation and scaling. **(d)** Translation of complex curve.

Figure 3.1.: Considered types of transformation: while (a) and (b) only affect the pose of the plane curve, (c) and (d) also affect its shape.

Contribution Our main contribution in this chapter is the *3D Random Hypersurface Model* (3DRHM), a new probabilistic model for extended objects in 3D which combines ideas from the elemental models from the previous chapter. Specifically, by assuming a probability for each transformed curve and ignoring (or approximating) the unknown information of "where" on the curve a measurement corresponds to, the new model can be seen as a combination of the Spatial Distribution Model and the Partial Information Model (or Greedy Association Model). In addition, it is closely related to the Random Hypersurface Model for region and group tracking from [63]. The resulting estimator

- is capable of estimating all parameters, including the object length,
- inherits the unbiasedness from the Partial Information Model,
- and can still be implemented using common recursive Bayesian estimation techniques such as a nonlinear Kalman filter.

For illustration, we explicitly develop estimators for a cylinder, torus, cone, and extruded complex curve. In simulations, we show that our approach outperforms state-of-the-art estimation techniques in terms of accuracy.

Remark 3.1. *This chapter builds on work presented in [151, 149, 156, 166, 160].*

3.1 Related Work

Let us briefly discuss related tracking approaches and modeling techniques. In doing so, we focus on works that simultaneously estimate pose and shape parameters of objects or scenes.

Random Hypersurface Models were proposed in [63] as a means for modeling extended objects in 2D, where measurements not only originate from the boundary of the object, but also from its interior. Based on RHMs, regions with different shape were modeled, such as ellipses [63], star-convex shapes [98], ellipse mixtures [99], as well as non-convex polygons [163]. We will heavily rely on the idea of RHMs when deriving the probabilistic model for transformed curves in this chapter. In the context of region tracking, there are also approaches using the popular Random Matrices approach [65, 80], where the extent of an object is represented as the mean and covariance matrix of a Gaussian distribution. Multiple random matrices were combined to model more complex shapes in 2D [100]. Using Extended Gaussian images [101] to represent shapes was proposed in [102, 103] for pose estimation and in [104] for surface reconstruction.

Spherical harmonics [105] were already used in medical applications [106] to represent complex shapes in 3D. Transforming a curve along another curve was proposed in [43], in order to reconstruct missing parts of a measured point cloud (see Figure 3.2a). In [107], the authors proceed one step further by generating a complex shape from back-projecting and intersecting silhouettes (see Figure 3.2b). Active contours [20] and active surfaces [108] can be used to reconstruct the shape of objects by minimizing some kind of energy function. However, active contours are typically used together with dense image measurements, as the energy terms depend on the number of measurements.

Another related line of work is estimating shapes that are connected via joints [109, 110]. These approaches essentially perform extended object tracking of multiple objects, which are connected via geometrical or physical constraints. Note that the models that are developed in this thesis can be easily incorporated in their frameworks.

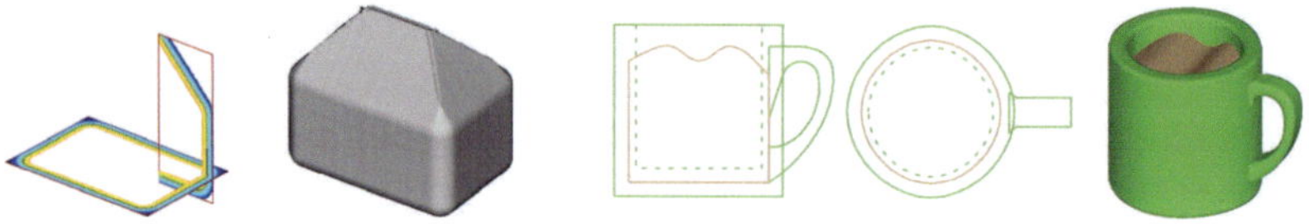

(a) Transformed curves [43] © 2012 IEEE.

(b) Backprojection of silhouettes [107] © 2010 Association for Computing Machinery, Inc. Reprinted by permission.

Figure 3.2.: Related Approaches.

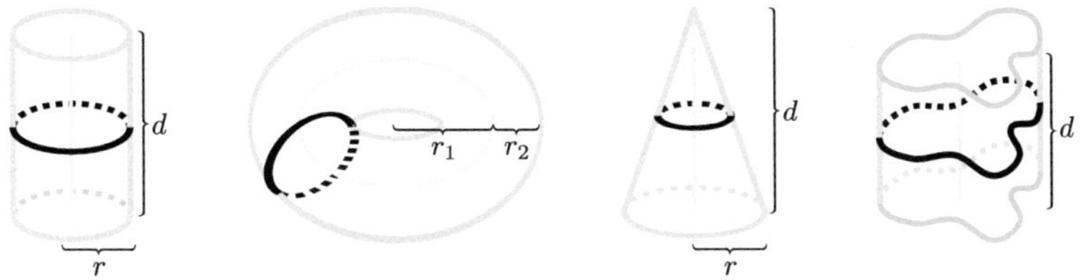

(a) Cylinder. **(b)** Torus. **(c)** Cone. **(d)** Extrusion.

Figure 3.3.: Geometric shapes, constructed by plane curve transformations.

3.2 Considered Types of Transformation

In this section, we show how to use plane curves to construct the surface of an object. A *plane curve* is one that can be embedded into a 2D plane, such as the circle in Figure 3.1(a-c). Let the parameters that are required to specify the pose and shape of the surface be aggregated in the state vector $\underline{x}$. Then, modeling a surface refers to the task of (i) specifying a function $\phi_x : S \to \mathbb{R}^2$ that lets us iterate through all points in the curve, and (ii) embedding it into 3D space by applying a transformation $\Phi_x : S \times U \to \mathbb{R}^3$. In particular, we consider transformations

$$\Phi_{x,u}(s) = \mathbf{R}_u \begin{bmatrix} f_u \cdot \phi_x(s) \\ 0 \end{bmatrix} + \underline{c}_u \ , \tag{3.1}$$

where $s \in S \subseteq \mathbb{R}$ iterates through the curve and $u \in U \subseteq \mathbb{R}$ controls the transformation. We will denote (3.1) as the *surface function.*

Using these parameters, the plane curve can be translated and rotated using the vector $\underline{c}_u \in \mathbb{R}^3$, and the 3×3 rotation matrix $\mathbf{R}_u$, respectively. The scalar $f_u \in \mathbb{R}$ allows scaling a given curve, and by using different curve functions $\phi_x(s)$, the shape itself can be modified. Note that in (3.1), we considered the object in its local coordinate system. Arbitrary object poses can be implemented by applying a rigid transformation $\mathbf{R}_x \Phi_{x,u}(s) + \underline{c}_x$ to the surface function. In the following, we derive specific instances of (3.1) for the shapes in Figure 3.3.

3.2.1 Translation (Cylinder)

Let us start with modeling the mantle of the cylinder in Figure 3.3a, which can be characterized by the state vector $\underline{x} = [r, d]^{\mathrm{T}}$, where r is the radius and d is the length. For the object coordinate system, let the bottom of the cylinder be centered on the origin, axis aligned, and let y_3 be the axis of extrusion. For the circular plane curve (black), we can use the function $\phi_x(s) = r \cdot [\cos(s), \sin(s)]^{\mathrm{T}}$ with $s \in [0, 2\pi)$. The translation can be modeled as a linear shift according to $\underline{c}_u = [0, 0, u \cdot d]^{\mathrm{T}}$ with $u \in [0, 1]$. The remaining transformation mechanisms for rotation and scaling are not needed and set to their respective identities $\mathbf{R}_u = \mathbf{I}$ and $f_u = 1$. Plugging all into the general formula (3.1) yields

$$\Phi_{x,u}(s) = \begin{bmatrix} r \cdot \cos(s) \\ r \cdot \sin(s) \\ u \cdot d \end{bmatrix} , \tag{3.2}$$

where each u refers to a circle in a plane that lies parallel to the y_1y_2-plane and is shifted along the y_3-axis.

3.2.2 Translation and Rotation (Torus)

By allowing translation and rotation, we can model more complex surfaces such as the torus in Figure 3.3b. Its surface can be specified by the state vector $\underline{x} = [r_1, r_2]^{\mathrm{T}}$ where r_1 is the central radius and r_2 is the lateral radius. For the object coordinate system, let the center of mass lie in the origin and the central circle lie in the y_1y_2-plane. For the circular plane curves (black), we can again use the function $\phi_x(s) = r_2 \cdot [\cos(s), \sin(s)]^{\mathrm{T}}$ with $s \in [0, 2\pi)$. The translation can be modeled as a circular function $\underline{c}_u = r_1 \cdot [\cos(u), \sin(u), 0]^{\mathrm{T}}$ with $u \in [0, 2\pi)$. Then, the rotation matrix $\mathbf{R}_u$ can be obtained using the tangent vector to the central circle at $\underline{c}_u$. Finally, by setting the scaling to $f_u = 1$, we arrive at

$$\Phi_{x,u}(s) = \begin{bmatrix} (r_1 + r_2 \cdot \cos(s)) \cdot \cos(u) \\ (r_1 + r_2 \cdot \cos(s)) \cdot \sin(u) \\ r_2 \cdot \sin(s) \end{bmatrix} . \tag{3.3}$$

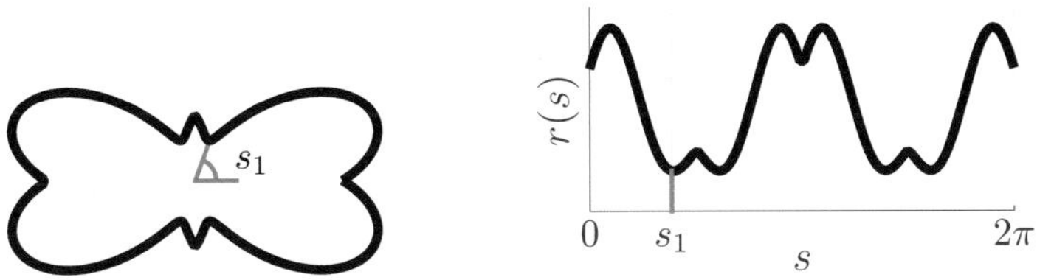

(a) Object contour. **(b)** Radius function.

Figure 3.4.: The polar function $r(s)$ specifies a radius for each angle s. The correspondence between polar function and shape contour is marked for a given s_1.

3.2.3 Translation and Scaling (Cone)

The cone in Figure 3.3c can be constructed in a similar way as the cylinder, except from an additional scaling term that controls the circle radius. The state vector is given by $\underline{x} = [r, d]^{\mathrm{T}}$, where r is the radius at the bottom and d is the height of the cone. Then, we can modify the cylinder model from (3.2) by replacing the formerly constant scaling factor by $f_u = 1 - u$, which yields the cone model

$$\Phi_{x,u}(s) = \begin{bmatrix} (1-u) \cdot r \cdot \cos(s) \\ (1-u) \cdot r \cdot \sin(s) \\ u \cdot d \end{bmatrix} , \tag{3.4}$$

where again $s \in [0, 2\pi)$ and $u \in [0, 1]$.

3.2.4 Translation of Star-convex Curve (Extruded Curve)

Instead of using circular curves, we could also use more general ones. In [98], it was proposed to use polar functions for star-convex curves in $\mathbb{R}^2$. Star-convex means that there is a point within the shape, where each line segment to any point on the boundary remains in the shape. This allows for a convenient representation by means of a polar function $r(s)$ that returns the radius for a given angle $s \in [0, 2\pi)$, as shown in Figure 3.4.

Specifically, $r(s)$ can be implemented by means of a Fourier series

$$r(s) = \frac{a_0}{2} + \sum_{m=1}^{M} a_m \cos(m \cdot s) + b_m \sin(m \cdot s) \tag{3.5}$$

that is controlled by a list of $2M + 1$ coefficients a, b.

Using this polar function, we can iterate through all points on the curve by $\phi_x(s) = r(s) \cdot [\cos(s), \sin(s)]^{\mathrm{T}}$. For the special case of $M = 0$, the corresponding function $r(s) = \frac{a_0}{2}$ specifies the constant radius of a circle. For a generalized cylinder based on star-convex curves, the state vector is given by the height d and the Fourier coefficients in the form of $\underline{x} = [d, a_0, a_1, b_1, \ldots, a_M, b_M]^{\mathrm{T}}$. Adapting the cylinder formula from (3.2), we obtain

$$\Phi_{x,u}(s) = \begin{bmatrix} r(s) \cdot \cos(s) \\ r(s) \cdot \sin(s) \\ u \cdot d \end{bmatrix} . \tag{3.6}$$

Next, we discuss the task of designing probabilistic models for these surfaces.

3.3 Probabilistic Model for Plane Curve Transformations

In this section, we derive a prototype likelihood $p(\underline{y}|\underline{x})$ for objects whose surface is constructed by transforming plane curves, and discuss solutions to the association problem. It turns out that, when using a PIM or a GAM, the resulting estimator is not capable of estimating the length parameter of the object, while it actually is when using an SDM. We study this issue for line segments, which are a special case of cylinders. Then, we introduce the Random Hypersurface Model (RHM), which will help us to overcome the length issue.

Likelihood Prototype Let us now derive a likelihood prototype $p(\underline{y}|\underline{x})$ for the considered objects from (3.1). For a given state vector $\underline{x}$, we have to model how likely it is for the surface $\Phi_{x,u}(s)$ with $u \in U$ and $s \in S$ to *produce* a measurement $\underline{y} \in \mathbb{R}^3$. As we assume additive Gaussian sensor noise, the generative measurement model can be written as

$$\underline{y} = \Phi_{x,u}(s) + \underline{v} \,, \tag{3.7}$$

where $\underline{v} \sim \mathcal{N}(\underline{0}, \mathbf{C}_v)$ is the noise term. This generative model can be rewritten as the likelihood

$$\begin{aligned} p(\underline{y}|\underline{x}) &= \int_U \int_S p(\underline{y}|\underline{x}, s, u) \cdot p(s, u|\underline{x}) \; \mathrm{d}s \; \mathrm{d}u \\ &= \int_U \int_S \underbrace{\mathcal{N}\left(\underline{y}; \Phi_{x,u}(s), \mathbf{C}_v\right)}_{\text{sensor model}} \cdot \underbrace{p(s, u|\underline{x})}_{\text{source model}} \; \mathrm{d}s \; \mathrm{d}u \end{aligned} \tag{3.8}$$

by assuming the probabilities of u and s to be known. As a reminder, the *sensor model* specifies the expected Gaussian sensor noise with covariance matrix $\mathbf{C}_v$ when measuring a specific source $\Phi_{x,u}(s)$, and the *source model* specifies how likely it is that this source is measured at all. When designing the source model $p(s, u|\underline{x})$, we are again faced with the *association problem* (Challenge 1), as it is generally not known from which point in the surface a measurement originated.

Solving the Association Problem In Chapter 2, we already discussed three elemental probabilistic models that solve the association problem, i.e., the Spatial Distribution Model, the Greedy Association Model and the proposed Partial Information Model. However, so far, we exclusively focused on shapes with a single boundary parameter s. Now, in (3.8), we additionally have to deal with the transformation parameter u. In order to explore the effect of this parameter in the probabilistic model, let us study line segments, which are a special case of plane curve transformations (3.1).

(a) Length issue for line segment.

(b) Same issue for cylinder.

Figure 3.5.: When greedily associating measurements to a line segment (or cylinder) the estimator cannot distinguish the true black length and the over-estimated red length.

3.3.1 Line Segments

A line segment of length $\underline{x} = [d]$ can be seen as a special case of a cylinder with radius $r = 0$. Hence, it can be modeled using the cylinder formula (3.2) according to

$$\Phi_{x,u}(s) = \begin{bmatrix} 0 \cdot \cos(s) \\ 0 \cdot \sin(s) \\ u \cdot d \end{bmatrix} = \begin{bmatrix} 0 \\ 0 \\ u \cdot d \end{bmatrix} ,$$

where $u \in [0, 1]$ scales a point along the y_3-axis. In consequence, each parameter u directly refers to a distinct point on the segment which renders $\Phi_{x,u}$ independent of the choice of the parameter s. This allows us to simplify the prototype likelihood (3.8) according to

$$\begin{aligned} p(\underline{y}|\underline{x}) &= \int_U p(\underline{y}|\underline{x}, u) \cdot p(u|\underline{x}) \, \mathrm{d}u \\ &= \int_U \mathcal{N}(\underline{y}; \Phi_{x,u}, \mathbf{C}_v) \cdot p(u|\underline{x}) \, \mathrm{d}u \,, \end{aligned} \tag{3.9}$$

where $\Phi_{x,u} := \Phi_{x,u}(s)$ is used as an abbreviation. In the following, we study the properties of the different probabilistic models for (3.9). For simplicity, we assume the noise to be isotropic according to $\mathbf{C}_v = \sigma^2 \cdot \mathbf{I}$.

Spatial Distribution Model The traditional way of evaluating the likelihood for line segments is assuming measurement sources to be uniformly distributed along the segment according to $p(u|\underline{x}) = 1$ for $U = [0, 1]$. Then, plugging $p(u|\underline{x})$ and $\Phi_{x,u}$ into (3.9) yields

$$p(\underline{y}|\underline{x}) = \int_0^1 \mathcal{N}(\underline{y}; [0, 0, u \cdot d]^{\mathrm{T}}, \mathbf{C}_v) \, du \,, \qquad (3.10)$$

where the integral can be solved in closed-form using the *Gaussian error function* [70]. Roughly speaking, an estimator based on (3.10) associates a measurement to each point on the segment and then minimizes their distances. In doing so, overestimated lengths are naturally penalized, as points far away on the segment have larger distance values.

Greedy Association Model When using a traditional curve fitting approach, the estimator minimizes the distance between measurements and their respective closest points on the line segment. An example association is depicted in Figure 3.5a. However, after a certain value, increasing the length further does not change the associations. Thus, there is no mechanism to penalize overestimated lengths and, for this reason, no estimator based on a GAM will be capable of accurately estimating the length of a line segment. Note that, analogously, this issue also applies to the cylinder in Figure 3.5b.

Partial Information Model When modeling line segments (or linear parts of a boundary), the PIM is locally equivalent to the GAM. That is, the estimator will also essentially minimize the distances between the measurements and their closest points on the line segment. This can be seen from Figure 3.6, where the l-levels lie parallel to the line segment, and do not change when varying the segment length. In consequence, a PIM-based estimator will find parameters so that all measurements lie on their closest l-level to the boundary and does not penalize overestimated lengths either.

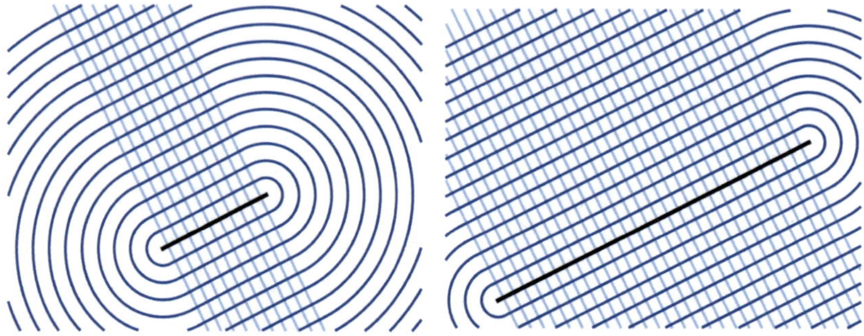

(a) Short line segment, isotropic noise. **(b)** Long line segment, isotropic noise.

Figure 3.6.: ls-parametrization for the Partial Information Model of a line segment.

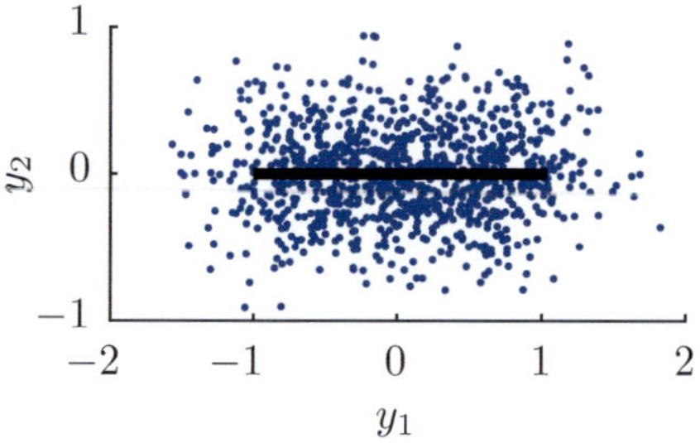

Figure 3.7.: Simulated measurements of a line segment.

Experimental Validation In order to illustrate the length issue, we performed a Monte Carlo simulation. Specifically, we consider the situation in Figure 3.7, where the parameters of the black line segment should be estimated based on 1000 noisy measurements. The segment is centered on $[0, 0]^{\mathrm{T}}$, axis aligned with angle 0, and has length 2. Measurement sources are uniformly drawn along the segment, and additively distorted with isotropic Gaussian noise with variance $\sigma^2 = 0.1$. We performed three experiments where, for each, we set all parameters to the ground truth except for one. Specifically, we compare the loglikelihood for varying values of (i) the horizontal position, (ii) the angle, and (iii) the length.

Results The results of the line segment experiments are shown in Figure 3.8. The right column shows the loglikelihoods and the left column shows snapshots for the parameter values that are marked by dashed, black lines. When looking at the loglikelihoods for the position and the angle in (b,d), it can be seen that all models yield the correct maximum at their respective ground truth values. When varying the length, it can be seen in (f) that the loglikelihood values for the SDM increase up to the true length of 2, and then decrease, which is the desired behavior. However, even though the values for the GAM and the PIM also increase up to the true length, they do not decrease for larger length values. Instead, they further increase up to a maximum value and then become constant, which is a completely undesired behavior. Generally, it can be said that when varying a parameter does not affect the likelihood, this parameter cannot be correctly found by the estimator.

Discussion In related work on *active contours* [20], it is proposed to implement artificial penalties for underdetermined shapes by introducing energy terms that affect the object boundary. However, this approach would introduce problematic shrinking parameters which cannot be set intuitively, as they depend on the number of measurements, the magnitude of the measurement noise, and on the distribution of measurement sources along the boundary. Another approach would be using negative information [167] or object silhouettes [152]. However, these approaches are based on other types of measurements which are out of the scope of this thesis. In conclusion, we must accept that estimating the length of line segments, and more general extrusions, will inherently require a certain amount of probabilistic association heuristics in the form of an SDM.

A similar issue occurs when estimating the extent of a region. For example when considering a filled circle, its radius can be estimated arbitrarily large, once all measurements lie in the region. In these situations, Random Hypersurface Models [63] can be used to overcome this issue.

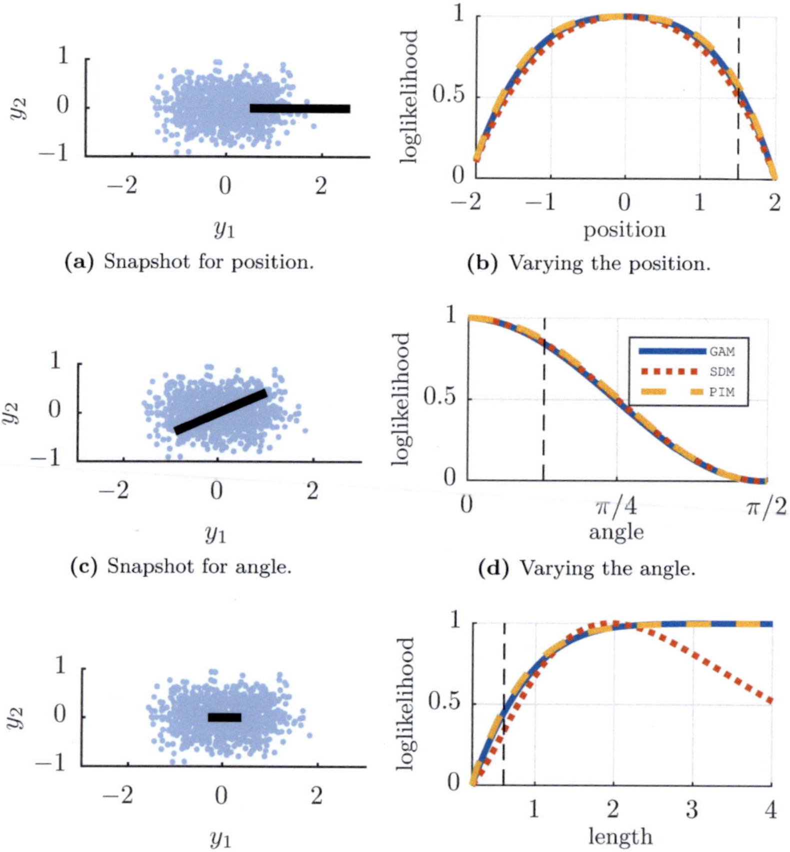

(a) Snapshot for position.

(b) Varying the position.

(c) Snapshot for angle.

(d) Varying the angle.

(e) Snapshot for length.

(f) Varying the length.

Figure 3.8.: Results of the line segment experiments. (a,c,e) show snapshots when varying the respective free parameter. (b,d,f) show the values of the loglikelihood.

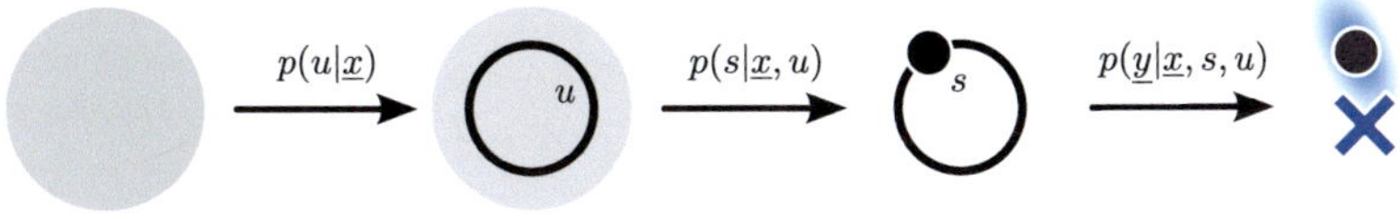

Figure 3.9.: Sketch of the Random Hypersurface Model for a filled circle in 2D. The shape is composed of scaled versions of a circle.

3.3.2 Random Hypersurface Model (RHM)

The *Random Hypersurface Model* (RHM) [63] is a probabilistic model for extended objects that combines two solutions to the association problem. Specifically, when the shape requires two parameters u and s to be described (e.g., a region in 2D), it is assumed that one parameter u has a known probability distribution, while the distribution of the other parameter s is unknown. To see what that means, let us consider a unit circle (with radius 1), which is centered on the origin. Using the function $\phi_{x,u}(s) = u \cdot [\cos(s), \sin(s)]^{\mathrm{T}}$ with $u \in U = [0, 1]$, and $s \in S = [0, 2\pi)$, we can describe the interior of the circular region. Plugging $\phi_{x,u}(s)$ into the likelihood prototype from (3.8) and substituting $p(s, u|\underline{x}) = p(s|\underline{x}, u) \cdot p(u|\underline{x})$ we obtain

$$p(\underline{y}|\underline{x}) = \int_U \int_S \mathcal{N}(\underline{y}; \phi_{x,u}(s), \mathbf{C}_v) \cdot p(s|\underline{x}, u) \, \mathrm{d}s \; p(u|\underline{x}) \, \mathrm{d}u \; , \qquad (3.11)$$

where $\mathbf{C}_v$ is the covariance matrix of the sensor noise, and the source model is divided into two parts. A visual explanation of (3.11) is shown in Figure 3.9.

For a fixed u, the parameter s iterates through all sources on a circle around the origin with radius u. For an RHM, it is assumed to be known how likely it is for each scaled version of the circle to be measured, but unknown how likely it is for points on these circles to be measured. In consequence, $p(u|\underline{x})$ can be seen as an SDM, and $p(s|\underline{x}, u)$ could me modeled using a GAM or a PIM. When deciding for a GAM for the parameter s, the term $p(s|\underline{x}, u)$ becomes a Dirac-δ distribution $\delta(s - \pi_{x,u}(\underline{y}))$ and (3.11) can be rewritten as

$$p(\underline{y}|\underline{x}) = \int_U \mathcal{N}(\underline{y}; \phi_{x,u}(\pi_{x,u}(\underline{y})), \mathbf{C}_v) \cdot p(u|\underline{x}) \, du \, .$$

In this formula, $\phi_{x,u}(\pi_{x,u}(\underline{y}))$ is a greedy estimate for the measurement source on the transformed curve according to

$$\pi_{x,u}(\underline{y}) = \arg\max_{s \in S} \mathcal{N}(\underline{y}; \phi_{x,u}(s), \mathbf{C}_v) \, . \tag{3.12}$$

Being a combination of different modeling approaches, the RHM inherits some of their individual properties. In particular, an RHM-based estimator for a filled circle is capable of estimating its radius while a GAM- or PIM-based estimator cannot [166]. Next, we show how we can adapt the ideas of RHMs to the length issue of 3D objects.

3.4 3D Random Hypersurface Model (3DRHM)

In this section, we derive a new type of Random Hypersurface Model for objects in 3D, which are modeled as transformed plane curves according to (3.1). As the major advantages of this model over the elemental models from Chapter 2, the resulting estimator (i) allows for estimating the object length, (ii) is unbiased when using a PIM-component, and (iii) allows for easier calculation compared to the SDM. In addition, it will still be possible to use 3DRHMs together with a nonlinear Kalman filter. The key idea refers to cutting the shape into *slices* and then assigning a "slice selection" probability to each slice, while the "slice likelihood" is modeled without assuming a probability distribution. Figure 3.9 and Figure 3.10 illustrate the relationship between traditional RHMs and 3DRHMs.

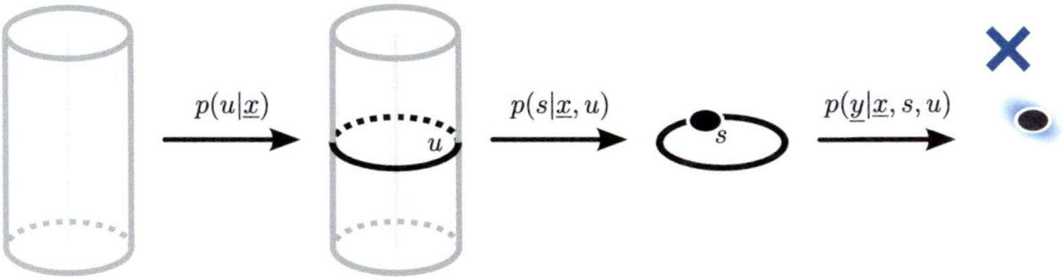

Figure 3.10.: Sketch of the new RHM for a cylinder in 3D. The cylinder is constructed from the extrusions of a circle. It is assumed to be known how likely it is for each extruded version of the circle to be measured.

3.4.1 Key Idea

Let us explain the key idea in more detail. As discussed in Section 3.2, each transformed plane curve is embedded into a plane in 3D, which we will refer to as *slice*. According to (3.1), each slice is specified by u and the curve itself is parametrized by s. As our studies in the previous section have revealed, we require probabilistic assumptions for modeling u, in order to accurately estimate the length of objects. Taking this insight into account, we can rearrange the likelihood prototype from (3.8) in a similar way as the traditional RHM from (3.11) according to

$$p(\underline{y}|\underline{x}) = \int_U \underbrace{\int_S \mathcal{N}(\underline{y}; \Phi_{x,u}(s), \mathbf{C}_v) \cdot p(s|\underline{x}, u) \, \mathrm{d}s}_{\text{slice likelihood } p(\underline{y}|\underline{x},u)} \quad \underbrace{p(u|\underline{x})}_{\text{slice selection}} \quad \mathrm{d}u \,. \quad (3.13)$$

Then, we assume the "slice selection" probability $p(u|\underline{x})$ to be known and the probability $p(s|\underline{x}, u)$ for a point on the transformed plane curve to be unknown. Hence, our tasks are (i) explicitly modeling $p(u|\underline{x})$ and (ii) deriving the "slice likelihood" without making assumptions about s. A visual explanation of both tasks is given in Figure 3.10.

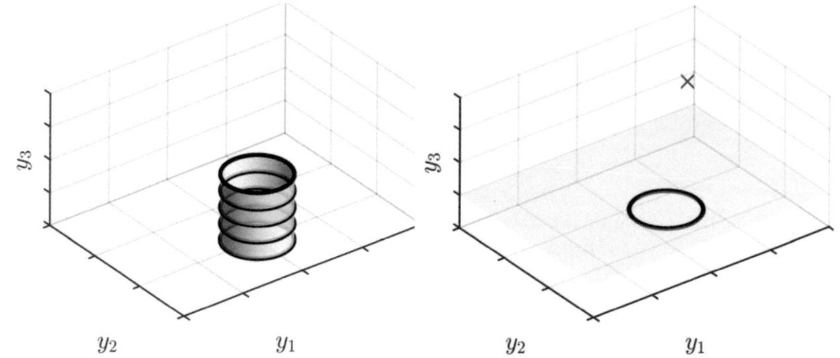

(a) Slice selection probability. **(b)** Slice likelihood.

Figure 3.11.: A "slice selection" probability (a) is defined for each slice. The "slice likelihood" (b) determines how likely its embedded black curve has produced the measurement.

3.4.2 Slice Selection Probability

Let us start with deriving the slice selection probability $p(u|\underline{x})$ in (3.13) that acts as the SDM-component in the 3DRHM. In Figure 3.11a, the cylinder for a given instance of the state vector $\underline{x}$ is shown together with exemplary slices. The slice selection probability rates for each u how likely a measurement $\underline{y}$ originates from the curve that is embedded into this slice. Mathematically, this distribution can be obtained by aggregating the individual probabilities of each point $\Phi_{x,u}(s)$ on the curve according to

$$p(u|\underline{x}) = \int_S p(s, u|\underline{x}) \, \mathrm{d}s \, .$$

An important special case occurs when all points on the object's mantle are assumed to have the same probability, i.e., when $p(s, u|\underline{x})$ is a uniform distribution. Then, $p(u|\underline{x})$ is proportional to the curve perimeter which results in a uniform distribution for the cylinder (3.2), torus (3.3) and star-convex cylinder (3.6). In contrast, the uniform distribution does not hold for the cone (3.4) as the perimeter scales linearly with u from bottom to top. Thus, $p(u|\underline{x})$ becomes a triangle distribution. Note that, for more general cases, where $p(s, u|\underline{x})$ cannot be assumed to be uniform, the distribution of slices could also be derived by taking into account sensor to object geometry [82]. For example when the viewing frustum (field of view) of a camera sensor is known, the visible part of the object could be modeled as a uniform distribution, while all other parts are set to 0.

3.4.3 Slice Likelihood

The slice likelihood $p(\underline{y}|\underline{x}, u)$ in (3.13) determines for a given state $\underline{x}$ and a given slice u, how likely the measurement $\underline{y}$ originated from the curve, which is embedded into this slice. This task is visually explained in Figure 3.11b. As an effect of the association problem (Challenge 1), the term $p(s|\underline{x}, u)$ appears in the slice likelihood

$$p(\underline{y}|\underline{x}, u) = \int_S \mathcal{N}(\underline{y}; \Phi_{x,u}(s), \mathbf{C}_v) \cdot p(s|\underline{x}, u) \, \mathrm{d}s \; , \tag{3.14}$$

and must be taken it into account. In contrast to the slice selection, where we modeled explicit probabilities for u, we do not want to make assumptions about the individual probabilities for s. Instead, we want to use a GAM or a PIM for solving the association problem.

3DRHM with GAM-Component (3DRHM-GAM) Deriving the GAM-component in order to model s is a straightforward application of Section 3.3.2, where $p(s|\underline{x}, u)$ becomes a Dirac-δ distribution $\delta(s - \pi_{x,u}(\underline{y}))$ and the slice likelihood (3.14) can be rewritten as

$$p(\underline{y}|\underline{x}, u) = \mathcal{N}(\underline{y}; \Phi_{x,u}(\pi_{x,u}(\underline{y})), \mathbf{C}_v) \; . \tag{3.15}$$

In this formula, $\Phi_{x,u}(\pi_{x,u}(\underline{y}))$ again is a greedy estimate for the measurement source on the transformed curve, analogously to (3.12), according to

$$\pi_{x,u}(\underline{y}) = \arg\max_{s \in S} \mathcal{N}(\underline{y}; \Phi_{x,u}(s), \mathbf{C}_v) \ .$$

Plugging the GAM-component (3.15) into the likelihood prototype from (3.13), we obtain

$$p(\underline{y}|\underline{x}) = \int_U \mathcal{N}(\underline{y}; \Phi_{x,u}(\pi_{x,u}(\underline{y})), \mathbf{C}_v) \cdot p(u|\underline{x}) \, \mathrm{d}u \ , \tag{3.16}$$

where the parameter s is greedily approximated using the measurement $\underline{y}$, and the parameter u needs to be modeled explicitly through $p(u|\underline{x})$. The corresponding measurement equation in classical notation is given by

$$\begin{aligned} \underline{y} &= h(\underline{x}, \underline{y}, u, \underline{v}) \\ &= \Phi_{x,u}(\pi_{x,u}(\underline{y})) + \underline{v} \ . \end{aligned}$$

As we will see in the evaluation, the 3DRHM with GAM-component (3DRHM-GAM) is a suitable model in situations, when the noise level is moderate. However, for higher noise levels, the GAM-component is subject to bias. In these cases, we can substitute it by a PIM-component in the slice likelihood.

3.5 PIM-Component

In this section, we derive a PIM-component for 3DRHMs that can be used as slice likelihood in (3.13) in situations with higher measurement noise. As a reminder, let us briefly review the key idea of the Partial Information Model (PIM) from Section 2.4. Based on a re-parametrization of the measurements in terms of "how well" they fit to the object boundary and "where" on the boundary they correspond to, we could design a probabilistic model for the valuable "how well" information only, while ignoring the unknown "where" information. In the following, we explain how to adapt this idea for deriving the PIM-component.

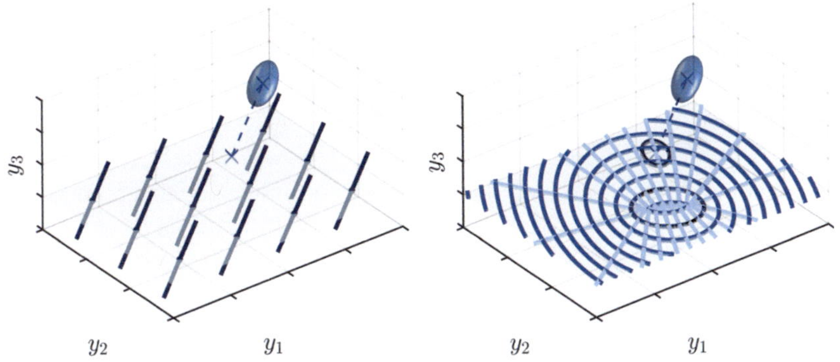

(a) t-coordinate.

(b) l- and s-coordinates.

Figure 3.12.: Constraint-induced parametrization of measurements with respect to a curve in a slice and the sensor noise.

First, we again need a constraint-induced parametrization for the measurements. In Section 2.4, we extended the boundary function $\phi_x(s)$ by a second parameter l, in order to specify the entire 2D domain by $\phi_x(l, s)$. As the measurements are in 3D this time, we need to extend $\Phi_{x,u}(s)$ to three parameters in the form of $\Phi_{x,u}(t, l, s)$. Again, $l \in L \subseteq \mathbb{R}$ and $s \in S \subseteq \mathbb{R}$ should express "how well" measurements fit to the curve and "where" on the curve they correspond to. A sketch of the l- and s-coordinates for a circular curve is illustrated in Figure 3.12b. In addition, the parameter $t \in T \subseteq \mathbb{R}$ fills the remaining degree of freedom and encodes "how well" measurements fit on the slice (see Figure 3.12a). Let us define that $t = l = 0$ denotes that a measurement fits perfectly (i.e., it is located on the curve) and increasing negative (positive) values t, l indicate that the measurement increasingly differs to the one (or the other) side. It can be seen that $\Phi_{x,u}(t, l, s)$ generalizes the previous definition, as $\Phi_{x,u}(0, 0, s) = \Phi_{x,u}(s)$ holds.

Second, we can use the constraint-induced parametrization $\Phi_{x,u}(l_y, l_y, s_y)$ of a measurement $\underline{y}$, in order to design a partial likelihood for the valuable information. Specifically, the variables l_y and t_y are valuable, as it is known that both are noisy observations of the true value 0. In consequence, we only have to remove the probabilistic assumptions about s_y from the full likelihood according to

$$\begin{aligned} p(t_y, l_y, s_y|\underline{x}, u) &= p(t_y, l_y|\underline{x}, s_y, u) \cdot p(s_y|\underline{x}, u) \\ &\approx p(t_y, l_y|\underline{x}, s_y, u) \ . \end{aligned} \tag{3.17}$$

By dropping $p(s_y|\underline{x}, u)$, we ignore the association heuristics and only rate how well a measurement fits to the slice and the curve. In the following we derive explicit formulas for $p(t_y, l_y|\underline{x}, s_y, u)$, which will be denoted as the PIM-component.

3.5.1 Constraint-induced Parametrization of Slice Curves

We start by formally developing the constraint-induced parametrization for a curve in a slice. The following considerations are closely related to those in Section 2.4.2. Again, we already know that the s-axis must lie in the curve as for $l = t = 0$, the s component lets us iterate through the curve via $\Phi_{x,u}(0, 0, s)$. In addition, we know that the s-axis lies in the slice. Thus, we have to specify the t- and l-axes in such a way that the measurement noise is independent in t_y, l_y, and s_y. From the measurement function in (3.7), it follows that measurements $\underline{y}$ from a source $\Phi_{x,u}(0, 0, s)$ occur according to

$$\underline{y} = \Phi_{x,u}(0, 0, s) + \underline{v} \ , \tag{3.18}$$

where $s \in S$ specifies the point on the curve and $\underline{v}$ is the additive noise variable. When expressing measurements in terms of $\Phi_{x,u}(t_y, l_y, s_y) = \underline{y}$ the generative model from (3.18) can be rewritten as

$$\begin{bmatrix} t_y \\ l_y \\ s_y \end{bmatrix} = \begin{bmatrix} 0 \\ 0 \\ s \end{bmatrix} + \begin{bmatrix} t_v \\ l_v \\ s_v \end{bmatrix} \ , \tag{3.19}$$

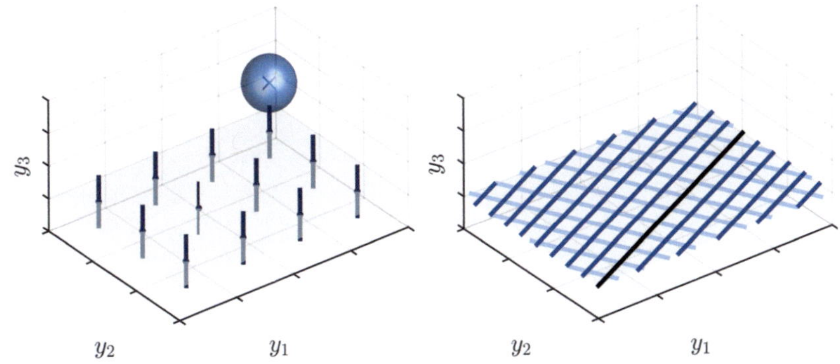

(a) t-coordinate. **(b)** l- and s-coordinates.

Figure 3.13.: Ideal constraint-induced parametrization of measurements where all dimensions become independent.

where the measurement noise $\underline{v}$ is also represented in terms of t_v, l_v and s_v. Analogously to our previous considerations, the axes will be independent when they coincide with the *principal components* of the Gaussian measurement covariance matrix $\mathbf{C}_v$ (which are always orthogonal). Hence, we can conclude that the t- and l-axes both must lie orthogonal to the s-axis, i.e, to the curve in the slice. Again, before we look at the general (anisotropic/nonlinear) case, let us study a special case where independence can be achieved.

The Ideal Case We consider a linear curve and isotropic Gaussian noise $\underline{v}$ in the Cartesian coordinate system with covariance matrix $\mathbf{C}_v = \sigma^2 \cdot \mathbf{I}$ (see Figure 3.13). As the tls-coordinate system is actually a rotated and translated version of the Cartesian coordinate system, the noise retains its isotropic characteristics. Thus, measurements $\underline{y}$ that originate from a source $\Phi_{x,u}(0, 0, s)$ according to (3.18) are independent in their t_y, l_y

and s_y component and we can write the likelihood from (3.14) as

$$
\begin{aligned}
&p(t_y, l_y, s_y | \underline{x}, u) \\
&= \int_S \mathcal{N}\left(\begin{bmatrix} t_y \\ l_y \\ s_y \end{bmatrix} ; \begin{bmatrix} 0 \\ 0 \\ s \end{bmatrix} , \begin{bmatrix} \sigma^2 & 0 & 0 \\ 0 & \sigma^2 & 0 \\ 0 & 0 & \sigma^2 \end{bmatrix} \right) \cdot p(s|\underline{x}, u) \, \mathrm{d}s \\
&= \underbrace{\mathcal{N}(t_y; 0, \sigma^2)}_{p(t_y|\underline{x},u)} \cdot \underbrace{\mathcal{N}(l_y; 0, \sigma^2)}_{p(l_y|\underline{x},u)} \cdot \underbrace{\int_S \mathcal{N}(s_y; s, \sigma^2) \cdot p(s|\underline{x}, u) \, \mathrm{d}s}_{p(s_y|\underline{x},u)} \ .
\end{aligned}
$$

Note that all information about the unknown parameter s is isolated in the term $p(s_y|\underline{x}, u)$ and, thus, when deriving the partial likelihood $p(t_y, l_y|\underline{x}, u) = p(t_y|\underline{x}, u) \cdot p(l_y|\underline{x}, u)$, we do not need to explicitly model $p(s|\underline{x}, u)$ anymore.

As an important observation, note that the t and l components are closely related to the signed Euclidean distance of points to the slice and to the curve, respectively. Specifically, for all measurements $\underline{y} = \Phi_{x,u}(t_y, l_y, s_y)$, their closest point on the slice and on the curve in terms of the Euclidean distance is given by $\Phi_{x,u}(0, l_y, s_y)$ and $\Phi_{x,u}(0, 0, s_y)$, respectively. Based on this observation, we can formally define the concepts "how well" and "where" measurements correspond to a slice (curve) according to:

- **"How well:"** all points on a level t_y have the same signed Euclidean distance to the slice.
- **"How well:"** all points on a level l_y have the same signed Euclidean distance to the curve.
- **"Where:"** all points on a level s_y have the same closest point $\Phi_{x,u}(0, 0, s_y)$ on the curve.

The General Case While for the line in the slice and isotropic noise perfect independence could be achieved, for a nonlinear constraint (and/or anisotropic noise), we find us in the same dilemma as for the general case in Section 2.4.2. On the one hand, the s-axis dictates that the t- and l-axes lie orthogonal to the slice and to the curve, respectively. On the other hand, the noise will only be independent if the axes coincide with the *principal components* of the Gaussian measurement covariance matrix. As a compromise, we again propose to sacrifice orthogonality of the *tls*-coordinate system, in order to come up with the parametrization in Figure 3.12, which retains the meaning of the axes for the Mahalanobis distance with respect to the noise covariance.

For the following derivations, let us assume the slice is centered on the origin and axis aligned in the y_1y_2-plane. Technically, this can be realized by transforming the measurements and the noise from the global frame into the local slice frame by applying (2.8). In particular, the local coordinates are given by $\underline{y} \leftarrow \mathbf{R}_u^{\mathrm{T}}\underline{y} - \mathbf{R}_u^{\mathrm{T}}\underline{c}_u$, $\underline{v} \leftarrow \mathbf{R}_u^{\mathrm{T}}\underline{v}$, and $\mathbf{C}_v \leftarrow \mathbf{R}_u^{\mathrm{T}}\mathbf{C}_v\mathbf{R}_u$. In addition, let the function $\phi_x(0,s)$ already include the scaling variable f_u so that $\phi_x(0,s) \leftarrow f_u \cdot \phi_x(0,s)$. Using these substitutions, we can rewrite the measurement function from (3.18) as

$$\underline{y} = \begin{bmatrix} \phi_x(0,s) \\ 0 \end{bmatrix} + \underline{v} \, .$$

Deriving the t-Component For deriving t_y of a point $\underline{y}$, we must calculate its minimum Mahalanobis distance to the y_1y_2-plane with respect to $\mathbf{C}_v$. The point $\underline{y}^0 = [y_1^0, y_2^0]^{\mathrm{T}}$ that minimizes this distance can be found by solving

$$\underline{y}^0 = \underset{y_1^0, y_2^0}{\arg\min} \begin{bmatrix} y_1 - y_1^0 \\ y_2 - y_2^0 \\ y_3 - 0 \end{bmatrix}^{\mathrm{T}} \cdot \mathbf{C}_v^{-1} \cdot \begin{bmatrix} y_1 - y_1^0 \\ y_2 - y_2^0 \\ y_3 - 0 \end{bmatrix} \, . \tag{3.20}$$

The closed-form solution of this optimization problem has the well-known form $\underline{y}^0 = \left(\mathbf{H}^{\mathrm{T}}\mathbf{C}_v^{-1}\mathbf{H}\right)^{-1}\mathbf{H}^{\mathrm{T}}\mathbf{C}_v^{-1}\underline{y}$ with $\mathbf{H} = \begin{bmatrix} 1 & 0 & 0 \\ 0 & 1 & 0 \end{bmatrix}^{\mathrm{T}}$. Based on (3.20) we define the function $\downarrow(\underline{y}) := \underline{y}^0$ that projects a point $\underline{y}$ to its closest point in the y_1y_2-plane, in terms of the Mahalanobis distance. An example of this projection is illustrated in Figure 3.12a. The Mahalanobis distance to this point is then given by

$$t_y = \eta_x(\underline{y}) := \pm \left(\left(\underline{y} - \begin{bmatrix} \underline{y}^0 \\ 0 \end{bmatrix} \right)^{\mathrm{T}} \mathbf{C}_v^{-1} \left(\underline{y} - \begin{bmatrix} \underline{y}^0 \\ 0 \end{bmatrix} \right) \right)^{\frac{1}{2}} , \tag{3.21}$$

where the sign indicates on which side of the slice the measurement lies.

Deriving the l- and s-Components In order to derive l_y and s_y of a measurement, we can essentially use their original formulas from Chapter 2, i.e., (2.23) and (2.22). However, besides the point $\underline{y}^0$ in the y_1y_2-plane, these formulas also require its covariance matrix $\mathbf{C}_v^0$, which can be calculated according to

$$\mathbf{C}_v^0 = \mathbf{H}^{\mathrm{T}} \mathbf{C}_v^{-1} \mathbf{H} \, . \tag{3.22}$$

An example of the projected covariance is illustrated in Figure 3.12b. Based on $\underline{y}^0$ from (3.20) and $\mathbf{C}_v^0$ from (3.22), we can now proceed to derive the s- and l-components using their original formulas. Then, s_y specifies the closest point $\phi_x(0, s_y)$ to $\underline{y}^0$ on the boundary by

$$\begin{aligned} s_y &= \pi_x(\downarrow(\underline{y})) \\ &:= \underset{s \in S}{\arg\min} \left((\underline{y}^0 - \phi_x(0,s))^{\mathrm{T}} (\mathbf{C}_v^0)^{-1} (\underline{y}^0 - \phi_x(0,s)) \right)^{\frac{1}{2}} , \end{aligned} \tag{3.23}$$

and l_y specifies the signed distance of $\underline{y}^0$ to this point by

$$\begin{aligned} l_y &= g_x(\downarrow(\underline{y})) \\ &:= \pm \left((\underline{y}^0 - \phi_x(0,s_y))^{\mathrm{T}} (\mathbf{C}_v^0)^{-1} (\underline{y}^0 - \phi_x(0,s_y)) \right)^{\frac{1}{2}} , \end{aligned} \tag{3.24}$$

where the sign indicates on which side of the curve the measurement lies. Again, note that the sign naturally comes into play as the l-axis is 0 on its intersection with the constraint. Based on (3.21), (3.23), and (3.24) we can finally define the desired parametrization according to

$$\begin{bmatrix} t_y \\ l_y \\ s_y \end{bmatrix} = \Phi_{x,u}^{-1}(\underline{y}) := \begin{bmatrix} \eta_x(\underline{y}) \\ g_x(\downarrow(\underline{y})) \\ \pi_x(\downarrow(\underline{y})) \end{bmatrix} , \tag{3.25}$$

It is important to note that this parametrization includes the ideal case as a special case of isotropic noise, where it holds that $\underline{y}^0 = [y_1, y_2]^\mathrm{T}$ and $\mathbf{C}_v^0 = \sigma^2 \cdot \mathbf{I}$.

3.5.2 Deriving the Partial Slice Likelihood

Prepared with the constrained-induced parametrization of measurements $\underline{y} = \Phi_{\underline{x},u}(t_y, l_y, s_y)$, we can now derive the partial slice likelihood $p(t_y, l_y|\underline{x}, u, s_y)$ from (3.17). For the following derivations, we use a simplified notation in order to improve readability. As all probability distributions (except from $p(\underline{v})$) depend on a given state $\underline{x}$ and a given slice $\underline{u}$, we will drop their symbols whenever possible, e.g., in $p(t_y, l_y|s_y) := p(t_y, l_y|\underline{x}, u, s_y)$.

Then, for deriving the partial slice likelihood $p(t_y, l_y|s_y)$, we can adapt the approach from Section 2.4.3 in the following straightforward way. First, the given s_y-value refers to the source $\Phi(0, 0, s_y)$. Second, this source refers to the generative model in (3.18). For the partial slice likelihood, we are interested in $t_y = 0 + t_v$ and $l_y = 0 + l_v$, which finally refer to

$$
\begin{aligned}
p(t_y, l_y|s_y) &= \iint\limits_{T\,L} p(t_y, l_y|s_y, t_v, l_v) \cdot p(t_v, l_v|s_y) \,\mathrm{d}l_v \,\mathrm{d}t_v \\
&= \iint\limits_{T\,L} \delta\left(\begin{bmatrix} t_y - (0 + t_v) \\ l_y - (0 + l_v) \end{bmatrix}\right) \cdot f_{t_v,l_v}(t_v, l_v) \,\mathrm{d}l_v \,\mathrm{d}t_v \\
&= f_{t_v,l_v}(t_y, l_y) \ .
\end{aligned}
$$

where $p(t_v, l_v|s_y) = f_{t_v,l_v}(t_v, l_v)$ is the joint distribution of the noise variables t_v and l_v. According to this formula, the partial slice likelihood essentially is the distribution $f_{t_v,l_v}(t_v, l_v)$ that describes the t-value and l-value of the sensor noise, evaluated in t_y and l_y.

Deriving the Partial Noise Then, analogously to Section 2.4.3, the next step is calculating the partial noise distribution $p(t_v, l_v | s_y)$. Again, we have to extract it from the original distribution of the sensor noise $p(\underline{v})$. In the first place, this requires expressing the variable $\underline{v}$ in terms of t_v, l_v, and s_v in order to derive the joint noise distribution $p(t_v, l_v, s_v | s_y)$. Then, by marginalizing out the s_v-component, we obtain the partial noise distribution

$$p(t_v, l_v | s_y) = \int_S p(t_v, l_v, s_v | s_y) \, \mathrm{d}s_v \; . \tag{3.26}$$

Let us again start with expressing $p(\underline{v})$ in terms of t_v, l_v, and s_v. Given the s_y-value of $\underline{y}$, hypothetical measurements $\tilde{\underline{y}}$ of the source $\Phi(0,0,s_y)$ occur according to the additive noise model $\tilde{\underline{y}} = \Phi(0,0,s_y) + \underline{v}$ from (3.18). We use the tilde symbol in order to distinguish the hypothetical measurements from the original measurement $\underline{y}$. By solving this equation for the noise $\underline{v}$ and applying the tls-parametrization to $\tilde{\underline{y}}$, we obtain

$$\begin{aligned} \underline{v} &= \tilde{\underline{y}} - \Phi(0,0,s_y) \\ &= \Phi(\tilde{t}_y, \tilde{l}_y, \tilde{s}_y) - \Phi(0,0,s_y) \\ &= \Phi(0 + t_v, 0 + l_v, s_y + s_v) - \Phi(0,0,s_y) \; . \end{aligned} \tag{3.27}$$

Based on this relationship, we can apply a change of variables to the distribution $p(\underline{v})$, which is known to be zero-mean Gaussian $\mathcal{N}(\underline{v}; 0, \mathbf{C}_v)$. Then, analogously to (2.28), we can apply the general formula for changing variables of a probability distribution according to

$$\begin{aligned} & p(t_v, l_v, s_v | s_y) \\ &= p(\underline{v}) \cdot \left| \det\left(\mathbf{J}_{\underline{v}}(t_v, l_v, s_v)\right) \right| \\ &= \mathcal{N}\left(\underline{v}; \underline{0}, \mathbf{C}_v\right) \cdot \left| \det\left(\mathbf{J}_{\underline{v}}(t_v, l_v, s_v)\right) \right| \\ &= \mathcal{N}\left(\Phi(0 + t_v, 0 + l_v, s_y + s_v) - \Phi(0,0,s_y); \underline{0}, \mathbf{C}_v\right) \cdot \left| \det\left(\mathbf{J}_{\underline{v}}(t_v, l_v, s_v)\right) \right| \end{aligned} \tag{3.28}$$

with the Jacobian matrix

$$\mathbf{J}_{\underline{v}}(t_v, l_v, s_v) = \begin{bmatrix} \frac{\partial \underline{v}}{\partial t_v} & \frac{\partial \underline{v}}{\partial l_v} & \frac{\partial \underline{v}}{\partial s_v} \end{bmatrix} . \tag{3.29}$$

Again, note that (3.28) is nothing else but the measurement noise $p(\underline{v})$ expressed in tls-coordinates, where the differential expression (3.29) accounts for the skewness of the coordinate system. Then, by marginalizing s_v out of $p(t_v, l_v, s_v|s_y)$ according to (3.26) we obtain the distribution of the partial noise

$$\begin{aligned} &p(t_v, l_v|s_y) \qquad (3.30) \\ &= \int_S \mathcal{N}\left(\Phi(t_v, l_v, s_y + s_v); \Phi(0,0,s_y), \mathbf{C}_v\right) \cdot \left| \det\left(\mathbf{J}_{\underline{v}}(t_v, l_v, s_v)\right) \right| \mathrm{d}s_v \\ &= f_{t_v,l_v}(t_v, l_v)\ . \end{aligned}$$

3DRHM with PIM-Component (3DRHM-PIM) Finally, by plugging t_y and l_y into the distribution of the partial noise (3.30), we obtain the partial slice likelihood (PIM-component)

$$\begin{aligned} &p(t_y, l_y|\underline{x}, u, s_y) \qquad (3.31) \\ &= \int_S \mathcal{N}\left(\Phi_{x,u}(t_y, l_y, s_y + s_v); \Phi_{x,u}(0,0,s_y), \mathbf{C}_v\right) \cdot \left| \det\left(\mathbf{J}_{\underline{v}}(t_y, l_y, s_v)\right) \right| \mathrm{d}s_v\,, \end{aligned}$$

where we returned to the full notation, i.e., explicitly writing out dependencies of $\underline{x}$ and u. The partial slice likelihood (3.31) has the same intuitive geometric interpretation as the partial likelihood (2.31) from Chapter 2. Essentially, it is the integral of a Gaussian (centered on the most likely source $\Phi_{x,u}(0,0,s_y)$) over all potential measurements that fit equally well (i.e., t_y and l_y) to the slice and curve.

By substituting the slice likelihood $p(\underline{y}|\underline{x}, u)$ in the likelihood prototype from (3.13) by the PIM-component $p(t_y, l_y|\underline{x}, s_y, u)$ (3.31), we obtain the 3D Random Hypersurface Model with PIM-component (3DRHM-PIM)

$$
\begin{aligned}
& p(\underline{y}|\underline{x}) \\
& \approx \int_U p(t_y, l_y|\underline{x}, u, s_y) \cdot p(u|\underline{x}) \, \mathrm{d}u \\
& = \int_U \int_S \mathcal{N}\left(\Phi_{x,u}(t_y, l_y, s_y + s_v); \Phi_{x,u}(0, 0, s_y), \mathbf{C}_v\right) \\
& \cdot \left| \det\left(\mathbf{J}_{\underline{v}}(t_y, l_y, s_v)\right) \right| \mathrm{d}s_v \cdot p(u|\underline{x}) \, \mathrm{d}u \, .
\end{aligned}
\tag{3.32}
$$

In this model, only the valuable "how well" information t_y and l_y of a measurement $\underline{y}$ is used for evaluating the slice likelihood $p(t_y, l_y|\underline{x}, u, s_y)$, while the parameter u needs to be modeled explicitly through $p(u|\underline{x})$. We will see in the evaluation that an estimator based on the 3DRHM-PIM still finds unbiased estimates, even in situations where the noise level is high.

Remark 3.2. *Note that all parameters t_y, l_y, and s_y of the constraint-induced parametrization are defined with respect to a given slice (and curve) and cannot exist without a given state $\underline{x}$ and transformation u. As a consequence of this dependence, we have to re-calculate t_y, l_y, and s_y for each instance of $\underline{x}$ and u.*

Measurement Equation The underlying generative model that yields the 3DRHM-PIM (3.32) can be obtained from the relationship in (3.19)

$$
\begin{bmatrix} t_y \\ l_y \end{bmatrix}_{x,u} = \begin{bmatrix} 0 + t_v \\ 0 + l_v \end{bmatrix}_{x,u} ,
$$

where we added indices in order to indicate the dependence of $\underline{x}$ and u (see Remark 3.2). We can rearrange this equation to a measurement equation in classical notation

$$\begin{aligned} \underline{0} = h(\underline{x}, \underline{v}, u, \underline{y}) &= \begin{bmatrix} t_y \\ l_y \end{bmatrix}_{x,u} - \begin{bmatrix} t_v \\ l_v \end{bmatrix}_{x,u} \\ &= \begin{bmatrix} \eta(\underline{y}) \\ g(\downarrow(\underline{y})) \end{bmatrix}_{x,u} - \underbrace{\begin{bmatrix} \eta(\Phi(0,0,\pi(\downarrow(\underline{y})))) + \underline{v}) \\ g(\downarrow(\Phi(0,0,\pi(\downarrow(\underline{y})))) + \underline{v})) \end{bmatrix}_{x,u}}_{A} \end{aligned} \tag{3.33}$$

by substituting t_y, l_y according to (3.25), and t_v, l_v according to (3.27). Formally, in this measurement equation, $\underline{x}$ is the state, $\underline{v}$ is non-additive Gaussian noise, u is non-additive, (potentially) non-Gaussian noise, $\underline{y}$ acts as a model parameter, and $\underline{0}$ is a constant *pseudo-measurement*. Note that the measurement equation (3.33) can immediately be used to derive a nonlinear Kalman filter update according to Algorithm A.1.

3.5.3 Implementation

Analogously to the PIM in Chapter 2, analytic solutions to the integrals in the 3DRHM-PIM (3.32) cannot be found. Thus, in order to derive a likelihood-based measurement update according to Algorithm A.2, we have to apply approximation techniques. In this section, we show how to get rid of both integrals by means of (i) moment matching and (ii) sampling. For the inner integral over $s \in S$, we propose to approximate the slice likelihood $p(t_y, l_y | \underline{x}, u, s_y)$ as a Gaussian by means of moment matching [92, 93]

$$\begin{aligned} &p(\underline{y}|\underline{x}) \\ &= \int_U \mathcal{N}\left(\begin{bmatrix} t_y \\ l_y \end{bmatrix}_{x,u} ; \mathrm{E}\left\{ \begin{bmatrix} t_v \\ l_v \end{bmatrix}_{x,u} \right\}, \mathrm{Var}\left\{ \begin{bmatrix} t_v \\ l_v \end{bmatrix}_{x,u} \right\} \right) \cdot p(u|\underline{x}) \, du \, . \end{aligned} \tag{3.34}$$

Specifically, mean and variance of the Gaussian are to be calculated by propagating the moments of the original noise variable $\underline{v}$ through the expression A in (3.33). Again, please note that these moments generally differ for each slice (except from special cases) and, thus, must be calculated for each u.

In order to evaluate the outer integral over $u \in U$, we propose to approximate $p(u|\underline{x})$ as a Dirac-mixture distribution according to

$$p(u|\underline{x}) = \sum_{j=1}^{J} \omega_j \cdot \delta(u - u_j) ,$$

by means of moment matching [111, 112], where ω_j with $j = 1 \ldots J$ are scalar weights, one for each Dirac-component. Using this approximation, we can apply the sifting property of the Dirac-δ distribution and further simplify (3.34) according to

$$p(\underline{y}|\underline{x}) \tag{3.35}$$
$$= \sum_{j=1}^{J} \omega_j \cdot \mathcal{N}\left(\begin{bmatrix} t_y \\ l_y \end{bmatrix}_{x,u_j}; \mathrm{E}\left\{\begin{bmatrix} t_v \\ l_v \end{bmatrix}_{x,u_j}\right\}, \mathrm{Var}\left\{\begin{bmatrix} t_v \\ l_v \end{bmatrix}_{x,u_j}\right\}\right) .$$

At this point, we have arrived at a tractable version of the RHM-PIM, which can be used, e.g., in a particle filter.

3.6 Modeling Guide

In this section, we take a more practical view and propose specific probabilistic models for the example objects from Section 3.2. In doing so, we want to identify the "simplest" model that still ensures two properties of the resulting estimator: (i) it should be capable of finding estimates for all parameters, and (ii) these estimates should be unbiased even in the presence of higher sensor noise. Both properties refer to issues that we have already discussed earlier in this thesis.

3.6.1 Potential Issues

Issue 1 (The estimator cannot find a parameter at all). *In order to enable the estimator to find the value of a parameter, the likelihood must produce different values when changing this parameter. However, when ignoring the distributions for* u, s, *and using distances instead (GAM and PIM), the likelihood could become invariant to parameter changes. We have discussed this issue for the length parameter of a line segment and a cylinder in Section 3.3.1. For these shapes, the closest distance of measurements to the object surface is identical for the true and any overestimated height parameter. Then, varying the height parameter does not affect the closest distances and, in turn, the value of the likelihood. As a result, the height is likely to be unobservable. This issue can be either resolved by introducing regularization terms or by incorporating knowledge about the distribution of measurement sources [70, 149, 156] in the fashion of SDMs and RHMs. In sum, when GAM- or PIM-based estimators are subject to unobservable parameters, switching to an 3DRHM-GAM, 3DRHM-PIM, or SDM may render the desired parameter observable.*

Issue 2 (The estimator finds a biased parameter). *It is well-known that when using a GAM, estimates of curvature parameters are likely to be biased in the presence of noise [113]. We have theoretically discussed this issue in Section 2.3.3 for a circle and a corner, and then showed numerical examples for a parabola in Section 2.6.2. Essentially, curvature causes that measurements of a given source on the boundary are more likely to occur on the concave side of the boundary. However, a GAM-based estimator will find a boundary that, roughly speaking, balances the probability mass on both sides [159], as it tries to minimize the distances to the curve. As the imposed balance is incorrect except for linear boundaries, the estimated boundary will be biased when it has a significant curvature within the magnitude of the noise. In these situations, we can use an SDM, PIM or 3DRHM-PIM [113, 159, 157] that do not suffer from this issue.*

3.6.2 Proposed Estimators

We can now design probabilistic models for the considered objects that will not cause these issues in the estimator. In doing so, we also propose a compatible recursive Bayesian estimators, including the unscented Kalman filter (UKF) [92], the smart sampling Kalman filter (S2KF) [93], and the progressive Gaussian filter (PGF) [97]. While UKF and S2KF both are nonlinear Kalman filters based on deterministic sampling (the latter with a variable number of samples), the PGF is a sophisticated nonlinear estimator that uses a particle-filter like measurement update.

Proposed Cylinder Estimator A cylinder is potentially subject to both issues, i.e., an unobservable length and a biased radius. In consequence, we propose to use an RHM-PIM according to (3.35), where the known distribution for u enables the length estimation and the PIM-component prevents bias. If measurements originate uniformly from the cylinder mantle, $p(u|\underline{x})$ can be modeled as $\mathcal{U}(0,1)$ with $\mathrm{E}\{u\} = \frac{1}{2}$ and $\mathrm{Var}\{u\} = \frac{1}{12}$. In this form [151], the RHM-PIM can be used with a nonlinear estimator, such as the PGF. However, we found in [149] that the structure of the measurement equation (3.33) causes that the state cannot be directly estimated when using a nonlinear Kalman filter. In order to allow for using these simpler estimators, we show in the next chapter how to exploit the reflectional symmetry of the cylinder.

Proposed Torus Estimator In contrast to the cylinder, the torus is not affected by Issue 1, as there is no length parameter and varying the radii will always have an effect on the closest distances of points to the surface. However, as both radii are subject to Issue 2, we propose to use a PIM according to (2.34). Thus, the torus parameters can be estimated with a standard UKF.

Proposed Cone Estimator Similar to the cylinder, the cone is subject to both issues, i.e., an unobservable height and a biased radius. In consequence, we again propose to use an RHM-PIM according to (3.35), where the known distribution for u enables the height estimation and the PIM component prevents bias. The probability $p(u|\underline{x})$ of each scaled circle is proportional to its perimeter $2\pi \cdot (1-u) \cdot r$ and scales linearly with u. As such, the variable u can be modeled as a triangle distribution between 0 and 1 with $\mathrm{E}\{u\} = \frac{1}{3}$ and $\mathrm{Var}\{u\} = \frac{1}{18}$. Thus, an S2KF can be used for estimation together with the measurement equation (3.33).

Proposed Extruded Curve Estimator Being essentially a cylinder, the extruded curve is subject to both issues, as well. However, as estimating higher shape detail is more relevant in low noise scenarios, we assume the curvature to be negligible within the magnitude of the noise. Given this situation, we propose to use an RHM-GAM according to (3.16) with $p(u|\underline{x}) = \mathcal{U}(0,1)$. In addition, instead of using the Mahalanobis distance-based projection of measurements to the boundary, we propose to approximate it by a polar projection according to [98], which can be calculated much faster. For estimation, we propose to use a PGF.

3.7 Evaluation

In this section, we evaluate the proposed probabilistic models in two estimation scenarios with synthetic data. Specifically, we consider the tasks of estimating a static cylinder, torus, and cone, and compare the results of the proposed approach to those of a publicly available estimation toolbox [41]. In a second scenario, we look at the task of tracking an unknown moving object based on a star-convex extrusion model, and evaluate the estimation quality for different degrees of modeled shape detail.

	Trad. Batch	Trad. Recursive		Prop. Recursive	
		Model	Filter	Model	Filter
Cylinder	LSGE	GAM	PGF	RHM-PIM	PGF
Torus	LSGE	GAM	PGF	PIM	UKF
Cone	LSGE	GAM	PGF	RHM-PIM	S2KF

Table 3.1.: Overview of the implemented estimators.

3.7.1 Estimating Pose and Shape of Static Objects

Let us first look at the task of estimating pose and shape of a static cylinder, torus, and cone. We conduct two experiments, one with low noise and another with high noise. For both experiments, we compare the "Proposed Recursive" approaches from Section 3.6.2 to the following traditional approaches.

Traditional Approaches For a static object, the "Traditional Batch" approach is processing all measurements using an instance of GAM (2.15) together with a maximum likelihood estimator. A reference implementation for cylinder, torus, and cone is publicly available in the LSGE toolbox [41]. For a potentially dynamic object, the "Traditional Recursive" approach is using an instance of GAM (2.15) together with a recursive Bayesian estimator such as a particle filter [46]. For the ease of a lower computational complexity, we use a similar PGF implementation [114] instead. A summary of all implemented estimation approaches is given in Table 3.1.

Experiments For ground truth, we model all objects at the position $[0.1, 0.4, 0.2]^{\mathrm{T}}$ with an orientation $[0, 0.5, 0]^{\mathrm{T}}$ in *axis-angle* representation. The shape parameters are set to $[r, d] = [1, 2]^{\mathrm{T}}$ (cylinder), $[r, d] = [1.5, 4]^{\mathrm{T}}$ (cone), and $[r_1, r_2]^{\mathrm{T}} = [1, 0.5]$ (torus). Then, we simulate 1250 measurements of each object by uniformly drawing measurement sources from the surface and then adding Gaussian sensor noise with $\mathbf{C}_v = 0.01 \cdot \mathbf{I}$ (low noise) and $\mathbf{C}_v = 0.1 \cdot \mathbf{I}$ (high noise).

	Low noise			High noise		
	T.B.	T.R.	P.R.	T.B.	T.R.	P.R.
Cylinder r	5.9	6.3	3.7	52	53	12
Torus r_1, r_2	8.0	8.3	6.1	86	90	31
Cone top	63	70	201	594	616	330

Table 3.2.: RMSE of selected parameters $\times 10^{-3}$ units.

We initialize all parameters with Gaussian random values, drawn from the ground truth using variances of $5 \cdot 10^{-2} \cdot \mathbf{I}$. In the recursive approaches, we incorporate a *random walk model* [46] into the prediction step, which inflates the state covariance matrix with process noise in order to prevent local minimums. We choose a logarithmically decreasing diagonal covariance in the magnitude from 10^{-2} to 10^{-12}. Measurement updates are performed in 250 steps with stacks of 5 measurements. The following results are obtained from 100 Monte-Carlo runs.

Results The average estimation results after processing all measurements are illustrated in Figure 3.14 for the low noise experiment, and in Figure 3.15 for the high noise experiment, respectively. It can be seen that all estimators can find the object orientation very accurately. This accuracy also applies to the position estimates, except from a random linear shift along the length axis (cylinder, cone) in the traditional approaches, which is due to their missing capability of estimating the length (Issue 1).

From the third column in Figure 3.14 and Figure 3.15, it can be seen that the proposed approach finds accurate parameters for all objects. Specifically, "Proposed Recursive" finds the height parameter of the cylinder and the cone (and is not subject to Issue 1). In addition, even in the presence of high noise, the radii still remain unbiased (and are not subject to Issue 2).

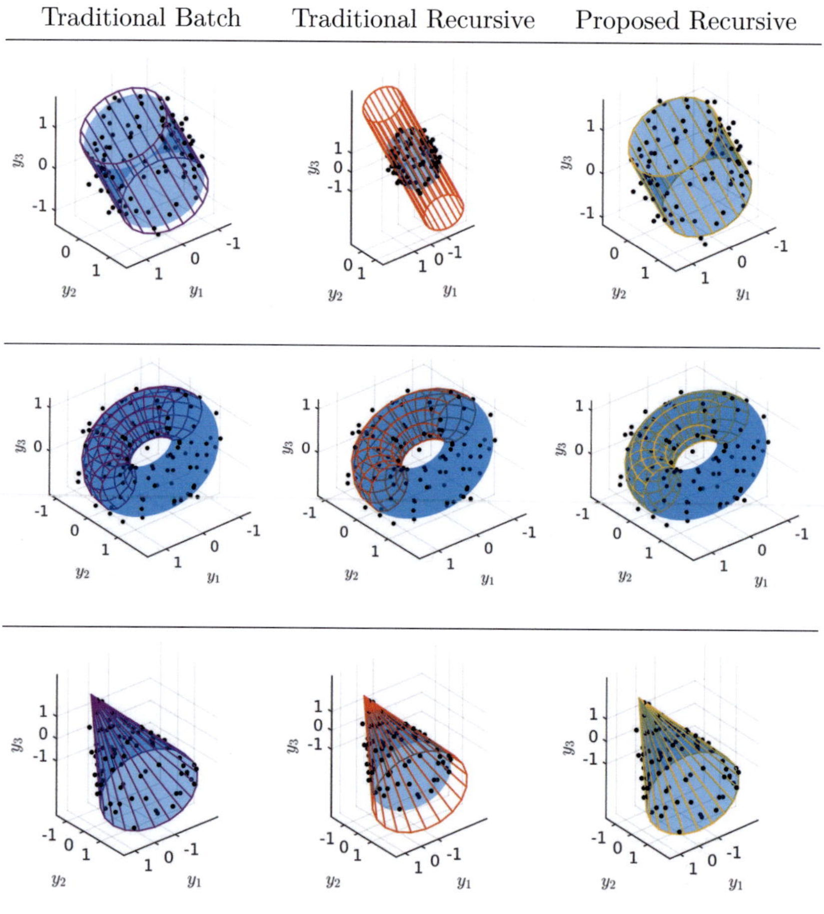

Figure 3.14.: Average estimates for 100 Monte Carlo runs of the low noise experiment. Exemplary measurements illustrate the noise level.

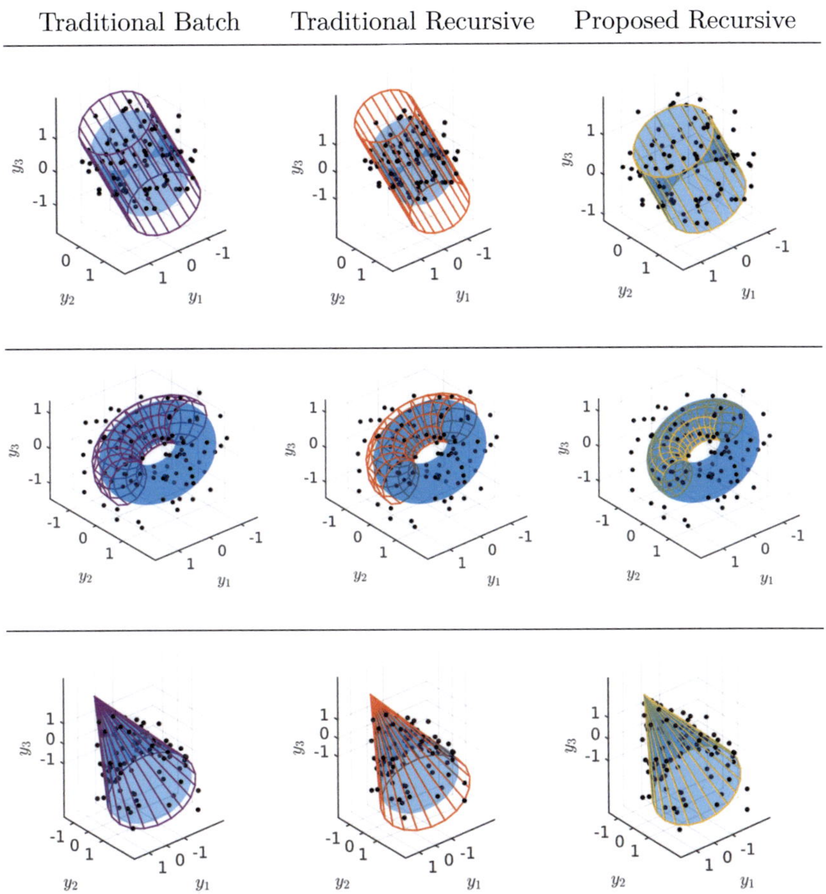

Figure 3.15.: Average estimates for 100 Monte Carlo runs of the high noise experiment. Exemplary measurements illustrate the noise level.

In contrast, the curvature parameters of the traditional approaches are biased for high noise, as Table 3.2 numerically confirms. This result can be explained by the PIM-component that accounts for the bias in "Proposed Recursive". However, evaluating the PIM is relatively sophisticated and might perform worse than a simpler GAM in some situations. An example can be found when considering the top of the cone, which is estimated more accurately by the traditional approaches for low noise.

In sum, traditional GAM-based approaches are suitable when the problematic length parameters are known in advance, and when the surface has a negligible curvature with respect to the magnitude of the noise. Otherwise, the experiments show that RHM and PIM can effectively compensate for Issue 1 and Issue 2, respectively. Note that in situations with low noise and the task of estimating length parameters, it might be also reasonable to combine an RHM with a GAM instead of a PIM. For the second evaluation, we consider such a scenario.

3.7.2 Tracking a Moving Box-Object

In this section, we illustrate the performance of the 3DRHM by means of a tracking example.

Experiment We consider the task of tracking a moving box. As a challenging aspect in this experiment, the estimator actually is not given any prior knowledge about the fact that the object is a box. As a reminder, this lack of knowledge was referred to as Challenge 2. Instead, the estimator assumes the object to be an extruded star-convex curve according to Section 3.6.2.

Figure 3.16 shows the track, together with the ground truth box with an edge length of $6 \times 4 \times 8$, drawn at some selected locations. While the box moves, a simulated sensor performs 250 point cloud measurements, where each of contains 25 noisy points. For the selected locations, exemplary measurements are drawn as black dots in Figure 3.16. The measurement sources are uniformly drawn from the four longer sides of the box and then distorted by adding Gaussian sensor noise with $\mathbf{C}_v = 5 \cdot 10^{-2} \cdot \mathbf{I}$.

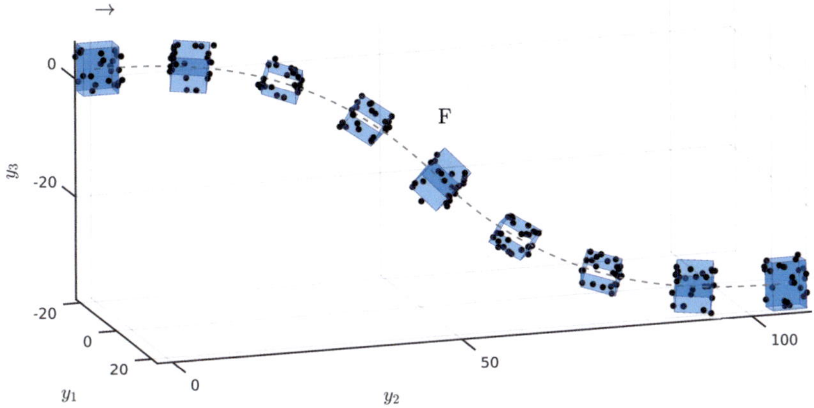

Figure 3.16.: Box tracking experiment. The box moves with constant speed along the S-shaped track while performing a rotation.

As the noise level is relatively low with respect to the object size, we decide for an RHM-GAM (instead of a RHM-PIM) together with a PGF according to Section 3.6.2. The state to be estimated consists of the Fourier-coefficients for the star-convex curve, the height, the pose, as well as the object's velocity. Then, for the evaluation, we consider four different number of Fourier coefficients: 1, 5, 9, and 13.

For initialization, all parameters (except from the Fourier coefficients) are set to Gaussian random values, drawn from the ground truth using variances of 10^{-2}. The Fourier coefficients are initialized as a circular curve with $a_0 = 5$ and $a_1 = b_1 = 0$. In order to predict the object location, we incorporate a *3D constant velocity model* [46] into the prediction step, with a process covariance in the magnitude of 10^{-5}. The following results are obtained from 100 Monte-Carlo runs.

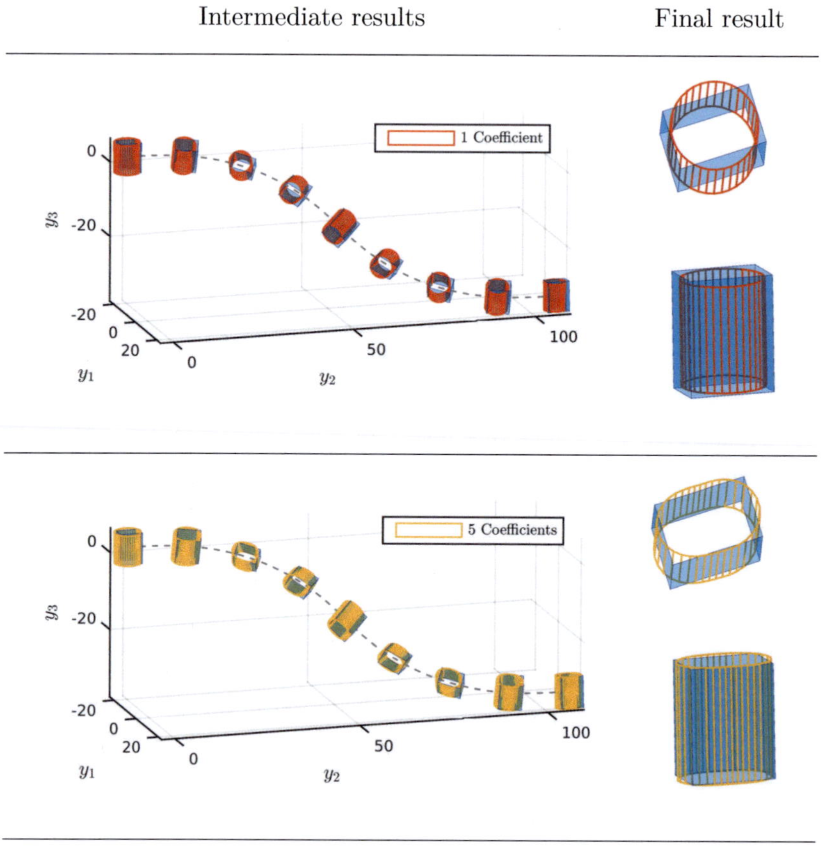

Figure 3.17.: Average results of the box-tracking example for different numbers of Fourier coefficients.

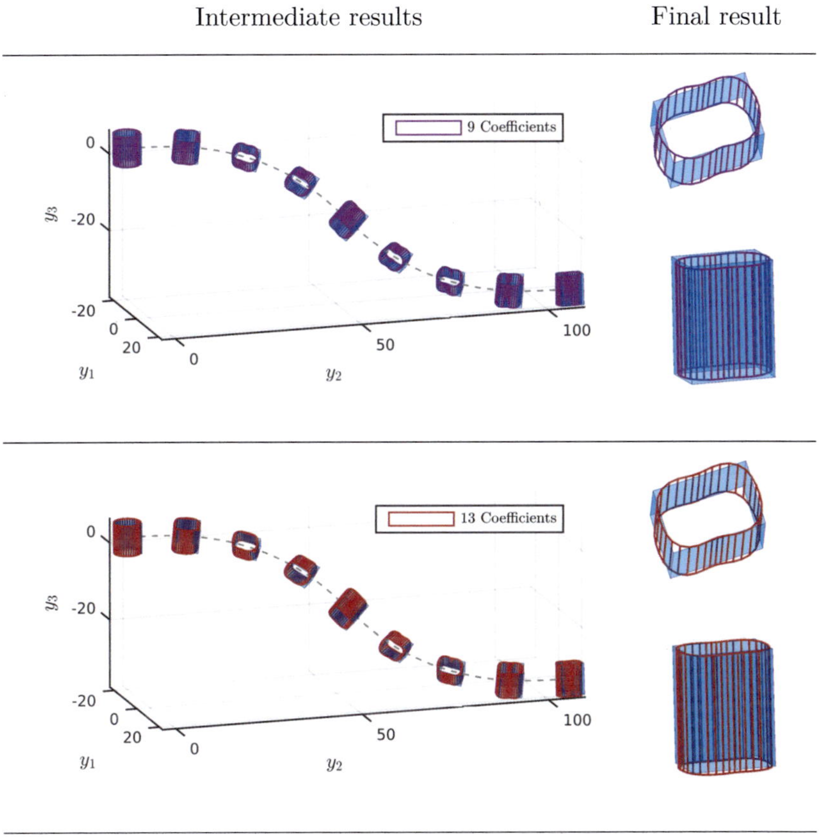

Figure 3.18.: Average results of the box-tracking example for different numbers of Fourier coefficients (continued).

Results Figure 3.17 and Figure 3.18 visualize the average intermediate and final results of the tracking example for different numbers of Fourier coefficients. From the figures, it can be seen that all approaches manage to find the orientation and position of the box quite accurate. In addition, all estimators find correct height parameters, thanks to the 3DRHM. As we would have expected, the major difference can be found in the shape, which becomes more accurate and detailed with increasing number of Fourier coefficients. The "1 Coefficient" approach, which only uses a radius, essentially results in a cylinder-estimator. In addition, the "5 Coefficients" approach already is capable of finding the proportions of the box. For more coefficients, the estimated shapes steadily approach the corners of the box. However, perfectly representing corners with Fourier series requires even higher coefficients, or, as we will discuss in the next chapter, assumptions about the object symmetry. Finally, note that there is no significant bias in the estimated shapes, even though we are using the 3DRHM with GAM-component here. This behavior is due to the low noise and demonstrates the eligibility of the 3DRHM-GAM.

3.8 Conclusions from Chapter 3

In this chapter, we have developed a tracking algorithm for 3D objects that can be constructed by transforming plane curves. In particular, we considered translation, rotation and scaling operations for the surface construction. However, when applying the elemental probabilistic models from Chapter 2 to these shapes, we encountered that only an estimator based on the Spatial Distribution Model would be capable of finding accurate values for all parameters. Unfortunately, SDMs for more complex shapes are computationally demanding.

We studied the origin of the estimation failure in the Greedy Association Model and the Partial Information Model by means of a simple line segment shape. Based on this analysis, we proposed a new probabilistic model for 3D shapes—the 3D Random Hypersurface Model. By assuming a probability for each transformed curve and ignoring (or greedily approximating) the unknown information of "where" on the curve a measurement corresponds to, this model is a combination of an SDM and a PIM (or GAM). The resulting estimator based on the 3DRHM inherited the capability of finding accurate values for all parameters from the SDM and, either the lower computational complexity from the GAM, or the unbiasedness from the PIM.

We confirmed these properties in the evaluation for four different shapes. Specifically, we modeled a cylinder, torus, cone, as well as an extruded star-convex curve. Compared to a state-of-the-art fitting approach, we could reduce the RMSE in the curvature parameters by 44%-77% in the presence of high noise. Moreover, in a tracking scenario, where the pose and shape of a moving box should be estimated (with no prior knowledge about its shape), we demonstrated the flexibility of the new 3DRHM.

CHAPTER 4

Exploiting Geometric Shape Symmetries

Contents

In this chapter, we develop an extension to the proposed tracking algorithms in order to make them more robust against occlusions and missing measurements. These issues (Challenge 3) are inherent when acquiring point clouds by depth sensors, as they always observe only one side of the target object at a time. Even when considering a sensor network, it is rather unlikely to observe an object as a whole. In this chapter, we deal with the question

how to compensate for missing measurements?

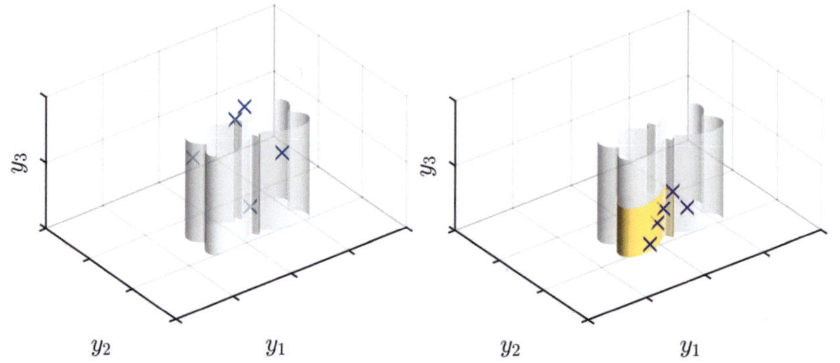

(a) Traditional model. **(b)** Symmetric model.

Figure 4.1.: Where traditional models (a) require modeling measurements $\underline{y}$ (blue) in the full domain, we propose to use symmetric representatives (purple) of these measurements $\underline{y}'$ (b).

The motivation of our approach is that many objects in everyday life have geometric symmetries, i.e., they look the same from different perspectives. For these objects, measurements from one part of the shape also contain information about their occluded counterparts. In the context of computer vision and point cloud processing, known geometric symmetries are already used as a compression tool for shapes [115], a means for improving segmentation [116], as well as a means for scan consolidation [117]. However, to the best of our knowledge, this is the first approach to explicitly incorporate geometric symmetries into probabilistic models for Bayesian extended object tracking.

Object symmetry can be interpreted as shape redundancy that allows it to be constructed from a fraction by some unfolding operation, such as mirroring. Conversely, under specific conditions, we can just fold the measurements and design the probabilistic model only in the reduced domain. This idea is illustrated in Figure 4.1. While the original probabilistic model in Figure 4.1a considers the full domain, the desired model in Figure 4.1b should operate on the folded measurements (purple) and one-eight of the shape (yellow) only. As the two major advantages, the simplified probabilistic model (i) inherently considers the object symmetry, and (ii) has a potentially lower computational complexity. However, transforming measurements has to be applied carefully, as it affects the sensor noise and the association heuristics of measurements to the boundary.

Contribution Our main contribution in this chapter is a scheme for simplifying probabilistic models for Bayesian extended object tracking, given a known object symmetry. We consider rotoreflectional symmetry, which is a generalization of radial and axial symmetry. *Aggregating* all measurements into the *non-redundant* part of the domain allows us to design simplified probabilistic models, which only need to be specified and evaluated using a fraction of the original object. The resulting estimator

- compensates for missing measurements by inferring unobserved shape geometry from symmetry, and
- has a generally reduced computational complexity.

In addition, and to our surprise, when applying symmetric simplification to the SDM for a line segment, its pose and length can be accurately estimated using a simple extended Kalman filter, where the original SDM required more sophisticated nonlinear filtering techniques. In order to demonstrate the power of our approach, we consider a line segment tracking scenario, and extend the moving-box tracking scenario from Chapter 3 by a permanent occlusion.

Remark 4.1. *This chapter builds on work presented in [158, 156].*

4.1 Related Work

There are many approaches related to computer vision that exploit geometric symmetries, e.g., surveyed in [5] and [118]. In the context of [118], our work would be classified as *model acquisition and representation*. In the following, we highlight related work that shares similarities with the approach in this thesis.

(a) Segmentation [116] © 2006 IEEE.

(b) Scan consolidation [117] © 2005 IEEE.

(c) Compression [115]. Printed with kind permission of the authors.

Figure 4.2.: Related approaches which exploit symmetry.

Reflectional symmetry was incorporated into an image-based tracking algorithm [116] that estimates the bounding box of a moving symmetric object (see Figure 4.2a). The popular *Scale-invariant feature transform* (SIFT) from [119] makes assumptions about symmetry, as it is invariant under rotation and scaling. Reflectional symmetry has also been exploited for segmentation purposes [120] and scan consolidation [117] (see Figure 4.2b). Rotational symmetry with respect to a skeleton was used in [121] in order to compensate for a significant lack of measurements. Simplifying a symmetric mesh was proposed in [115], where the authors incorporate symmetry in the data structure of the mesh in order to remove redundancies (see Figure 4.2c). Treating symmetric multimodalities with directional statistics [122] is also a related field of research, as well as symmetric measurement functions [123] that consider symmetry in the sense of invariance to switching specific parts of the state. In [124], symmetric measurement equations were used together with Gaussian kernels in the context of multi-object tracking.

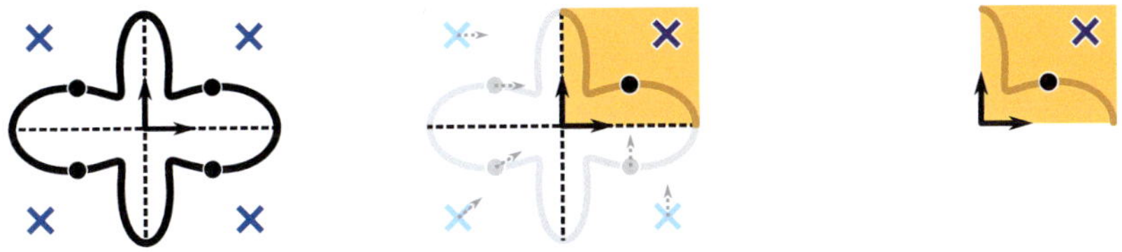

(a) Symmetric equivalents. (b) Aggregation function. (c) Symmetric representatives.

Figure 4.3.: The aggregation function $T(\underline{y})$ transforms all points $\underline{y}$ in the domain to their symmetric representatives in the non-redundant part (yellow).

4.2 Considered Types of Symmetry

In this section, we explain the types of symmetry to be considered in this thesis, and introduce their mathematical formulations. While there are many ways to describe geometric symmetries in general [118], we treat symmetry of as the repetition of a *non-redundant part* of the shape. In other words, the domain is partitioned into a number of symmetric parts and it is sufficient to know the object shape in only one of them in order to infer the rest.

Formally, symmetry can be described by an *aggregation function* $T : \mathbb{R}^d \to \mathbb{R}^d$ that is idempotent with $T(T(\underline{y})) = T(\underline{y})$, and maps each point $\underline{y} \in \mathbb{R}^d$ in the domain on its *symmetric representative* $\underline{y}' := T(\underline{y})$ in the non-redundant part. In the following, we will denote all points, which are mapped on the same representative as its *symmetric equivalents.* A visual explanation of these concepts is given in Figure 4.3 for a 2-axial symmetry. As can be seen, all information to recover the object shape is contained in the non-redundant part, e.g., the first quadrant for the 2-axial symmetry. The blue crosses and the filled black circles serve to emphasize that both measurements and sources can be aggregated by $T(\cdot)$. In the following, we discuss in detail what types of 2D and 3D symmetry are considered in this thesis.

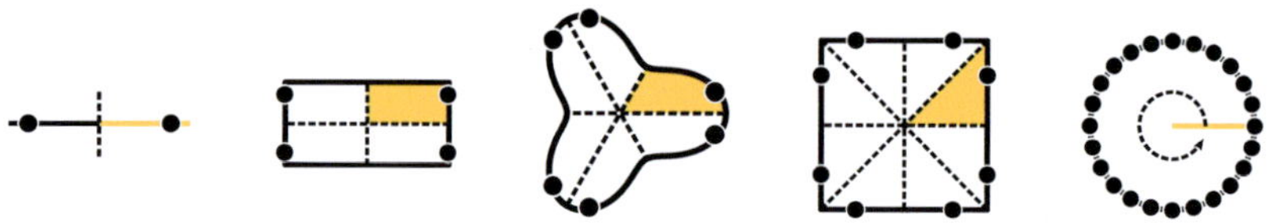

(a) 1-axial (b) 2-axial (c) 3-axial (d) 4-axial (e) radial

Figure 4.4.: Symmetry examples: The non-redundant part of each shape is marked in yellow. One representative and its symmetric equivalents are marked as filled black circles.

4.2.1 2D Symmetry

In 2D, we focus on rotoreflections with $2n$-fold rotation angle, which means a shape is generated by reflecting its non-redundant part with respect to $n \in \mathbb{N}_1$ rotated axes that intersect in the origin. The corresponding 2D symmetries of some selected shapes are visualized in Figure 4.4, and their non-redundant parts are marked in yellow. Rotoreflections include special cases such as axial symmetries in Figure 4.4(a-d), as well as radial symmetry for $n \to \infty$ in Figure 4.4e. Next, we derive formulas for appropriate aggregation functions $T(\,\cdot\,)$.

General Rotoreflection When dealing with rotoreflections in 2D, polar coordinates offer a convenient representation. The conversion of a point $\underline{y}$ from Cartesian coordinates $\underline{y} = [y_1, y_2]^{\mathrm{T}}$ into its corresponding representation in polar coordinates is defined as

$$\begin{aligned} \theta(\underline{y}) &= \operatorname{atan2}(y_2, y_1) \ , \\ r(\underline{y}) &= \sqrt{y_1^2 + y_2^2} \ , \end{aligned} \tag{4.1}$$

where $\theta(\underline{y})$ is the angle to the y_1-axis and $r(\underline{y})$ is the Euclidean norm of $\underline{y}$. For a rotoreflection, its $2n$-fold rotation angle is given by

$$\Theta = \frac{\pi}{n} \ ,$$

which means that each of the n axes of symmetry is rotated about Θ. In terms of polar coordinates, we then define the non-redundant part to lie in the period from 0 to Θ. The corresponding aggregation function $T(\cdot)$ should map all points onto their equivalents in this part. This mapping only requires a modulo operation on the angle $\theta(\underline{y})$ according to

$$\theta(\underline{y}, n) = \begin{cases} \mathrm{mod}(\theta(\underline{y}), \Theta) & \text{if } \lfloor \frac{\theta(\underline{y})}{\Theta} \rfloor \text{ is even} \\ \Theta - \mathrm{mod}(\theta(\underline{y}), \Theta) & \text{if } \lfloor \frac{\theta(\underline{y})}{\Theta} \rfloor \text{ is odd} , \end{cases} \tag{4.2}$$

while leaving the radius $r(\underline{y})$ untouched. The final aggregation function then is given by

$$T(\underline{y}) = \begin{bmatrix} r(\underline{y}) \cdot \cos(\theta(\underline{y}, n)) \\ r(\underline{y}) \cdot \sin(\theta(\underline{y}, n)) \end{bmatrix} . \tag{4.3}$$

Special Cases The general aggregation function (4.3) for rotoreflections includes several special cases. For example, given a reflectional symmetry with respect to the y_2-axis (see Figure 4.4a), the non-redundant part is a half-plane, and the aggregation function

$$T(\underline{y}) = [|y_1|, y_2]^{\mathrm{T}}$$

aggregates points $\underline{y}$ according to their absolute values $|y_1|$. Analogously, the aggregation function for a 2-axial symmetry (see Figure 4.3 and Figure 4.4b) maps each point $\underline{y}$ to the first quadrant, according to

$$T(\underline{y}) = [|y_1|, |y_2|]^{\mathrm{T}} . \tag{4.4}$$

A rotoreflection with $n \to \infty$ axes causes the non-redundant part to collapse into a ray, e.g., the positive y_1-axis, where the aggregation function can be written as

$$T(\underline{y}) = [\|\underline{y}\|, 0]^{\mathrm{T}} ,$$

and maps each point $\underline{y}$ to this axis, according to its Euclidean distance $\|\cdot\|$ to the origin.

4.2.2 3D Symmetry

For rotoreflections in 3D, cylindrical coordinates are chosen. The conversion of a point $\underline{y}$ from Cartesian coordinates $\underline{y} = [y_1, y_2, y_3]^{\mathrm{T}}$ into cylindrical coordinates is very similar to the 2D case. First, (4.1) can be used to derive polar coordinates for the y_1- and y_2-component and second, the height component is immediately given by y_3. Symmetry in y_1 and y_2 can be incorporated by applying (4.3). For symmetry of the y_3 component, we allow a reflection with respect to the y_1y_2-plane, which results in taking the absolute value of y_3. Then, an aggregation function with reflectional symmetry in the height can be defined as

$$T(\underline{y}) = \begin{bmatrix} y_1 \\ y_2 \\ |y_3| \end{bmatrix} . \tag{4.5}$$

As a brief remark, the shape in the motivating example in Figure 4.1 has both a 2-axial symmetry in y_1y_2 and a reflectional symmetry in y_3.

4.3 Simplified Probabilistic Models for Symmetric Objects

In this section, we develop symmetric versions of the elemental probabilistic models, i.e., the Spatial Distribution Model (SDM), the Greedy Association Model (GAM), and the Partial Information Model (PIM). It will turn out that due to their structural differences, each model needs individual treatment. Based on the studies in this section, we will subsequently develop a symmetric version of the 3D Random Hypersurface Model (3DRHM).

Formal Problem Statement We consider the task of estimating the parameters $\underline{x}$ of an extended object based on the likelihood prototype

$$p(\underline{y}|\underline{x}) = \int\limits_{S} \mathcal{N}(\underline{y}; \phi_x(s), \mathbf{C}_v) \cdot p(s|\underline{x}) \, \mathrm{d}s \, ,$$

which was introduced in (2.10). In this formula, the term $\phi_x(s)$ with $s \in S$ represents the boundary function which specifies each point on the object boundary, $p(s|\underline{x})$ is a probability distribution that models how likely it is for each source on the boundary to be measured, and $\mathbf{C}_v$ is the covariance matrix of the Gaussian sensor noise. As a reminder, we showed in Chapter 2 that the elemental probabilistic models essentially differ in the assumptions they make about $p(s|\underline{x})$.

We assume that knowledge is given about the object shape being symmetric in relation to the aggregation function $T(\,\cdot\,)$. From this symmetry follows that, for each point $\phi_x(s)$ on the boundary, its symmetric representative lies also on the boundary. In consequence, it holds that

$$T(\phi_x(s)) = \phi_x(s') \ , \tag{4.6}$$

where $s' \in S' \subseteq S$ is the index of the symmetric representative. Then, the non-redundant part of the boundary can be specified by $S' := \{s \in S \mid T(\phi_x(s)) = \phi_x(s)\}$. The task now is to find simpler expressions for the elemental probabilistic models by incorporating the symmetric relationship (4.6). We start the derivations with two simplifying assumptions, which will be removed subsequently: (i) we consider a 1D boundary which is embedded in the 2D domain, and (ii) we assume the sensor noise to be isotropic.

4.3.1 Key Idea

A straightforward approach to incorporate symmetry into a tracking algorithm consists of unfolding the non-redundant part of the shape in order to generate the full shape, and then use it in one of the probabilistic models in its original form. However, we observed that under specific conditions, the likelihood $p(\underline{y}|\underline{x})$ for a symmetric shape is symmetric too, and it holds that

$$p(\underline{y}|\underline{x}) = p(\underline{y}'|\underline{x}) \ ,$$

where $\underline{y}' = T(\underline{y})$ is the symmetric representative of $\underline{y}$ in the non-redundant part. This observation motivated us to fold the measurements to the non-redundant part $T(\mathbb{R}^d)$ instead of unfolding the non-redundant boundary to the full domain $\mathbb{R}^d$ (see Figure 4.3).

Expected Benefits First, in GAMs and PIMs, where the most likely point on the boundary has to be found for each measurement, the computational complexity could be significantly reduced by only focusing on a fraction of the domain. As an intuitive example, let us assume the boundary function $\phi_x(s)$ would be implemented by a polygon with N edges in total. Finding the most likely point on this polygon for a given measurement then would require processing all N edges. If we could only consider the boundary in the non-redundant part, we could potentially reduce the number of required edges to the fraction $\frac{N}{2n}$, where n is the number of axes for the rotoreflection. In turn, this reduction of complexity could be either used to speed up calculations, or to increase the number of edges (i.e. the shape detail) by keeping the calculation effort.

Second, in SDMs, the folding operation coincidentally aggregates not only the symmetric equivalents of each measurement source $\phi_x(s)$ but also their individual probabilities $p(s|\underline{x})$. This introduces ignorance on the symmetric parts of the object, and, in sampling-based estimators where a Gaussian is to be evaluated for a set of points on the boundary, the resolution of these points could be significantly increased.

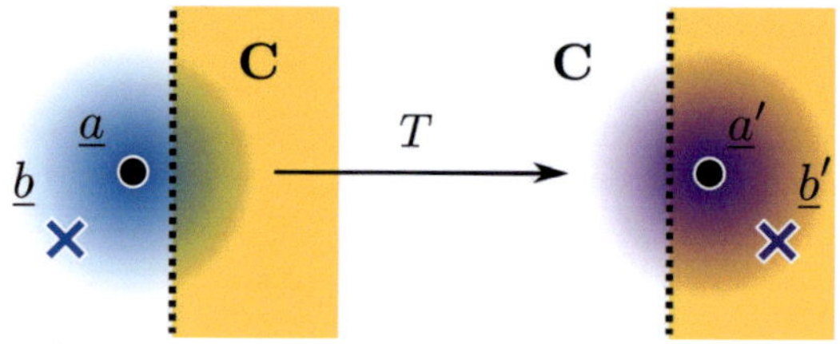

Figure 4.5.: Property 1: Symmetry of the Gaussian distribution for reflection.

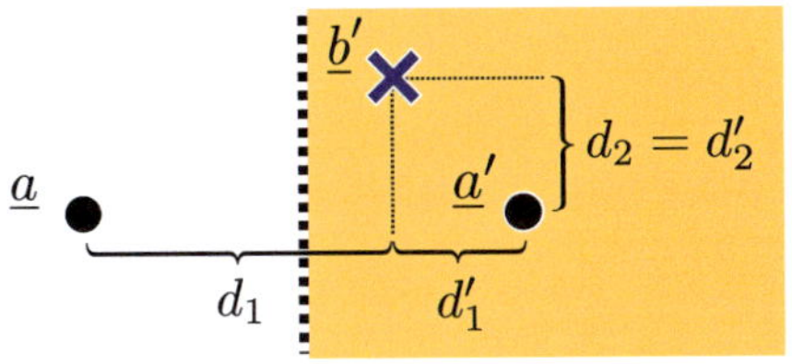

Figure 4.6.: Property 2: The Euclidean distance of a symmetric representative $\underline{b}'$ to the symmetric equivalents of another point $\underline{a}$ is minimum for its symmetric representative $\underline{a}'$.

Approach to Achieve Symmetric Simplification We want to specify the object boundary only in the non-redundant part of the domain through a (potentially) simpler boundary function $\phi'_{\underline{x}}(s')$ with $s \in S'$ and then use $\underline{y}' = T(\underline{y})$ in the estimator. Our tasks are now

1. proving that $p(\underline{y}|\underline{x}) = p(\underline{y}'|\underline{x})$ holds, i.e., the likelihood produces the same value for all symmetric equivalents, and
2. ensuring that for the symmetric representative $\underline{y}'$, all calculations can be performed in the non-redundant part of the domain, i.e., the symmetric parts are not required.

For these derivations, we will employ the following two properties.

Property 1: Symmetry of the Gaussian Distribution Consider a Gaussian distribution $\mathcal{N}(\underline{b}; \underline{a}, \mathbf{C})$ with mean $\underline{a}$ and isotropic covariance matrix $\mathbf{C}$ that is evaluated in $\underline{b}$. Given an aggregation function $T(\cdot)$ that implements a rotoreflection, the symmetric representatives for $\underline{a}$ and $\underline{b}$ can be derived according to $\underline{a}' = T(\underline{a})$ and $\underline{b}' = T(\underline{b})$. Given that $\underline{a}$ and $\underline{b}$ both lie in the same symmetric part it will always hold that

$$\mathcal{N}(\underline{b}; \underline{a}, \mathbf{C}) = \mathcal{N}\left(\underline{b}'; \underline{a}', \mathbf{C}\right) .$$

This relationship is visually explained in Figure 4.5. The isotropic covariance matrix is not affected by the aggregation. □

Property 2: Minimum Euclidean Distance to Symmetric Points Consider a point $\underline{b}'$ in the non-redundant part, and the symmetric equivalents of another point $\underline{a}$. Then it follows that the Euclidean distance between $\underline{b}'$ and the symmetric representative $\underline{a}' = T(\underline{a})$ is always shorter than the distance between $\underline{b}'$ and $\underline{a}$. In Figure 4.6 the proof for this relationship is illustrated. As can be seen, $\underline{a}$ and $\underline{a}'$ are symmetric with respect to the dashed black line, and the non-redundant part is colored in yellow. Let $d = \|\underline{b}' - \underline{a}\|$ and $d' = \|\underline{b}' - \underline{a}'\|$ denote the Euclidean distances between the point $\underline{b}'$ and $\underline{a}$, $\underline{a}'$. For the individual components of these distances it is always true that $d_2 = d_2'$ and $d_1 \geq d_1'$. From this relationship, it follows that

$$d = \sqrt{(d_1)^2 + (d_2)^2} \geq \sqrt{(d_1')^2 + (d_2')^2} = d'$$

holds, which means that the distance d' is always smaller than d. □

Even though we only proved the validity of the properties for one reflection axis, they immediately generalize to arbitrary rotoreflections by successively processing one axis after another. Let us now start simplifying the probabilistic models. We start with the GAM, which allows for a straightforward incorporation of symmetry, and then look at the more challenging SDM and PIM.

4.3.2 Symmetric Greedy Association Model

We consider an object with boundary function $\phi_x(s)$ for $s \in S$. As a reminder, for a measurement $\underline{y}$ and a state $\underline{x}$, the GAM (2.15) is given by $p(\underline{y}|\underline{x}) = \mathcal{N}(\underline{y}; \phi_x(\pi_x(\underline{y})), \mathbf{C}_v)$, where $\pi_x(\underline{y})$ refers to the source with the shortest Euclidean distance to the measurement. Let the object have a rotoreflectional symmetry according to the aggregation function $T(\,\cdot\,)$ and let $\underline{y}' = T(\underline{y})$ be the symmetric representative of the measurement $\underline{y}$. In order to use the symmetric representative $\underline{y}'$ in the likelihood, we have to show that

$$\begin{aligned} p(\underline{y}|\underline{x}) &= \mathcal{N}(\underline{y}; \phi_x(\pi_x(\underline{y})), \mathbf{C}_v) \\ &= \mathcal{N}(\underline{y}'; \phi_x(\pi_x(\underline{y}')), \mathbf{C}_v) \\ &= p(\underline{y}'|\underline{x}) \end{aligned} \tag{4.7}$$

holds. For the proof, we can exploit Property 1 and Property 2 in the following way. The identity in (4.7) immediately follows from Property 1 for $\underline{y}$ and $\phi_x(\pi_x(\underline{y}))$ lying in the same symmetric part. Property 2, in turn, ensures this condition by stating that the closest symmetric equivalent of a point to another is the one that lies in the same symmetric part. In consequence, we can define and evaluate (4.7) exclusively in the non-redundant part.

Simplification First, we define $\phi'_x(s)$ as an arbitrary boundary function in the non-redundant part that might exploit one of the expected benefits mentioned in Section 4.3.1 (e.g., a polygon with more vertices). Then, we substitute $\phi_x(s)$ by $\phi'_x(s)$ in (4.7) and write

$$\begin{aligned} p(\underline{y}|\underline{x}) &= \mathcal{N}(\underline{y}'; \phi'_x(\pi_x(\underline{y}')), \mathbf{C}_v) \\ &= \mathcal{N}(T(\underline{y}); \phi'_x(\pi_x(T(\underline{y}))), \mathbf{C}_v) \, . \end{aligned} \tag{4.8}$$

The corresponding simplified generative model is given by

$$\begin{aligned} \underline{0} &= h(\underline{x}, \underline{y}, \underline{v}) \\ &= T(\underline{y}) - \phi'_x(\pi_x(T(\underline{y}))) - \underline{v} \, . \end{aligned}$$

4.3.3 Symmetric Spatial Distribution Model

Again, we consider an object whose boundary is specified by $\phi_x(s)$ with $s \in S$. The SDM (2.10) is given by $p(\underline{y}|\underline{x}) = \int_S \mathcal{N}(\underline{y}; \phi_x(s), \mathbf{C}_v) \cdot p(s|\underline{x}) \, \mathrm{d}s$, where $p(s|\underline{x})$ explicitly specifies how likely it is for each source on the object boundary to be measured. Let the object again be symmetric with respect to $T(\cdot)$ and let $\underline{y}' = T(\underline{y})$ be the symmetric representative of the measurement $\underline{y}$. Unfortunately, evaluating the SDM for different symmetric equivalents may produce different values in the likelihood

$$\begin{aligned} p(\underline{y}|\underline{x}) &= \int_S \mathcal{N}(\underline{y}; \phi_x(s), \mathbf{C}_v) \cdot p(s|\underline{x}) \, \mathrm{d}s \\ &\neq \int_S \mathcal{N}(\underline{y}'; \phi_x(s), \mathbf{C}_v) \cdot p(s|\underline{x}) \, \mathrm{d}s \\ &= p(\underline{y}'|\underline{x}) \, , \end{aligned}$$

as $\underline{y}$ and $\phi_x(s)$ do not always lie in the same symmetric part (see Figure 4.7a), and $p(s|\underline{x})$ is not necessarily symmetric. In consequence, the original SDM is generally not symmetric, not even for symmetric shapes. However, we can derive a symmetric version of the SDM by aggregating symmetric measurement sources.

Aggregation For this purpose, let $s' \in S'$ denote measurement sources $\phi_x(s')$ in the non-redundant part. In addition, let $s \in [s']$ refer to their symmetric equivalents through

$$[s'] := \{ s \in S \mid T(\phi_x(s)) = \phi_x(s') \} \, . \tag{4.9}$$

In a next step, we derive the marginalized probability distribution $p(s'|\underline{x})$ for the representatives according to

$$p(s'|\underline{x}) = \sum_{s \in [s']} p(s|\underline{x}) \, . \tag{4.10}$$

For the example in Figure 4.7b, $p(s_1|\underline{x})$ and $p(s_2|\underline{x})$ would be summed up by (4.10). The intuitive interpretation of this aggregation is as follows: Where $p(s|\underline{x})$ formerly specified how likely each individual source $\phi_x(s)$ on the object boundary is measured, $p(s'|\underline{x})$ specifies how likely any (no matter which) of the symmetric equivalents of $\phi_x(s')$ is measured.

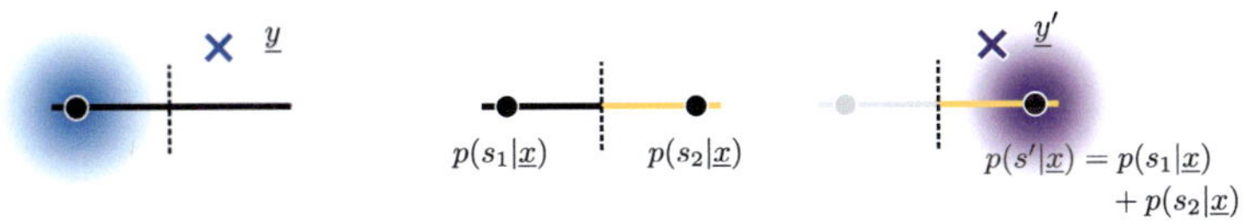

(a) original SDM. **(b)** Aggregation. **(c)** SDM with symmetry.

Figure 4.7.: Process of deriving a symmetric version of an SDM.

Simplification This ignorance, in turn, lets us define and evaluate an SDM exclusively in the non-redundant part, according to

$$p(\underline{y}|\underline{x}) = \int_{S'} \mathcal{N}(T(\underline{y}); \phi'_x(s'), \mathbf{C}_v) \cdot p(s'|\underline{x}) \, \mathrm{d}s' \, . \tag{4.11}$$

where we again substituted the boundary function $\phi_x(\,\cdot\,)$ by a simpler one $\phi'_x(\,\cdot\,)$. A visualization is given in Figure 4.7c. However, note that (4.11) is only an approximation of the original SDM as we waived the capability of defining individual probabilities for sources in the different symmetric parts. The corresponding measurement equation is given by

$$\begin{aligned} \underline{0} &= h(\underline{x}, \underline{y}, s', \underline{v}) \\ &= T(\underline{y}) - \phi'_x(s') - \underline{v} \, . \end{aligned}$$

4.3.4 Symmetric Partial Information Model

Once more, we consider an object whose boundary is specified by $\phi_x(s)$ with $s \in S$. The PIM $p(l_y|\underline{x}, s_y)$ according to (2.31) is an approximation for the original likelihood $p(\underline{y}|\underline{x})$, where $l_y = g_x(\underline{y})$ is the Euclidean distance to the closest source $\phi_x(0, s_y)$ on the boundary, which is referred to by $s_y = \pi_x(\underline{y})$. For this purpose, we extended the boundary function by the second parameter l_y. Evaluating $p(l_y|\underline{x}, s_y)$ then requires integrating the Gaussian distribution of the sensor noise along the l_y-level, as visually explained in Figure 4.8a.

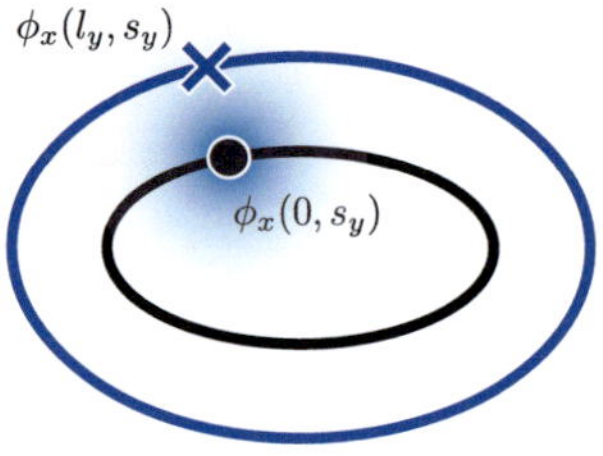

(a) PIM without symmetry.

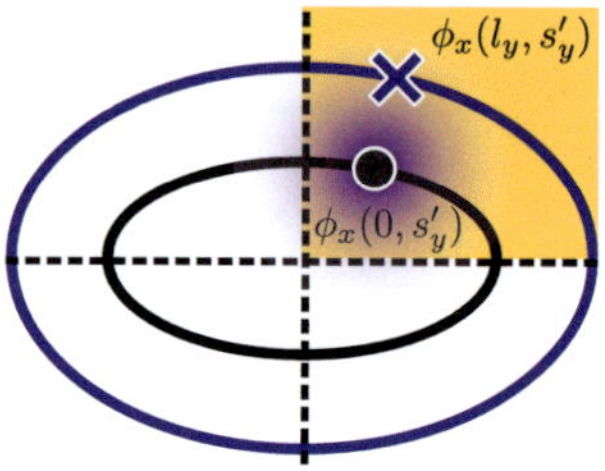

(b) PIM with symmetry.

Figure 4.8.: Evaluating the PIM requires integrating along the entire l_y-level.

Let the object again be symmetric with respect to $T(\,\cdot\,)$ and let $\underline{y}' = T(\underline{y})$ be the symmetric representative of the measurement $\underline{y}$. From Property 2, it follows that all symmetric equivalents of a measurement $\underline{y}$ have the same Euclidean distance $l_y = l'_y$ to the boundary and it holds that

$$T(\phi_x(l_y, s_y)) = \phi_x(l_y, s'_y)\ . \tag{4.12}$$

As this aggregation does not affects l_y at all, evaluating (2.31) produces identical values for all symmetric equivalents $p(l_y|\underline{x}, s_y) = p(l_y|\underline{x}, s'_y)$. This identity is visually explained in Figure 4.8, where the same l_y-level is to be integrated. However, as this integration runs through all symmetric parts, it is not possible to evaluate it in the non-redundant part without applying non-trivial folding operations to the Gaussian.

Approximation Even though the original PIM requires modeling the object in the full domain, we found that its Gaussian approximation (2.35) is symmetric

$$\begin{aligned} p(l_y|\underline{x}, s_y) &= \mathcal{N}\left(l_y; \mathrm{E}\{l_v\}, \mathrm{Var}\{l_v\}\right) \\ &= p(l_y|\underline{x}, s'_y) \end{aligned}$$

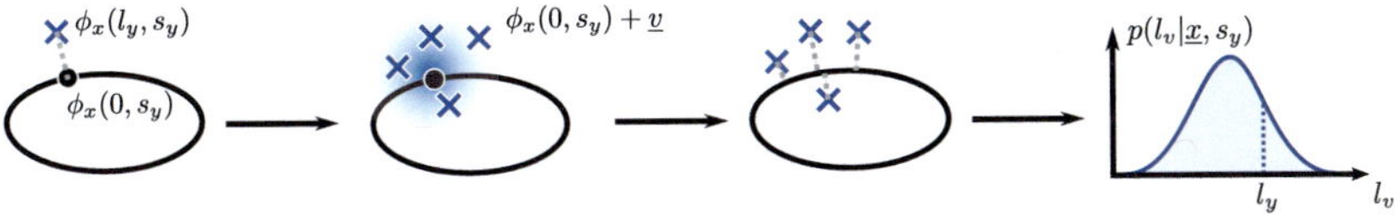

(a) Without symmetry.

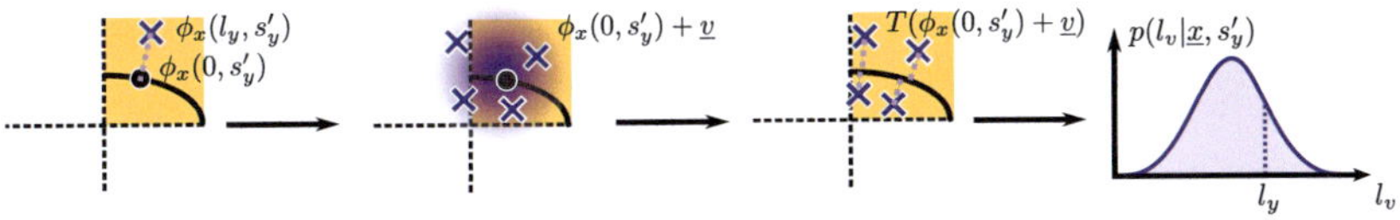

(b) With symmetry.

Figure 4.9.: Sampling-based approximation of the PIM with and without symmetry.

as well, and can be exclusively evaluated in the non-redundant part. As a brief reminder, the approximated PIM is based on moment matching of the partial noise $l_v = g_x(\phi_x(0, s_y) + \underline{v})$, which encodes the expected distribution of Euclidean distances when measuring $\phi_x(0, s_y)$. The Euclidean distance, in turn, can be calculated exclusively in the non-redundant part, according to Property 2. In the following, we detail the sampling-based approach (2.36).

In particular, we show that the calculations for a measurement $\underline{y}$ and its symmetric representative $\underline{y}'$ result in identical distributions for l_v. Figure 4.9 provides a direct visual comparison. As can be seen in Figure 4.9b, all steps are equivalent, except for the aggregation $T(\phi_x(0, s_y) + \underline{v})$ in the third step for the symmetric approach. This folding operation is required, as the simulated sensor noise may produce simulated measurements outside of the non-redundant part. However, we are only interested in the l_y-values of these measurements, which are not affected by folding according to (4.12). In consequence, it holds that

$$\begin{aligned} \mathrm{E}\{l_v\} &= \mathrm{E}\{g_x(\phi_x(0, s_y) + \underline{v})\} \\ &= \mathrm{E}\big\{g_x(T(\phi_x(0, s'_y) + \underline{v}))\big\} \ , \end{aligned} \tag{4.13}$$

which, analogously, holds for the variance $\mathrm{Var}\{l_v\}$.

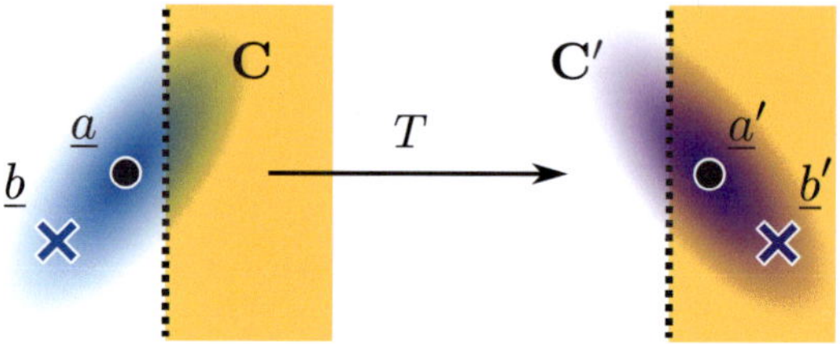

Figure 4.10.: Property 1: Equivalence of the Gaussian distribution with its reflected counterpart.

Simplification In consequence, we can substitute the boundary function $\phi_x(\,\cdot\,)$ in (4.13) by a simpler one $\phi'_x(\,\cdot\,)$ that only needs to be specified in the non-redundant part and use

$$\begin{aligned}\mathrm{E}\{l_v\} &= \mathrm{E}\big\{g_x(T(\phi'_x(0, s'_y) + \underline{v}))\big\} \\ &= \mathrm{E}\big\{g_x(T(\phi'_x(0, \pi_x(T(\underline{y})) + \underline{v}))\big\}\ .\end{aligned}$$

Finally, the corresponding measurement equation is given by

$$\begin{aligned}0 &= h(\underline{x}, \underline{v}, \underline{y}) \\ &= g_x(T(\underline{y})) - g_x(T(\phi'_x(\pi_x(T(\underline{y}))) + \underline{v}))\ .\end{aligned}$$

4.3.5 Discussion

In addition to the technical descriptions and derivations from the previous section, there are some interesting facts about our approach that should be noted.

Implementation As all symmetric considerations are encapsulated in the likelihood (or measurement equation), the proposed simplifications do not require any adaptations to the estimator being used. Specifically, the Bayes update can still be derived by using Algorithm A.2 (or Algorithm A.1) by means of simply switching to the symmetric version of the likelihood (or measurement equation).

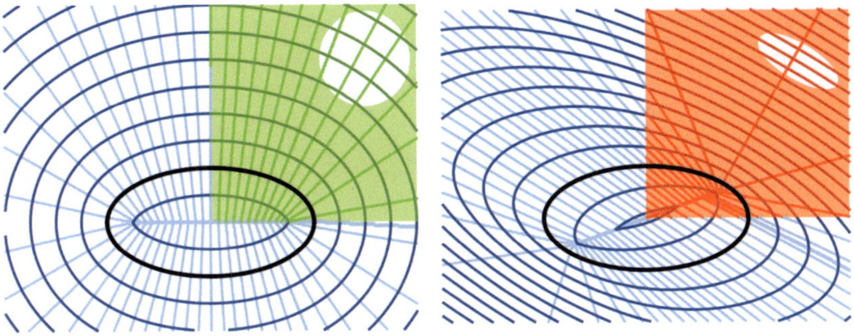

(a) Isotropic sensor noise.

(b) Anisotropic sensor noise.

Figure 4.11.: Symmetry of ellipse for isotropic and anisotropic sensor noise.

Anisotropic Noise When approaching to apply symmetric simplification in the presence of anisotropic noise, the properties, which have been discussed in Section 4.3.1 do not longer hold in their original form. In particular,

- Property 1 still holds for anisotropic Gaussian distributions, but the covariance matrix $\mathbf{C}$ is to be rotoreflected as well (see Figure 4.10), and
- Property 2 does not hold for the Mahalanobis distance, due to its anisotropy.

Both changes have consequences in the probabilistic models. For example, as Property 2 is not fulfilled, there is no guarantee that the closest measurement source of a measurement lies in the same symmetric part. Figure 4.11 visually explains what that means for an elliptical boundary. For isotropic noise, the s-levels in Figure 4.11a (which relate points to their closest measurement source), do not leave their symmetric parts. In contrast, for anisotropic noise, some s-levels run through multiple symmetric parts, as can be seen in Figure 4.11b. Moreover, the l- and s-levels are not even symmetric with respect to the object geometry, which makes the situation even more complicated.

However, symmetric simplification can be still applied by, e.g., approximating its distribution with an isotropic one. Unfortunately, this rather pragmatic approach would introduce another additional approximation. A more sophisticated idea would be adapting the aggregation function $T(\,\cdot\,)$ so that it folds points to their symmetric representatives according to their respective ls-values, instead of their Cartesian coordinates.

Higher Dimensions It is also possible to apply symmetric simplification to measurements of higher dimensionality. For example when considering shape estimation and tracking in 3D, the derivations are analog to those in 2D. Note that symmetric simplification could even be applied to measurements with higher dimensionality. That is, when the shape color is considered as a measurement as well and is symmetric with respect to the object geometry, we can easily add a color vector $\underline{c}$ to the original measurement vector $\underline{y}$. Then, aggregation can be applied in the form of $T([\underline{y}^{\mathrm{T}}, \underline{c}^{\mathrm{T}}]^{\mathrm{T}})$, where the spatial component is mapped to its representative in the non-redundant part and the color remains untouched. This type of generalization also applies related features such as normals or curvature, as long as they are symmetric with respect to the object geometry.

Generalization The proposed approach is a general solution to exploit symmetries in probabilistic models and is not restricted to shape estimation and tracking. Whenever a likelihood function fulfills the symmetric relationship $p(\underline{y}|\underline{x}) = p(\underline{y}'|\underline{x})$ for a measurement $\underline{y}$ and some kind of symmetric representative $\underline{y}' = T(\underline{y})$, we can potentially find simpler expressions for the probabilistic model. However, note that incorporating symmetry will always yield an implicit measurement equation in the form of

$$\underline{0} = h(\underline{x}, \underline{y}, \underline{v}) \ ,$$

as the original measurement $\underline{y}$ is internally treated as its symmetric representative $T(\underline{y})$, whose calculation requires knowledge of the state parameters $\underline{x}$.

4.4 Simplified 3D Random Hypersurface Model

In this section, we develop a symmetric version of the 3DRHM from Chapter 3. As a brief reminder, we consider objects whose surface can be constructed by transformed plane curves according to the function $\Phi_{x,u}(s)$. This function has been defined in (3.1) and takes two parameters, where $u \in U$ controls the transformation of the curve, and $s \in S$ iterates through the curves.

The 3DRHM is a probabilistic model that describes, how a given sensor will measure points from the surface of an object. For this purpose, the probability distribution of u is explicitly modeled in the fashion of SDMs (slice selection), and the distribution of s is ignored, just as in GAMs or PIMs (slice likelihood). For the symmetric considerations in this section, we focus on the 3DRHM-GAM from (3.16), which is given as

$$p(\underline{y}|\underline{x}) = \int_U \underbrace{\mathcal{N}(\underline{y}; \Phi_{x,u}(\pi_{x,u}(\underline{y})), \mathbf{C}_v)}_{\text{slice likelihood}} \cdot \underbrace{p(u|\underline{x})}_{\text{slice selection}} \, du \,, \qquad (4.14)$$

with $\Phi_{x,u}(\pi_{x,u}(\underline{y}))$ being the greedy approximation of the true measurement source for each transformed curve.

Due to the inherent separation of the 3DRHM-GAM into SDM (slice selection) and GAM (slice likelihood), we can consider their symmetric simplification individually. Figure 4.12 exemplary illustrates the meaning for both types of symmetry. That is, the extruded star-convex curve object is symmetric with respect to its length axis (see Figure 4.12a), which allows for exploiting symmetry in the slice selection. In addition, the 2-axial symmetry of each transformed curve, which is illustrated in Figure 4.12b, can be exploited in the slice likelihood. In the remainder of this section, we first consider symmetry in the slice selection and then in the slice likelihood. Note that, even though both types of symmetry will be discussed separately, they are not mutually exclusive, which means that the estimator can take advantage of both types simultaneously, as initially motivated in Figure 4.1.

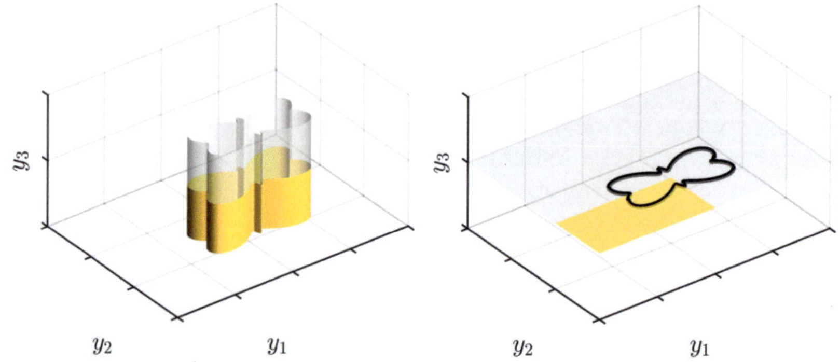

(a) Symmetric slice selection. **(b)** Symmetric slice likelihood.

Figure 4.12.: The 3DRHM can be subject to two types of symmetry: for the slice selcetion, and for the slice likelihood.

4.4.1 Symmetric Slice Selection

Symmetry in the slice selection technically means that the object shape is composed of slices with identical curves. For example when folding the extruded star-convex curve object in Figure 4.12a with respect to the y_1y_2-plane, each curve u is reflected exactly onto another identical curve u'. Assuming this folding operation to be encoded in the aggregation function $T(\,\cdot\,)$, symmetry in the slice selection can be expressed as

$$T\left(\Phi_{x,u}(s)\right) = \Phi_{x,u'}(s)\ .$$

That is, the aggregation function $T(\,\cdot\,)$ maps a point $\Phi_{x,u}(s)$ on the curve in a slice u to its symmetric representative $\Phi_{x,u'}(s)$ on the curve in the slice u' that lies in the non-redundant part. Note that the parameter s is not affected by this aggregation.

For the 3DRHM, we assume the parameter u to be modeled according to an SDM with known probability distribution of $p(u|\underline{x})$. In order to simplify (4.14), we can derive a symmetric SDM according to Section 4.3.3, which is an approximation of the original SDM. For this purpose, we have (i) identify the indices $u \in [u']$ of all symmetric equivalents of a symmetric representative $\Phi_{x,u'}(s)$ according to (4.9), and (ii) aggregate the values of their probability distribution according to (4.10)

$$p(u'|\underline{x}) = \sum_{u \in [u']} p(u|\underline{x}) \ .$$

Simplification The simplified model according to (4.11) is given by

$$p(\underline{y}|\underline{x}) = \int_{U'} \mathcal{N}(T(\underline{y}); \Phi'_{x,u'}(\pi_{x,u'}(T(\underline{y}))), \mathbf{C}_v) \cdot p(u'|\underline{x}) \, \mathrm{d}u' \ , \quad (4.15)$$

where Φ could be replaced by Φ', which only needs to be modeled in the non-redundant part. The simplified measurement equation that corresponds to (4.15) is given by

$$\begin{aligned} \underline{0} &= h(\underline{x}, \underline{y}, u', \underline{v}) \\ &= T(\underline{y}) - \Phi'_{x,u'}(\pi_{x,u'}(T(\underline{y})) - \underline{v} \ . \end{aligned}$$

In the following, we simplify the SDM of a line segment, which is the most simple example for a shape that takes advantage of symmetric slice selection.

Example 4.1 (Symmetric Line Segment)**.** *As previously discussed in Section 3.3, a line segment SDM can be seen as a 3DRHM for a cylinder with radius* 0*. Within this interpretation, the curve in each slice u is a point $\Phi_{x,u}$. For a line segment with length d, which is centered on the origin, the boundary function is given by*

$$\Phi_{x,u} = \begin{bmatrix} 0 \\ 0 \\ u \cdot \frac{d}{2} \end{bmatrix} \ , \quad (4.16)$$

where $u \in U = [-1, 1]$ iterates the point along the segment. We intentionally set the center to the origin, for a convenient incorporation of symmetry. For $p(u|\underline{x})$, we assume a uniform distribution with value $\frac{1}{2}$ for all $u \in U$. As the line segment is symmetric with respect to the $y_1 y_2$-plane, we can use the aggregation function $\underline{y}' = T(\underline{y}) = [y_1, y_2, |y_3|]^{\mathrm{T}}$ from (4.5), in order to map points to the non-redundant part.

For simplification, we have to identify all symmetric equivalents according to (4.9)*. This identification yields* $[u'] = \{u, -u\}$ *with* $u' \in U' = [0,1]$*. Then, the original probabilities* $p(u|\underline{x})$ *of the symmetric equivalents are aggregated to* $p(u'|\underline{x})$ *by summing them up according to* (4.10)*. As all* u' *refer to two elements* $-u$ *and* u*, the aggregation yields* $p(u'|\underline{x}) = \frac{1}{2} + \frac{1}{2} = 1$*. Finally, the simplified model can be obtained by plugging* (4.16) *and* $p(u'|\underline{x})$ *into* (4.15) *according to*

$$p(\underline{y}|\underline{x}) = \int_0^1 \mathcal{N}([y_1, y_2, |y_3|]^{\mathrm{T}}; [0, 0, u \cdot \tfrac{d}{2}]^{\mathrm{T}}, \mathbf{C}_v) \, \mathrm{d}u' \ , \qquad (4.17)$$

with $\mathbf{C}_v$ *being the covariance matrix of the isotropic sensor noise. Please note that we have not replaced the boundary function* Φ*, as there does not exist a simpler one. Nevertheless, in Section 4.5, we will show that* (4.17) *outperforms its non-symmetric version from* (3.10)*.*

4.4.2 Symmetric Slice Likelihood

Symmetry in the slice likelihood means that the curve within each slice is symmetric. For example the star-convex curve object in Figure 4.12b has a 2-axial symmetry. Assuming the symmetry to be encoded in $T(\cdot)$, symmetry in a slice can be expressed as

$$T\left(\Phi_{x,u}(s)\right) = \Phi_{x,u}(s') \ .$$

That is, the aggregation function $T(\cdot)$ maps a point $\Phi_{x,u}(s)$ on the curve in a given slice to its symmetric representative $\Phi_{x,u}(s')$ in the non-redundant part in the same slice. In doing so, the parameter u is not affected by this aggregation.

For the 3DRHM-GAM, we assume the parameter s to be modeled according to a GAM, which means that it is approximated by its most likely estimate $s \approx \pi_{x,u}(\underline{y})$. In order to simplify (4.14), we can derive a symmetric GAM according to Section 4.3.2. For this purpose, we just have to substitute the measurement $\underline{y}$ by its symmetric representative $\underline{y}' = T(\underline{y})$.

Simplification The simplified model according to (4.8) is given by

$$p(\underline{y}|\underline{x}) = \int_U \mathcal{N}(T(\underline{y}); \Phi'_{x,u}(\pi_{x,u}(T(\underline{y}))), \mathbf{C}_v) \cdot p(u|\underline{x}) \, du \,,$$

where we can again substitute the boundary function Φ by a simpler one Φ'. The corresponding measurement equation is given by

$$\begin{aligned} \underline{0} &= h(\underline{x}, \underline{y}, u, \underline{v}) \\ &= T(\underline{y}) - \Phi'_{x,u}(\pi_{x,u}(T(\underline{y}))) - \underline{v} \,. \end{aligned}$$

In the following, we simplify the GAM-component of a 3DRHM for an extruded star-convex curve.

Example 4.2 (Symmetric Star-convex Curve). *We consider the extruded star-convex curve from Section 3.2.4, which is specified by*

$$\Phi_{x,u}(s) = \begin{bmatrix} r(s) \cdot \cos(s) \\ r(s) \cdot \sin(s) \\ u \cdot \frac{d}{2} \end{bmatrix} \,,$$

and where $r(s)$ is a polar function (3.5) *that determines the radius for each angle $s \in [0, 2\pi)$, and $u \in [-1, 1]$ shifts the curve between bottom and top. In this representation, the object is centered on the origin, and has a length of d. Now, instead of exploiting symmetry of the parameter u, we are interested in exploiting symmetry of s. For this example, we assume that prior knowledge is available that the star-convex curve has a 2-axial symmetry* (4.4) *according to $\underline{y}' = T(\underline{y}) = [|y_1|, |y_2|, y_3]^{\mathrm{T}}$. The corresponding non-redundant part is the first quadrant with angles (for the polar representation) between* 0 *and $\frac{\pi}{2}$, as illustrated in Figure 4.13. We can use* (4.2) *for transforming arbitrary points with angle s to the non-redundant according to $s' = \theta(\phi_x(s), n)$, where $n = 2$ is the number of symmetry axes.*

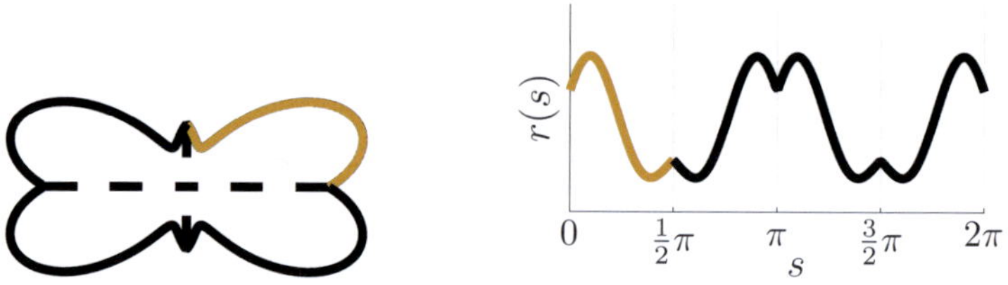

(a) Object contour. (b) Radius function.

Figure 4.13.: Star-convex object with 2-axial symmetry, represented by a polar function. The non-redundant part of the boundary is colored yellow.

Then, we can simplify the GAM by substituting the original boundary function $\Phi_{x,u}(s)$ *by another one* $\Phi'_{x,u}(s')$ *that is exclusively defined and evaluated in the non-redundant part. Specifically, we can employ an alternative radius function* $r'(s')$ *in*

$$\Phi'_{x,u}(s') = \begin{bmatrix} r'(s') \cdot \cos(s') \\ r'(s') \cdot \sin(s') \\ u \cdot \frac{d}{2} \end{bmatrix} , \tag{4.18}$$

where s' *must only be considered in* $[0, \frac{\pi}{2}]$. *For this purpose, we can modify the period of the Fourier series from* (3.5) *according to the number of symmetry axes*

$$r'(s') = \frac{a_0}{2} + \sum_{m=1}^{M} a_m \cos(m \cdot n \cdot s') + b_m \sin(m \cdot n \cdot s') ,$$

as discussed in [158]. Finally, the simplified model can be obtained by plugging (4.18) *and* $p(u'|\underline{x})$ *into* (4.15) *according to*

$$p(\underline{y}'|\underline{x}) = \int_{-1}^{1} \mathcal{N}\left(\begin{bmatrix} |y_1| \\ |y_2| \\ y_3 \end{bmatrix} ; \begin{bmatrix} r'(\pi_{x,u}(\underline{y}')) \cdot \cos(\pi_{x,u}(\underline{y}')) \\ r'(\pi_{x,u}(\underline{y}')) \cdot \sin(\pi_{x,u}(\underline{y}')) \\ u \cdot \frac{d}{2} \end{bmatrix} , \mathbf{C}_v \right) \cdot p(u|\underline{x}) \, \mathrm{d}u \, . \tag{4.19}$$

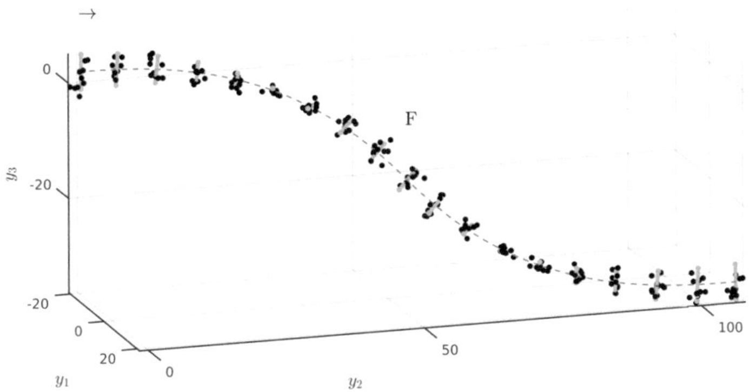

Figure 4.14.: Line segment tracking experiment. The line segment moves with constant speed along the S-shaped track while performing a rotation.

4.5 Evaluation

In this section, we evaluate the symmetric probabilistic models in two estimation scenarios with synthetic data. First, we consider the task of tracking a moving line segment and compare the traditional non-symmetric model to the symmetric one. In a second scenario, we look again at the task of tracking the moving box from Section 3.7.2 and show how symmetry in this scenario can help to compensate for missing measurements (Challenge 3).

4.5.1 Tracking a Moving Line Segment

Let us first look at the task of tracking a moving line segment.

Experiment Figure 4.14 shows the track, together with the ground truth line segment with a length of 6, drawn at selected locations. While the object moves, a simulated sensor performs 250 point cloud measurements, where each cloud consists of 10 points. For the selected locations, exemplary measurements are drawn as black dots. The measurement sources were uniformly drawn from the segment and then distorted by additive Gaussian sensor noise with $\mathbf{C}_v = 5 \cdot 10^{-1} \cdot \mathbf{I}$. For the evaluation, we consider four tracking algorithms.

- **SDM PGF:** The state-of-the-art approach to line segment tracking [64, 149] is using a Spatial Distribution Model (3.10) together with a particle filter. We set up a comparable approach based on a PGF [97]. In doing so, we approximate the uniform distribution over $p(u|\underline{x})$ by a Dirac-Mixture with 51 equidistant samples.
- **SDM EKF:** In order to demonstrate that the SDM for a line segment cannot adequately be used together with a linear filter, we additionally set up a tracking algorithm based on an extended Kalman filter [46].
- **SYM-SDM PGF:** For this approach, we just replace the SDM in "SDM PGF" with its symmetric version from (4.17).
- **SYM-SDM EKF:** For this approach, we also just replace the SDM in "SDM EKF" with its symmetric version from (4.17).

The state to be estimated consists of length, pose, and velocity. For initialization, all parameters are set to Gaussian random values, drawn from the ground truth using variances of $5 \cdot 10^{-2}$. The length parameter was additionally distorted by a value of 4, to simulate a bad initialization procedure. For predicting the object location, we incorporate a *3D constant velocity model* [46] into the prediction step, with a process noise covariance matrix in the magnitude of $10^{-5} \cdot \mathbf{I}$. The following results are obtained from 100 Monte-Carlo runs.

Results The average estimates over all runs are drawn in Figure 4.16 and Figure 4.17 and allow for visual comparison of the approaches. A numerical comparison is given in Figure 4.15, where the RMSE for position, orientation and segment length are depicted. As can be seen, all approaches show an almost identical performance in estimating the position and orientation. However, there is a significant difference when comparing the RMSE of the estimated length parameter in Figure 4.15c.

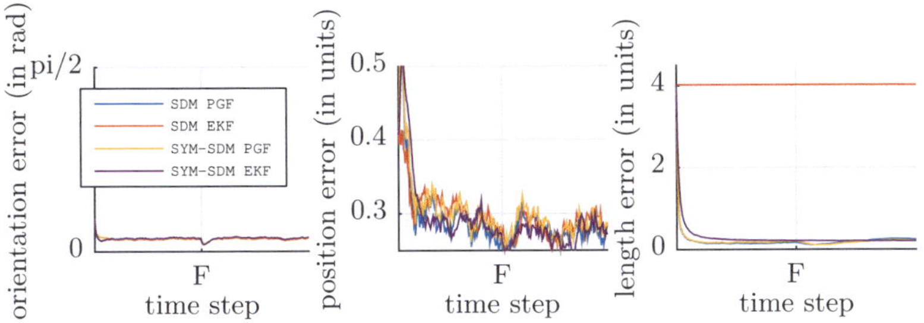

(a) Orientation. **(b)** Position. **(c)** Length.

Figure 4.15.: Numerical result of the line segment evaluation.

Specifically, all approaches are capable of estimating the length of the line segment except from "SDM EKF". We found in [149] that this issue is due to the fact that the linearization in the EKF drops any correlation between position and length parameter. Thus, the length parameter is not affected by the estimator at all. In contrast, its symmetric version "SYM-SDM EKF" is capable of estimating the length, and yields almost comparable accuracy to the PGF approaches. This is a remarkable result, as the complexity of the EKF is far lower than the complexity of a PGF. As an interesting observation, note that the symmetric and non-symmetric PGF approach both yield almost identical accuracy in all estimated parameters.

This evaluation shows that position, orientation and length of a moving line segment can be indeed estimated by a simple EKF when incorporating its reflectional symmetry. To our knowledge, this is the first EKF-based approach, which achieves this result.

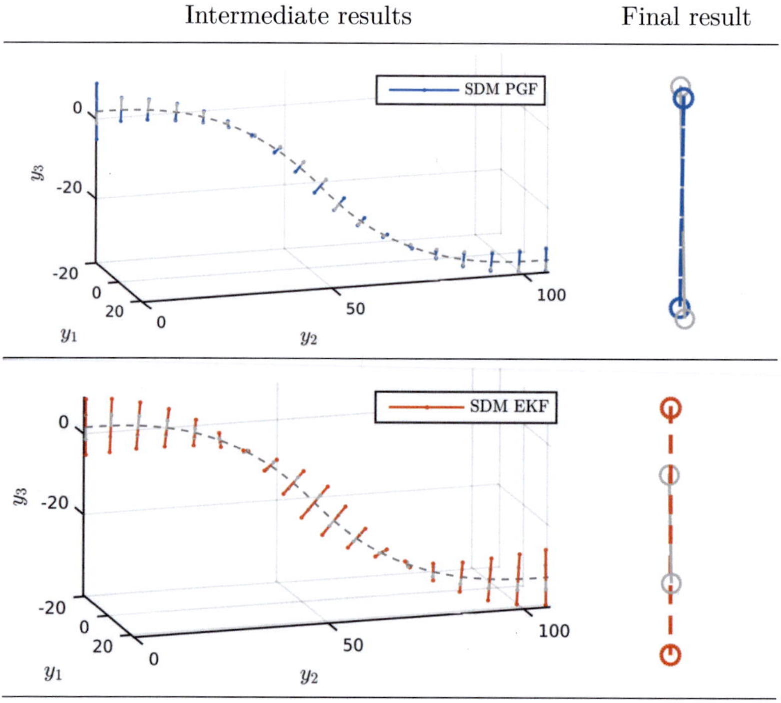

Figure 4.16.: Average estimates of the line segment evaluation.

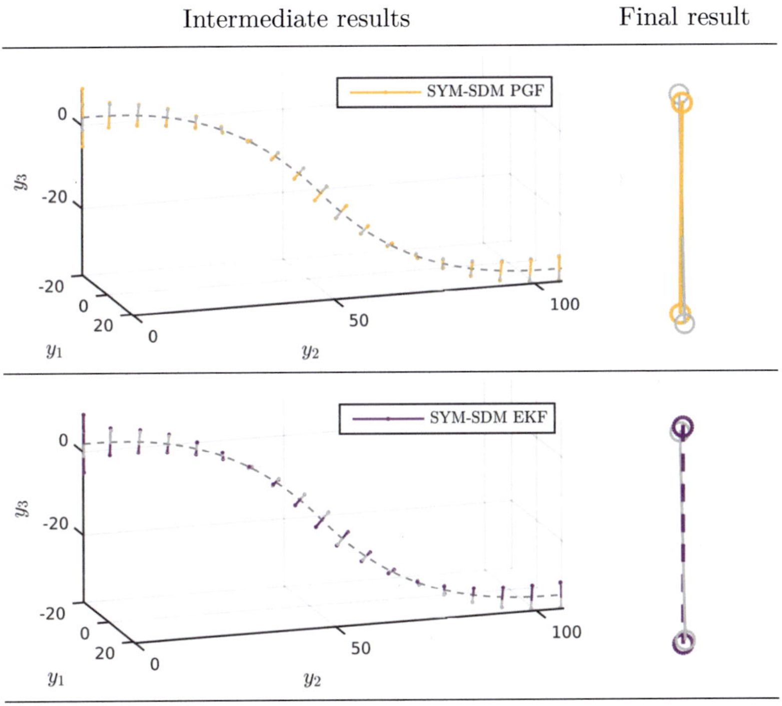

Figure 4.17.: Average estimates of the line segment evaluation (continued).

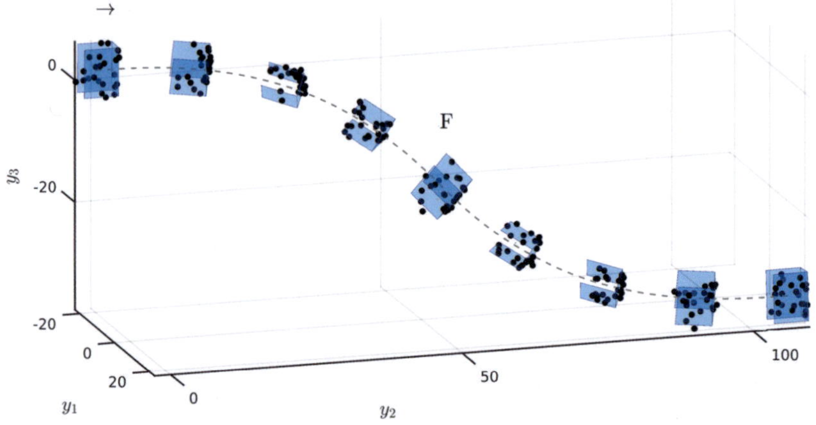

Figure 4.18.: Occluded box tracking experiment. The box moves with constant speed along the S-shaped track while performing a rotation.

4.5.2 Tracking a Moving Box-Object with Occlusion

In this section, we illustrate the performance of the symmetric version of 3DRHMs by means of a tracking example with a permanent occlusion. In particular, we want to demonstrate how symmetry can compensate for missing measurements (Challenge 3).

Experiment We consider the task of tracking the moving box from Section 3.7.2. Again, the estimator should track the object in the form of an extruded star-convex curve. In contrast to the previous tracking experiment, we modify two aspects:

1. an occlusion causes that measurements originate only from three sides of the box, and
2. we compare three estimators, which differ in the number of symmetry axes, they impose.

Figure 4.18 shows the track, together with the ground truth box with an edge length of $6 \times 4 \times 8$, drawn at selected locations. While the box moves, a simulated sensor performs 250 point cloud measurements, where each of contains 25 noisy points. For the selected locations, exemplary measurements are drawn as black dots in Figure 3.16. The measurement sources are uniformly drawn from only three sides of the box and then distorted by adding Gaussian sensor noise with $\mathbf{C}_v = 5 \cdot 10^{-2} \cdot \mathbf{I}$.

For estimation, we use a symmetric 3DRHM-GAM together with a PGF according to (4.19). The state to be estimated consists of the Fourier-coefficients for the star-convex curve, the height, the pose, as well as the object's velocity. Then, for the evaluation, we consider three different numbers of Fourier coefficients 5, 9, and 13, as well as three different types of symmetry, ranging from no symmetry, over 1-axial symmetry, up to 2-axial symmetry. In consequence, we consider $3 \cdot 3 = 9$ configurations for the comparison. As the box is composed of shifted rectangles, which are symmetric with respect to 2 axes, we expect the configurations with "2-axial" symmetry to yield the best estimation performance. In addition, as representing corners of a rectangle require higher order Fourier coefficients [158], the configurations with "13 Coeffs" will probably yield the best results.

Initialization procedure and dynamic model are identical to those in the previous box experiment in Section 3.7.2. The following results are obtained from 100 Monte-Carlo runs.

Results The average intermediate and final results for the nine model configurations are shown in Figure 4.19-4.21. As can be seen from the figures, position, orientation, and length estimates yield comparable results throughout all configurations. However, when comparing the shapes, there are significant differences. These differences can be seen in (i) the way the estimator compensates for the unobserved side, and (ii) the detail of the estimated shape.

Let us first focus the discussion on the first aspect. As expected, the configurations with “2-axial” symmetry compensate best for the unobserved (left) side, as they assume it to be an exact copy of the right side. However, surprisingly, the configurations with “1-axial” symmetry yield the poorest reconstruction of the unobserved side. This is due to the fact that the estimator (randomly) assumes the symmetry axis to lie parallel to the longer edges of the rectangle. From this behavior, we can conclude that we should always choose the highest possible number of symmetry axes in order to achieve the best compensation for missing measurements.

As can be visually confirmed, incorporating “more symmetry” also improves the shape detail for the same number of Fourier coefficients. In particular, each figure includes three configurations with identical numbers of coefficients but different types of symmetry. Then, from the first to the third rows, the number of symmetry axes increases, as well as the quality of the estimated shape for the observed sides. In addition, the computational complexity in each figure can be regarded as equal — except from applying the aggregation function, which for this example simply consist of taking the absolute value of each measurement (in object coordinates). In sum, the results confirm our initial expectation that a higher number of symmetry axes yields both a better reconstruction of the unobserved side and more shape detail.

4.6 Conclusions from Chapter 4

In this chapter, we have developed extensions to the previously discussed probabilistic models in order to make the estimator more robust against occlusions and missing measurements (Challenge 3). We saw that, under specific conditions, folding measurements into a small fraction of the original domain according to the object symmetry does not change the values of the likelihood. This observation allowed us to model the shape exclusively in this non-redundant part of the domain and evaluate symmetric representatives of the measurements in this reduced domain.

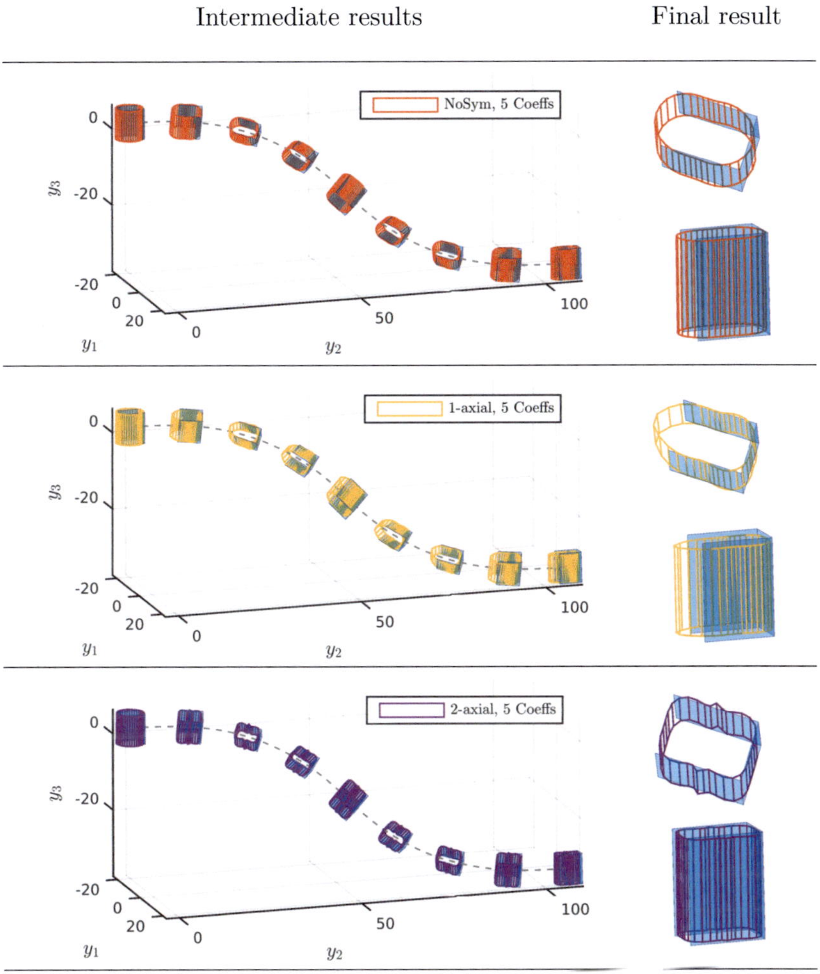

Figure 4.19.: Average results of the occluded box tracking example for 5 Fourier coefficients and different symmetries.

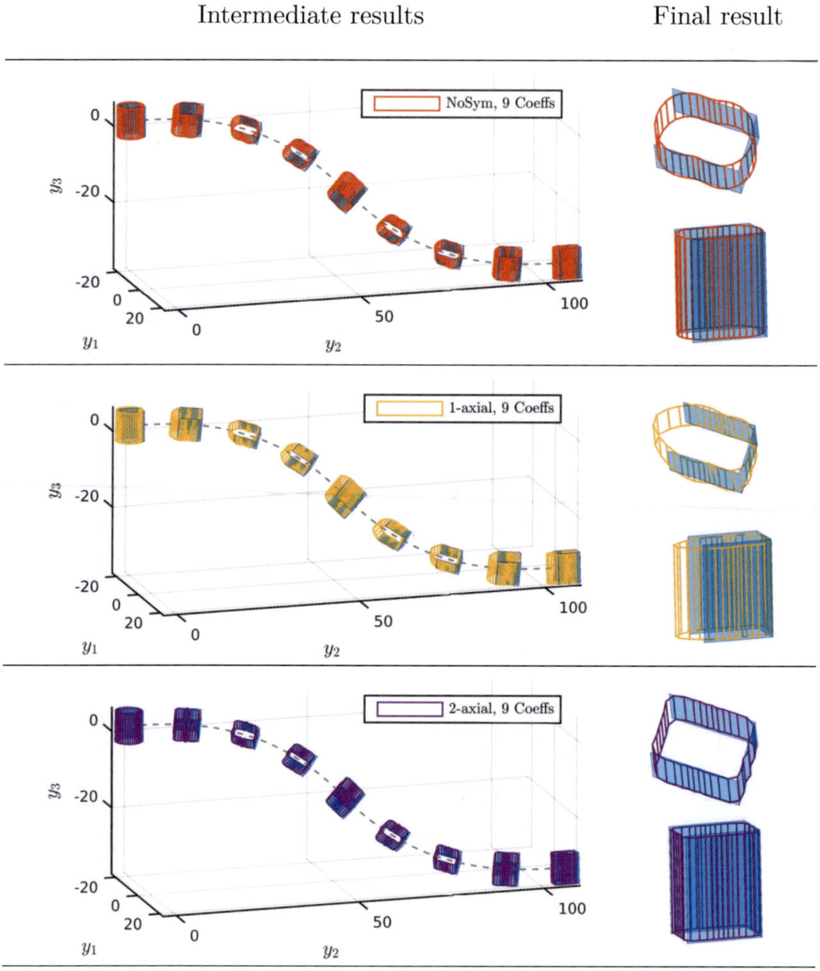

Figure 4.20.: Average results of the occluded box tracking example for 9 Fourier coefficients and different symmetries.

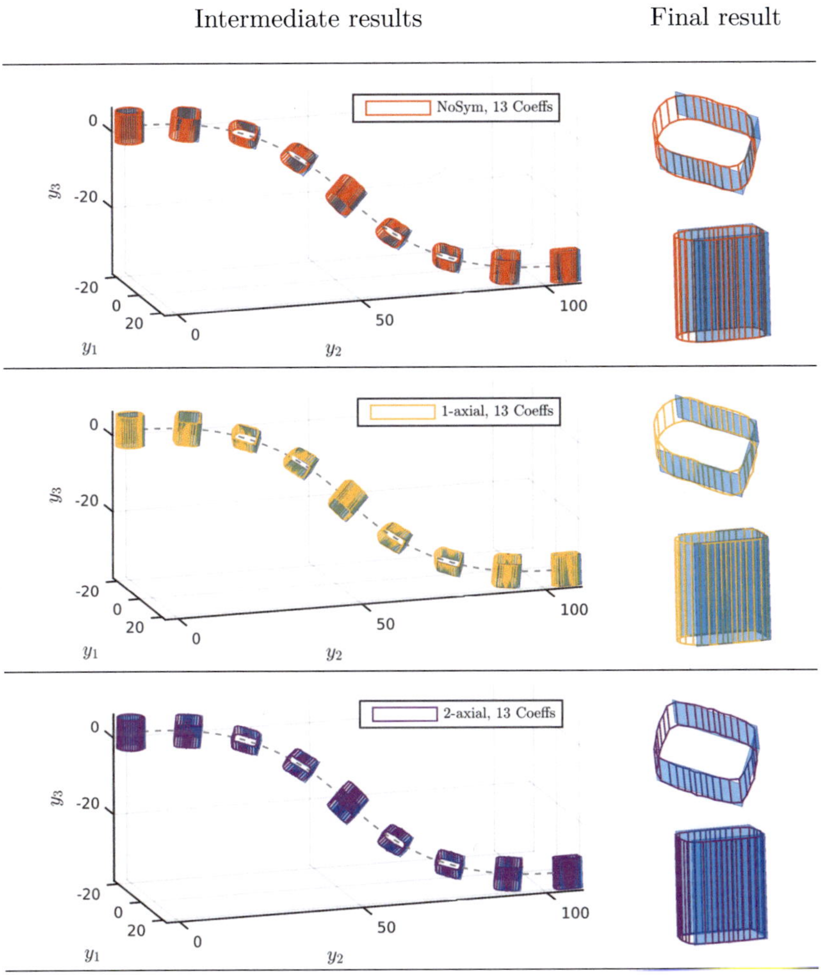

Figure 4.21.: Average results of the occluded box tracking example for 13 Fourier coefficients and different symmetries.

As a desired effect, each measurement forced the estimator to adjust the shape in the entire domain instead of only adjusting it locally. Depending on the specific probabilistic model, object shape, and the parametrization, our approach allows for

- introducing symmetry constraints upon the estimated shape,
- modeling a more detailed shape while keeping or even reducing the number of shape parameters,
- reducing the model complexity by reducing the domain of the integration variables, and
- increasing robustness against partial occlusion.

Our experiments demonstrated that, when correctly applied, we can improve the estimator even for simple objects such as a line segment. As a remarkable result, incorporating the reflectional symmetry of the line segment allowed us to simultaneously estimate its position, orientation, and length with a standard extended Kalman filter.

CHAPTER 5

Evaluation in a Multi-Kinect Network

Contents

In this chapter, we evaluate the practical use of the proposed algorithms in tracking experiments with real data. For this purpose, we use a sensor network based on four Microsoft Kinect cameras of the 2nd generation. The network is part of the telepresence system from Chapter 1.

Contribution There are two major contributions in this chapter. First, we derive a probabilistic sensor model that allows for assessing the quality of each measurement in a 2nd gen Kinect point cloud. This model relies on the accuracy analysis from [16] and is derived by propagating the uncertainty of the depth images to 3D Cartesian space with respect to the intrinsic camera parameters. Second, we transfer the synthetic tracking experiments from the previous chapters to real life in order to validate the theoretical results.

Remark 5.1. *This chapter builds on work on the 1st gen Kinect [154].*

(a) Kinect 1 color.

(b) Kinect 2 color.

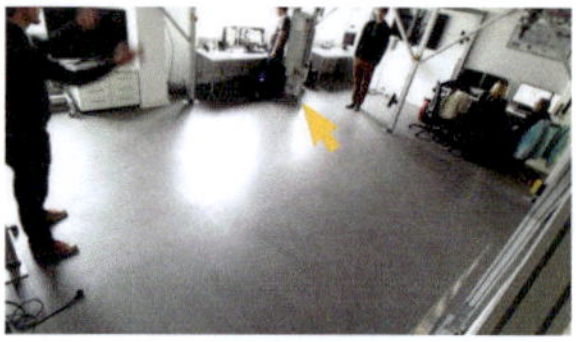

(c) Kinect 3 color.

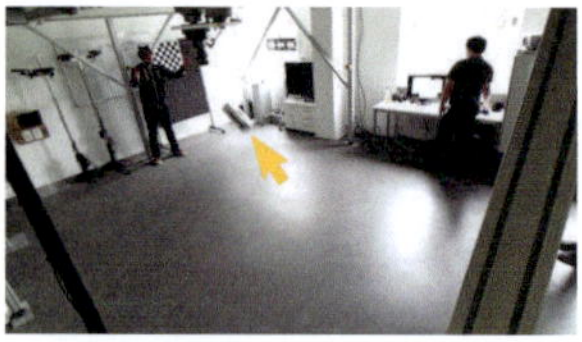

(d) Kinect 4 color.

Figure 5.1.: Raw color data. The object to be tracked is marked by a yellow arrow.

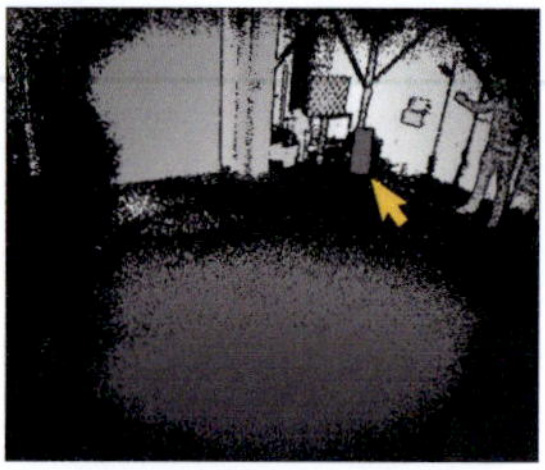

(a) Kinect 1 depth.

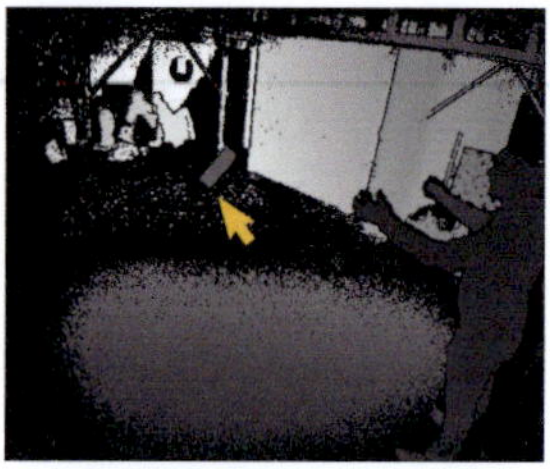

(b) Kinect 2 depth.

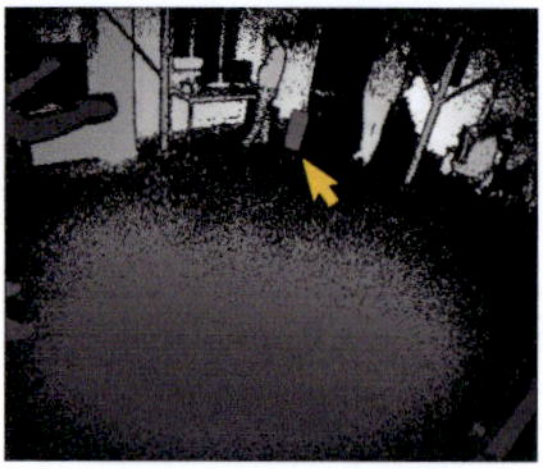

(c) Kinect 3 depth.

(d) Kinect 4 depth.

Figure 5.2.: Raw depth data. The object to be tracked is marked by a yellow arrow.

Figure 5.3.: 3D point cloud, combined from the data of the four Kinects in Figure 5.1 and Figure 5.2.

5.1 Experimental Setup

A multi-Kinect network is a specific instance of an RGBD-camera network, where RGBD means that each sensor observes a color (RGB) and a depth (D) image from the scene. Each Kinect produces RGB and D images at a speed of 30 frames per second in a resolution of 1920×1080 pixels and 512×424 pixels, respectively. Figure 5.1 and Figure 5.2 show example frames of a box tracking scene, as seen by the Kinect network.

While the RGB-images provide an intuitive understanding of the situation, depth images require explanation. Essentially, a depth image is an intensity image, where the intensity of each pixel encodes the range from the image plane of the camera to the observed point in space. In particular, for the example data, darker intensities indicate closer ranges, except from black pixels, which mark invalid range measurements. By *unprojecting* pixels from the image plane into space according to their range, we can recover the 3D position of the surface points in the observed scene. Together with the RGB-image, the corresponding color can be assigned to each 3D point in order to create a colored point cloud. In Figure 5.3, the 3D point cloud for the data in Figure 5.1 and Figure 5.2 is visualized.

In order to enable the tracking algorithm to fuse data from multiple Kinects, it is important to adequately assess the quality of the points. For this purpose, we take a closer look at the measurement principle of the Kinect.

5.2 Sensor Model

In this section, we derive a probabilistic sensor model to assess the quality for Kinect point clouds. We will end up with an algorithm that assigns a Gaussian random variable

$$\underline{v}_i \sim \mathcal{N}(\underline{0}, \mathbf{C}_{v_i})$$

to each measured 3D point $\underline{y}_i$. It is assumed that $\underline{y}_i$ was produced from a point $\underline{z}_i$ on the surface of the object distorted by $\underline{v}_i$ according to (2.4). In order to derive the characteristics of $\mathbf{C}_{v_i}$, we rely on the accuracy analysis of the depth images from [16], in order to propagate the given uncertainty of the depth image to the 3D points. It is assumed that no unexpected sources of noise, e.g., interference by Kinects with overlapping fields of view, are present.

5.2.1 Deterministic Pinhole Model

Let each depth image be indexed by image coordinates $(u, v) \in \{1, \ldots, 512\} \times \{1, \ldots, 424\}$ and let the depth value in meters be denoted by γ. In the following, we derive a deterministic model to transform a 2D pixel in the depth image $[u, v, \gamma]^\mathrm{T}$ to its corresponding 3D point $\underline{y} = [y_1, y_2, y_3]^\mathrm{T}$ using the pinhole model [125]. For a given calibration matrix (*camera intrinsics*)

$$\mathbf{K} = \begin{bmatrix} f_u & 0 & c_u \\ 0 & f_v & c_v \\ 0 & 0 & 1 \end{bmatrix} ,$$

with focal length f_u, f_v, and principal point $[c_u, c_v]^\mathrm{T}$, it holds that $\gamma \cdot [u, v, 1]^\mathrm{T} = \mathbf{K} \cdot \underline{z}$. From this equation, $\underline{y}$ can be recovered by multiplying $\mathbf{K}^{-1}$ from the left according to

$$\begin{bmatrix} y_1 \\ y_2 \\ y_3 \end{bmatrix} = \begin{bmatrix} \frac{u-c_u}{f_u} \\ \frac{v-c_v}{f_v} \\ 1 \end{bmatrix} \cdot \gamma \, . \tag{5.1}$$

5.2.2 Probabilistic Pinhole Model

Using (5.1), we can now propagate a given uncertainty for $[u, v, \gamma]^\mathrm{T}$ to its corresponding uncertainty for $\underline{y}$.

Initial Assumptions A major factor that contributes to the depth image distortion is the Johnson–Nyquist noise [126], which is a form of additive Gaussian-distributed noise and affects the brightness of each pixel in the IR-image of the Kinect, which is internally used to calculate the depth via time-of-flight. This noise directly affects the depth values γ. There are additional sources of noise depending on several values, such as incidence angle, material, distance, sensor artifacts, interference with other sensors or illumination sources, among others. Due to these unpredictable factors, the uncertainty $p(\gamma)$ for each depth value cannot be modeled exactly. However, given the range to the sensor γ, and θ being the angle between line of sight and normal to the intersecting surface, [16] found an approximate formula for the depth variance

$$\sigma_\gamma^2 = \left(1500 - 500\gamma + 300\gamma^2 + 100\gamma^{\frac{3}{2}} \frac{\theta^2}{(\frac{\pi}{2} - \theta)^2}\right)^2 \, .$$

As we do not exactly know the incidence angle, we approximate it conservatively with $\theta \approx \frac{\pi}{3}$. In a similar way to the depth, we conservatively approximate the distributions $p(u)$ and $p(v)$ according to [154]. Assuming pixel positions generally to be very accurate and the noise to be uncorrelated, we model uniform distributions between adjacent pixels with means $\hat{u}$, $\hat{v}$, and variances $\sigma_u^2 = \sigma_v^2 = \frac{1}{3}$.

Propagating the Uncertainty Let the means for depth and pixel positions be directly taken from the values $[\hat{u}, \hat{v}, \hat{\gamma}]^{\mathrm{T}}$ provided by the sensor. The propagation then requires two steps. First, σ_{γ}^2 together with the uncertainties σ_u^2, σ_v^2 are propagated through the deterministic model (5.1) to calculate a covariance matrix for $[y_1, y_2, y_3]^{\mathrm{T}}$. In particular, we are looking for the individual components of the covariance matrix

$$\mathbf{C}_v = \begin{bmatrix} \mathrm{Var}\{y_1\} & \mathrm{Cov}\{y_1, y_2\} & \mathrm{Cov}\{y_1, y_3\} \\ \mathrm{Cov}\{y_1, y_2\} & \mathrm{Var}\{y_2\} & \mathrm{Cov}\{y_2, y_3\} \\ \mathrm{Cov}\{y_1, y_3\} & \mathrm{Cov}\{y_2, y_3\} & \mathrm{Var}\{y_3\} \end{bmatrix} . \tag{5.2}$$

Second, by means of moment matching, we obtain the desired Gaussian distribution $p(\underline{v})$.

Let us start with the propagation. Please note that we assume u, v, and γ to be mutually independent, i.e., their covariances are 0. According to the deterministic pinhole model (5.1) the variances of y_1 and y_2 are

$$\begin{aligned} \mathrm{Var}\{y_1\} &= \mathrm{Var}\left\{ \frac{u - c_u}{f_u} \cdot \gamma \right\} \\ &= \frac{(\hat{u} - c_u)^2 \sigma_{\gamma}^2 + \hat{\gamma}^2 \sigma_u^2 + \sigma_{\gamma}^2 \sigma_u^2}{f_u^2} , \end{aligned}$$

$$\mathrm{Var}\{y_2\} = \frac{(\hat{v} - c_v)^2 \sigma_{\gamma}^2 + \hat{\gamma}^2 \sigma_v^2 + \sigma_{\gamma}^2 \sigma_v^2}{f_v^2} ,$$

respectively, where we exploit the fact that $\mathrm{Var}\{A \cdot B\}$ can be written as $\mathrm{E}\{A\}^2 \cdot \mathrm{Var}\{B\} + \mathrm{E}\{B\}^2 \cdot \mathrm{Var}\{A\} + \mathrm{Var}\{A\} \cdot \mathrm{Var}\{B\}$. The variance of y_3 simply is given by $\mathrm{Var}\{y_3\} = \sigma_{\gamma}^2$. For the covariance between y_1 and y_2, we obtain

$$\begin{aligned} \mathrm{Cov}\{y_1, y_2\} &= \mathrm{Cov}\left\{ \frac{u - c_u}{f_u} \cdot \gamma, \frac{v - c_v}{f_v} \cdot \gamma \right\} \\ &= \frac{\hat{u} - c_u}{f_u} \cdot \frac{\hat{v} - c_v}{f_v} \sigma_{\gamma}^2 , \end{aligned}$$

where we use the relationship $\text{Cov}\{A \cdot B, C \cdot B\} = \text{E}\{A\} \cdot \text{E}\{C\} \cdot \text{Var}\{B\}$ for A, B, C being mutually independent. The remaining covariances can be calculated according to

$$\begin{aligned}\text{Cov}\{y_1, y_3\} &= \text{Cov}\left\{\frac{u - c_u}{f_u} \cdot \gamma, \gamma\right\} \\ &= \frac{\hat{u} - c_u}{f_u} \sigma_\gamma^2 ,\end{aligned}$$

$$\text{Cov}\{y_2, y_3\} = \frac{\hat{v} - c_v}{f_v} \sigma_\gamma^2 ,$$

exploiting that $\text{Cov}\{A \cdot B, B\} = \text{E}\{A\} \cdot \text{Var}\{B\}$ for A, B being mutually independent. These terms specify the covariance matrix (5.2) for the point $\underline{y}$. By interpreting $\mathbf{C}_{v_i}$ as the covariance matrices of the Gaussian random variables $\underline{v}_i \sim \mathcal{N}(0, \mathbf{C}_{v_i})$ for each individual point of the cloud, we finally arrive at the desired sensor model. Typically, the individual variances lie in the magnitude of 10^{-4} m. Using this sensor model, we can proceed with evaluating the tracking algorithms.

5.3 Practical Evaluation

In this section, we first consider tracking a lightsaber, which is used by a person, and, subsequently, we look at tracking the pose and shape of a box while it is thrown. By means of these examples, we discuss the properties of the proposed tracking approach and compare it to the traditional tracking approach based on the *iterative closest point* algorithm [17] which is included in the Point Cloud Library [30].

Figure 5.4.: Lightsaber scene.

5.3.1 Tracking a Lightsaber

In the first experiment, we consider the task of tracking a moving lightsaber. In Figure 5.4, selected frames of the captured 2.5 s sequence are overlaid, in order to illustrate the motion. For the tracking experiment, we assume the lightsaber to be an instance of a line segment whose pose and length we are interested in.

Preprocessing For extracting point clouds of the lightsaber from the depth images, we create a binary mask for each depth image based on clipping planes. In this mask, "1"-values mark all pixels that originate from points inside the tracking volume while "0"-values mark irrelevant pixels. The segmentation procedure then finds connected 1-clusters in the mask, where each cluster is a candidate to either originate from (i) the target object, (ii) the person, or (iii) clutter. In order to identify the desired clusters, we can exploit that the position variance of the lightsaber clusters should be very high in one dimension (along its axis) and very low in the remaining two dimensions. Thus, we apply a *principal component analysis* (PCA) on each cluster and only keep clusters whose maximum variance value is 50 times higher than the second highest

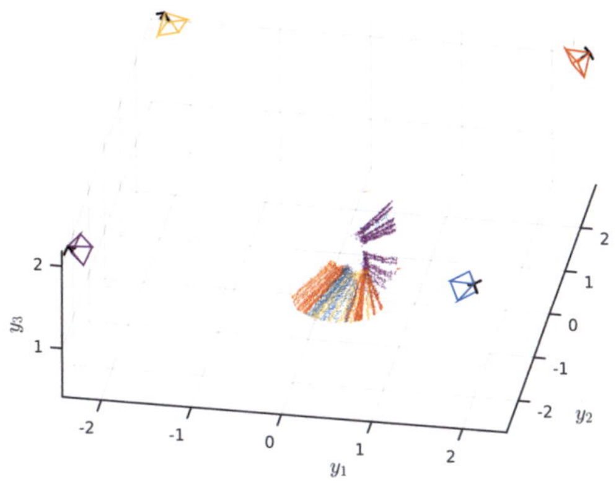

Figure 5.5.: Selected point cloud measurements of the lightsaber. Colors indicate the correspondence of measurements to the respective sensor.

value. From the extracted point clouds, up to 200 points (depending on the total amount) are randomly selected and serve as input for the tracking algorithms. Point cloud measurements for selected time steps are visualized in Figure 5.5. It can be seen that the sensor network is necessary in this tracking experiment as none of the sensors can observe the object throughout the entire sequence.

Tracking Algorithms For evaluation, we consider two tracking algorithms.

- **Proposed Approach:** Following the studies in Section 4.5.1, we would propose to design a tracking algorithm based on a symmetric SDM together with an EKF, in order to allow for length estimation. However, as it often happens that measurements only originate from a small and unpredictable fraction of the object, exclusively using an SDM would fail [156]. To alleviate this issue, we switch to a GAM after the first 10 measurement updates. In both cases, the state vector consists of the saber pose and length, as well as parameters for the first order derivatives (velocity) of the pose parameters. Between the measurement update steps we apply prediction steps according to a constant velocity model and the elapsed real time. The covariance matrix for the process noise is set to a diagonal matrix with $10^{-8} \cdot \mathbf{I}$ for position, $10^{-9} \cdot \mathbf{I}$ for rotation, 10^{-4} for length, and $10^{-6} \cdot \mathbf{I}$ (and $10^{-7} \cdot \mathbf{I}$) for the derivatives of the position (and rotation). For the measurement noise, we incorporate the probabilistic sensor model from Section 5.2.

- **Iterative Closest Point:** The traditional tracking approach for the considered scenario is applying ICP, which estimates pose transformations between one point cloud to another one. In particular, we use a publicly available MATLAB implementation [127], which is similar to the one used in the Point Cloud Library [30]. In order to set up ICP together with the point clouds from different sensors, we apply the following modification. First, for each sensor, the most recently measured point cloud is stored. Then, when a new point cloud is measured, ICP is performed with the point cloud of the corresponding sensor. Finally, (i) the previously stored point cloud from the "active" sensor is replaced by the new one, and (ii), the estimated pose transformation is applied to all point clouds in the "inactive" sensors. It is important to note that ICP does not support length estimation out of the box, and applying it to each measured point cloud individually would fail, as the point clouds often originate only from a fraction of the lightsaber. In consequence, we only consider pose estimates for this approach.

Initialization For the proposed approach, the initial state is set to a line segment according to the following procedure. The center is set to the mean of the first measured point cloud. The axis is derived as the direction of the highest variance of the initial measurements using a PCA. Finally the length of the segment is set to the maximum distance of the points along the axis. The initial state covariance is set to a diagonal matrix of $10^{-8} \cdot \mathbf{I}$. For the ICP algorithm, the initial pose is set in the same way, except for the length parameter (length is not estimated by the ICP approach) and the state covariance matrix, which are not required.

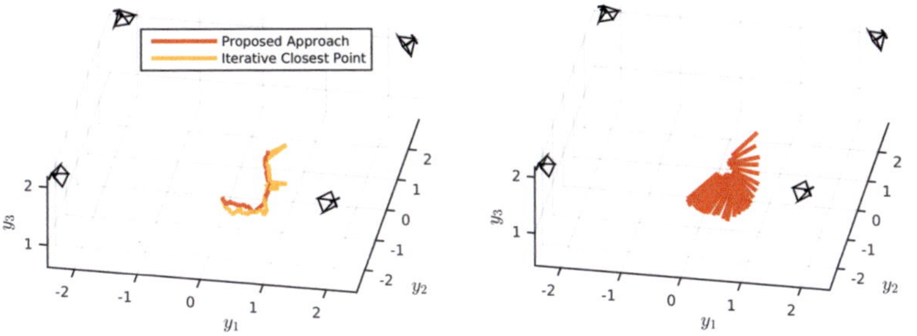

(a) Estimated trajectory.

(b) Estimated line segments from the proposed approach.

Figure 5.6.: Estimation result in a 3D visualization.

Results The estimation result is illustrated in Figure 5.6 for both approaches. When comparing the estimated trajectories in Figure 5.6a, it can be seen that the one obtained by the proposed approach is much smoother. This is due to the fact that the ICP-based tracking algorithm tries to find transformations between succeeding point cloud measurements. However, it sometimes occurs that these point clouds originate from different parts of the object, even for a single sensor. In these situations, the ICP approach incorrectly assumes a heavy motion of the object which results in a spike in the trajectory. Instead, the proposed approach relies on a geometric model of the object, which can compensate for the missing measurements. Figure 5.6b visualizes the estimated object pose together with its geometry for selected time steps. It is interesting to compare these estimates with the measurements in Figure 5.5. In particular, at the end of the maneuver, when there is a period of time without any measurements, the proposed approach is still capable of extrapolating the trajectory using the estimated motion parameters.

Finally, in Figure 5.7, the estimated lightsaber is superimposed on the frames of one Kinect. In particular, we consider the blue colored sensor from Figure 5.5. By means of the image sequence, it can be verified that the proposed tracking approach produces very accurate estimates. This result is extraordinary as it is obtained by using a simple EKF.

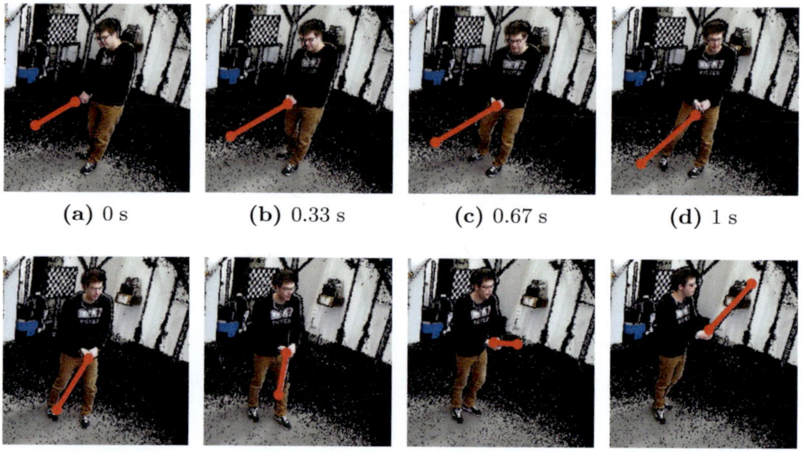

(a) 0 s (b) 0.33 s (c) 0.67 s (d) 1 s

(e) 1.33 s (f) 1.67 s (g) 2 s (h) 2.33 s

Figure 5.7.: Estimates projected on the frames of one Kinect for selected time steps. Black holes indicate parts of the scene which cannot be observed by the depth camera.

5.3.2 Tracking a Thrown Box

In the second experiment, we consider the task of tracking a box while it is thrown in the air. In Figure 5.8, frames of the captured 0.75 s sequence are overlaid for selected time steps, in order to illustrate the trajectory. As can be seen from the figure, the box rotates while it follows the parabolic path. For the tracking experiment, we intentionally do not want to incorporate any prior information about the object pose and shape (except from its symmetry).

Preprocessing For extracting the box point clouds from each Kinect, we again create a binary mask for each depth image based on clipping planes. In this mask "1"-values mark all pixels that originate from inside the tracking volume and "0"-values to the rest. The segmentation procedure is easier than for the lightsaber, as there is no person in the tracking

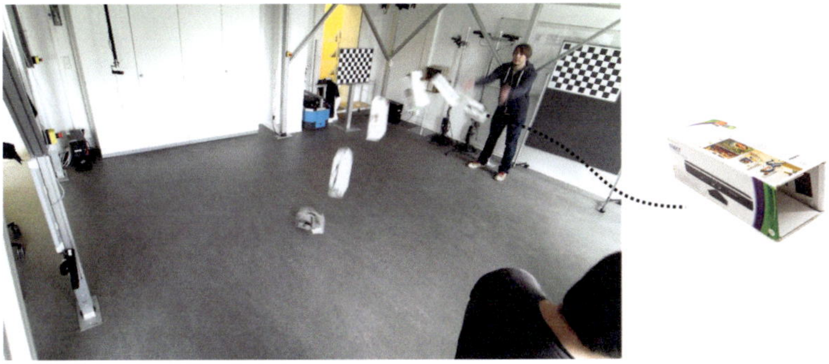

Figure 5.8.: "Thrown box" scene.

volume. Thus, it is sufficient to identify the biggest connected 1-cluster in the mask and assume it to correspond to the object. From the extracted point clouds, up to 200 points (depending on the total amount) are randomly selected and serve as input for the tracking algorithms. Point cloud measurements for selected time steps are visualized in Figure 5.9.

Tracking Algorithms We again consider two tracking algorithms.

- **Proposed Approach:** According to Section 4.5.2 we model the object using a symmetric 3DRHM-GAM for a star-convex extruded curve. For estimation, we use a PGF. The state to be estimated consists of the object pose, height, 5 Fourier-coefficients for the star-convex curve, as well as parameters for the first order derivatives (velocity) of the pose parameters. For the curve, we incorporate knowledge about its 2-axial symmetry. Between the measurement update steps, we again apply prediction steps according to a constant velocity model.

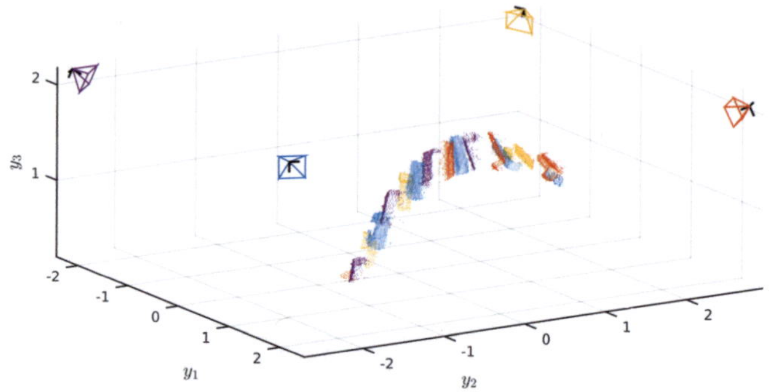

Figure 5.9.: Selected point cloud measurements of the moving box. Colors indicate the correspondence of measurements to the respective sensor.

The covariance matrix of the process noise is set to a diagonal matrix with a variance of $10^{-7} \cdot \mathbf{I}$ for position, $10^{-8} \cdot \mathbf{I}$ for rotation, 10^{-11} for height, $10^{-14} \cdot \mathbf{I}$ for the Fourier coefficients, and $10^{-4} \cdot \mathbf{I}$ (and $10^{-5} \cdot \mathbf{I}$) for the derivatives of the position (and rotation). For the measurement noise, we again incorporate the probabilistic sensor model from Section 5.2.

- **Iterative Closest Point:** For the traditional tracking approach we again use the ICP-based pose tracking approach from the lightsaber experiment.

Initialization For the proposed approach, the initial state is set to a cylinder according to the same procedure as used for the line segment. The center is set to the mean of the initial measurements. The axis is derived as the direction of the highest variance of the initial measurements using a PCA. Radius and height are set according to the maximum distance of points orthogonal and along the cylinder axis. The initial covariance is set to the diagonal matrix $10^{-8} \cdot \mathbf{I}$. The initial pose for ICP is set in the same way, except for radius and length which are not estimated, and state covariance matrix, which is again not required.

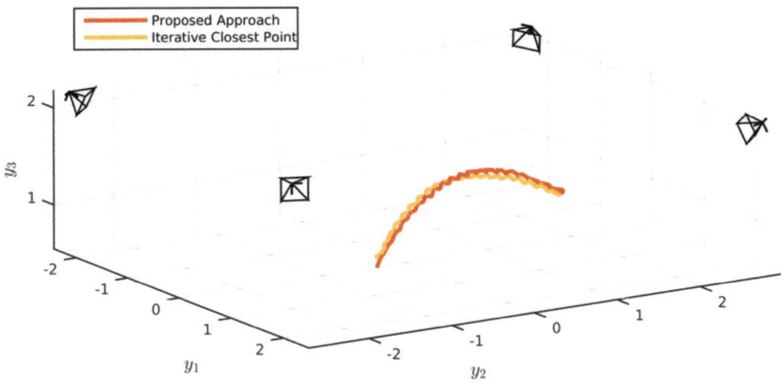

Figure 5.10.: Estimated trajectory for both approaches.

Results The estimated trajectories are drawn in Figure 5.10 for both approaches. At a first glance, the results look quite similar. However, in the more detailed view in Figure 5.11, it can be seen that the pose estimates of the proposed 3DRHM approach are slightly smoother compared to the ICP approach. This is due to the fact that the proposed approach explicitly takes into account the uncertainty of its estimated parameters which incorporates

- a sensor model that assesses the quality of the observed point clouds,
- a motion model that predicts the trajectory, and
- a shape model that adapts to the object geometry.

The additional shape estimate is probably the major advantage of the proposed approach over ICP. The process of estimating the shape can be seen in Figure 5.12. At the beginning of the toss, the estimated shape is cylindrical, according to its initialization. Then, as increasingly more data becomes available, the shape adapts to the cuboid. In total, our algorithm manages to find the correct shape in less than a second. The intermediate object estimates are projected on the frames for all Kinects in Figure 5.13. By comparing these estimates to Figure 5.8, the correctness of the tracking result can be visually verified.

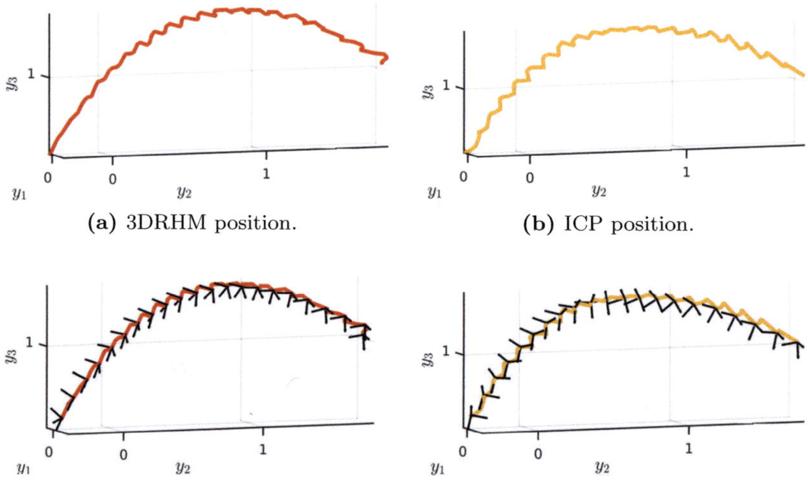

(a) 3DRHM position. (b) ICP position.

(c) 3DRHM rotation. (d) ICP rotation.

Figure 5.11.: Position and rotation estimates for both approaches.

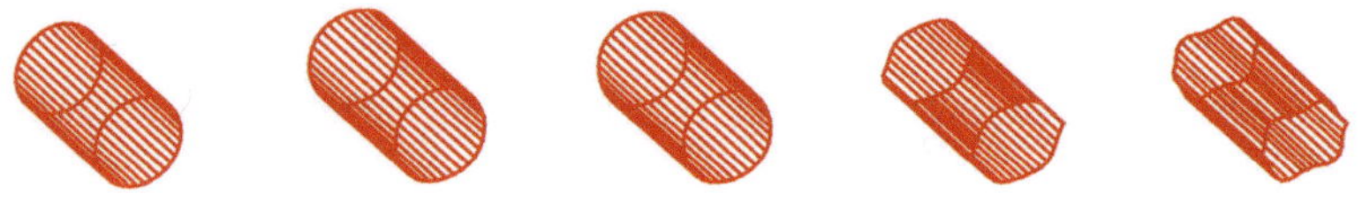

(a) 0 ms (b) 173 ms (c) 347 ms (d) 520 ms (e) 707 ms

Figure 5.12.: Respective shape estimates for the time steps shown in Figure 5.13.

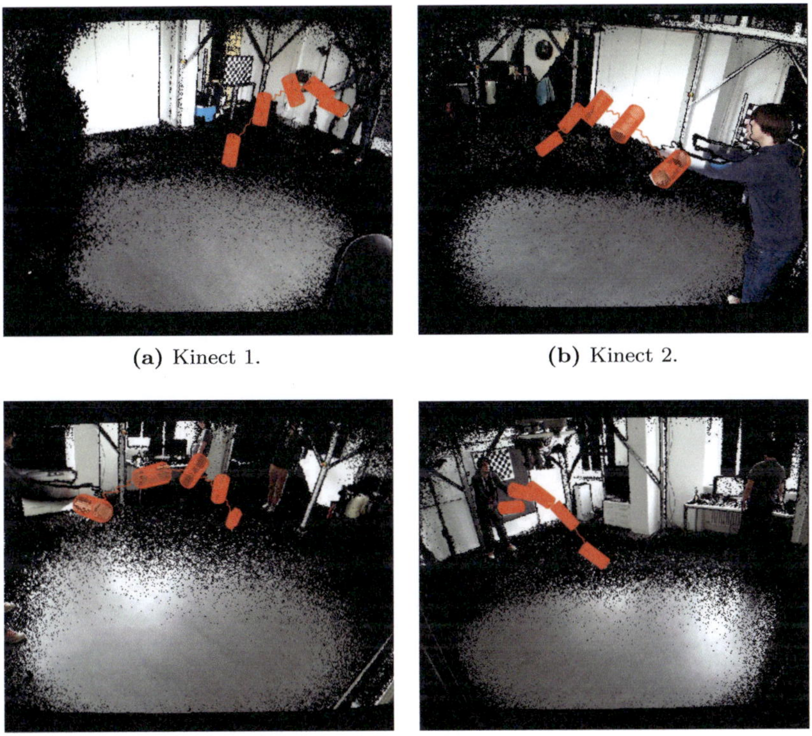

(a) Kinect 1. (b) Kinect 2.

(c) Kinect 3. (d) Kinect 4.

Figure 5.13.: Shape estimates for selected time steps, projected on the colored depth image of each Kinect. Black holes again indicate parts of the scene, which cannot be observed by the depth camera.

In summary, the presented results validate our previous observations from the box tracking experiment in Section 4.5.2, i.e., that the proposed approach can adapt to an a priori unknown shape, while symmetry compensates for missing measurements.

5.4 Conclusions from Chapter 5

In this chapter, we evaluated the proposed tracking algorithm in real-data tracking experiments. For this purpose, we set up a multi-Kinect network and derived a probabilistic sensor model to assess the quality of the point cloud measurements from each sensor. This sensor model describes the quality of each point measurement by means of its expected value and covariance matrix expressed as a Gaussian distribution. The experiments showed the performance of the proposed algorithm. In particular, we demonstrated that our approach outperforms the traditional ICP-based approach in terms of accuracy and robustness when tracking a lightsaber and a box in free fall. For the latter, our approach managed to find the correct shape in less than a second, despite of its fast motion and rotation, which is a remarkable result.

CHAPTER 6

Conclusions

Contents

Extended object tracking blurs the boundary between the fields of traditional shape reconstruction and pose tracking research. In this thesis, we studied an instance of extended object tracking, where objects with a priori unknown shape were to be tracked by a network of consumer 3D cameras such as Microsoft Kinect. As a motivation, consider a telepresence system where a user needs to naturally interact with the virtual environment by using arbitrary physical objects from her or his local environment. Most state-of-the-art tracking approaches for this situation would either require a polygonal model to be specified in advance, or apply a version of ICP to the foreground point cloud which, however, only works with dense measurements and low noise. Instead, we proposed to simultaneously estimate the shape, pose, and motion parameters of an object using a flexible geometric model together with a recursive Bayesian estimator, which allowed us to explicitly incorporate all involved sources of uncertainty.

6.1 Summary

We started with a thorough derivation of a likelihood prototype for extended objects. Evaluating this likelihood was challenging, as the sensor noise prevents an exact association of the measured points to their originating sources on the object (Challenge 1). We discussed the traditional approaches to this association problem, such as modeling a probability distribution over all potential sources (SDM), or greedily associating each point to its "closest" point on the boundary (GAM). However, these approaches were generally biased in situations where either the assumed source distribution was incorrect, or the noise level was high.

In order to overcome these drawbacks, we developed a new probabilistic model called the **Partial Information Model** (PIM), where the key idea essentially was to remove the problematic association heuristics. Specifically, we expressed the measurements in a transformed coordinate system, which allowed us to specify a probabilistic model for "how well" the measurements fit to the boundary without explicitly associating them to measurement sources. An estimator based on the PIM

- needs no explicit probability distribution for measurement sources,
- is unbiased according to [73],
- can deal with anisotropic sensor noise, and
- can be used together with a nonlinear Kalman filter.

Using a PIM instead of an SDM or a GAM can reduce the RMSE for curvature parameters up to a full order of magnitude.

In order to model arbitrary 3D objects flexibly (Challenge 2), we proposed to construct the surface of an object by translating, rotating and scaling plane curves, such as a cylinder by translating a circle. When developing an estimator for line segments being a special case of this construction method, we encountered that, while the computationally demanding SDM was capable of finding accurate values for the length, the GAM or

PIM would fail to do so. We studied the origin of this issue and found that, in order to estimate parameters which do not have an effect on the measurement association, we inherently require assumptions about the probability distribution of measurement sources.

Based on this analysis, we proposed a hybrid probabilistic model for 3D shapes, called the **3D Random Hypersurface Model** (3DRHM), which combines an SDM with PIM or GAM and is closely related to the homonymous model for 2D region tracking [98]. Specifically, we assumed a probability for each transformed curve, and ignored (or approximated) the unknown information of "where" on the curve a measurement corresponds to. The resulting estimator

- is capable of estimating all parameters, including the object length,
- has a lower computational complexity than the SDM,
- inherits the unbiasedness from the PIM, and
- can still be used together with a nonlinear Kalman filter.

We confirmed these properties in the evaluation for a cylinder, torus, cone, and an extruded star-convex curve. In particular, compared to a state-of-the-art fitting approach, we could reduce the RMSE in the curvature parameters by 44%-77% in the presence of high noise.

As an important property, the proposed tracking approach should be robust against occlusions and missing measurements (Challenge 3), as these issues are inherent when acquiring point clouds with depth sensors. In order to deal with this challenge, we proposed to **exploit geometric symmetries** of the object to be tracked. As the key observation, we saw that, under specific conditions, folding measurements into a small fraction of the original domain according to the object symmetry did not change the values of the likelihood. Thus, we proposed to specify the shape exclusively in this non-redundant part of the domain and evaluate the folded measurements by also using only a small fraction of the shape. Depending on the specific probabilistic model, object shape, and the parametrization, our approach allows for

- introducing symmetry constraints upon the estimated shape,

- modeling more detailed shapes with fewer parameters,
- reducing the overall complexity of the tracking task, and
- increasing robustness against occlusion.

Our approach even improves the tracking algorithm for a simple line segment, making it possible to use a standard *extended Kalman filter* for simultaneously estimating its length and pose.

In order to evaluate our tracking approach in real situations, we set up a sensor network, and conducted several experiments. We considered the task of tracking a lightsaber used by a person and the task of tracking a box while it was in free fall. As a remarkable result, our approach managed to find the box shape in less than a second, despite of its fast motion and rotation. In summary, the experiments confirmed our theoretic results and, moreover, showed the practical value of this thesis.

6.2 Outlook

In this thesis, we have addressed fundamental aspects and challenges of extended object tracking in 3D. Our results form a solid theoretical and practical platform for further research and developments. These include, but are not limited to

- using higher level sensor information, such as silhouettes, normals or curvature. As these features must be extracted from neighboring points, including them is an instance of modeling dependencies between measurements,
- alternatively, explicitly incorporating dependencies between individual points on a more general level by using, e.g., random finite sets [128, 129],
- incorporating color or intensity measurements, which may also be observed by the sensor,
- deriving closed-form solutions for the measurement update through approximation techniques,

- modeling more complex transformations for the 3D shapes. For instance, the curves could be translated along more general splines, or could change even their shape,
- investigating other approaches for boundary parametrization, which are known in shape analysis [5]. Using spherical harmonics for modeling complex shape geometry in 3D [105] would be a promising approach,
- exploring more general types of symmetry, such as repetitions and patterns,
- detecting the number of symmetry axes automatically, for example by using an Interacting Multiple Model (IMM) approach [48], where each model has a different number of symmetry axes and a probability of being the correct one. An IMM would also be reasonable for automatically detecting model complexity in the form of adding and removing shape parameters,
- applying the PIM to multi-target tracking tasks by assuming each target to be a potential measurement source.

Finally, I want to reiterate my thanks to all the people who contributed to this thesis.

APPENDIX A

Approximation of the Bayes' Update

A.1 Nonlinear Kalman Filter Update

When the prior knowledge about the state parameters is given as a Gaussian distribution

$$p(\underline{x}) = \mathcal{N}(\underline{x}; \underline{\mu}_x^p, \mathbf{C}_x^p) , \tag{A.1}$$

and the measurement function (2.3) is nonlinear, the key idea is to approximate the likelihood by the Gaussian

$$p(\underline{y}|\underline{x}) \approx \mathcal{N}(\underline{y}; \underline{\mu}_{y|x}, \mathbf{C}_{y|x}) , \tag{A.2}$$

where $\underline{\mu}_{y|x}$ and $\mathbf{C}_{y|x}$ are mean and covariance matrix of the measurement function $\underline{y} = h(\underline{x}, \underline{v})$ for a given state $\underline{x}$ with respect to $\underline{v}$. Note that for n measurements $\underline{y}_1, \ldots, \underline{y}_n$, we obtain

$$\begin{aligned} p(\underline{y}_1, \ldots, \underline{y}_n|x) &= \prod_{i=1}^{n} p(\underline{y}_i|x) \\ &\approx \mathcal{N}(Y; \underline{\mu}_{Y|x}, \mathbf{C}_{Y|x}) \end{aligned} \tag{A.3}$$

with $Y = [\underline{y}_1^{\mathrm{T}}, \ldots, \underline{y}_n^{\mathrm{T}}]^{\mathrm{T}}$ being the measurements stacked as a vector. Note that (A.2) and (A.3) are also functions of the parameters $\underline{x}$.

Then, given a set of measurements, a nonlinear Kalman filter update can be calculated according to the following procedure. We assume that the joint distribution $p(\underline{x}, Y) = p(\underline{y}_1, \ldots, \underline{y}_n | \underline{x}) \cdot p(\underline{x})$ is Gaussian, which lets us obtain the Gaussian posterior distribution $p(\underline{x}|Y) = \mathcal{N}(\underline{x}; \underline{\mu}_x, \mathbf{C}_x)$. The moments of this posterior distribution can be calculated according to the Kalman filter formulas

$$\begin{aligned} \underline{\mu}_x &= \underline{\mu}_x^p + \mathbf{K}(Y - \underline{\mu}_Y) \,, \\ \mathbf{C}_x &= \mathbf{C}_x^p - \mathbf{K}\mathbf{C}_Y\mathbf{K}^{\mathrm{T}} \,, \end{aligned} \tag{A.4}$$

with $\mathbf{K} = \mathbf{C}_{xY}\mathbf{C}_Y^{-1}$ being denoted as the Kalman gain. The basic algorithm for the nonlinear Kalman filter update is summarized in Algorithm A.1. There are several techniques to calculate the terms in

---

Algorithm A.1 Bayes' update using a nonlinear Kalman filter.

Input: prior distribution of state $p(\underline{x})$ according to (A.1) and measurements $\underline{y}_1, \ldots, \underline{y}_n$

Output: posterior distribution of state $p(\underline{x}|\underline{y}_1, \ldots, \underline{y}_n)$

1: **calculate** mean $\underline{\mu}_Y$, covariance matrix $\mathbf{C}_Y$ and cross-covariance matrix $\mathbf{C}_{xY}$;
2: **calculate** posterior mean $\underline{\mu}_x$ and covariance $\mathbf{C}_x$ according to (A.4)
3: **return** $p(\underline{x}|\underline{y}_1, \ldots, \underline{y}_n) = \mathcal{N}(\underline{x}; \underline{\mu}_x, \mathbf{C}_x)$

Line 1, ranging from analytic propagation of the state and measurement uncertainty through $h(\underline{x}, \underline{v})$ [130], over explicit linearization [131], up to implicit sampling-based linearization techniques [92, 93].

A.2 Particle Filter Update

If the prior distribution $p(\underline{x})$ over the state parameters is not necessarily Gaussian, a particle filter update [132] for $\underline{y}_1, \ldots, \underline{y}_n$ can be calculated according to the following procedure. The key idea is to approximate $p(\underline{x})$ as a set of particles $x_1, \ldots, x_M$ in the form of

$$p(\underline{x}) \approx \sum_{m=1}^{M} \beta_m \cdot \delta(\underline{x} - \underline{x}_m) , \tag{A.5}$$

where each particle is weighted by a scalar $\beta_m \in [0, 1]$. Then, the posterior distribution $p(\underline{x}|\underline{y}_1, \ldots, \underline{y}_n)$ can be calculated according to the Bayes' update from (2.1)

$$p(\underline{x}|\underline{y}_1, \ldots, \underline{y}_n) \approx \sum_{m=1}^{M} \beta_m \cdot p(\underline{y}_1, \ldots, \underline{y}_n|\underline{x}_m) \cdot \delta(\underline{x} - \underline{x}_m) . \tag{A.6}$$

The very basic algorithm for the particle filter update is summarized in Algorithm A.2. Note that there are approaches that incorporate more

Algorithm A.2 Bayes' update using a particle filter.

Input: prior distribution of state $p(\underline{x})$ and measurements $\underline{y}_1, \ldots, \underline{y}_n$
Output: posterior distribution of state $p(\underline{x}|\underline{y}_1, \ldots, \underline{y}_n)$
1: **represent** prior distribution $p(\underline{x})$ by particles in the form of (A.5);
2: **calculate** posterior distribution $p(\underline{x}|\underline{y}_1, \ldots, \underline{y}_n)$ according to (A.6);
3: **return** $p(\underline{x}|\underline{y}_1, \ldots, \underline{y}_n)$;

sophisticated techniques such as advanced resampling techniques [133], or progressive updates [97, 134, 135], to name only a few. Nevertheless, particle filters typically require an exponentially increasing number of particles with respect to the state dimension D. A thorough overview and discussion on particle filter techniques is given in [136, 137].

Bibliography

[1] M. Minsky, "Telepresence," *OMNI magazine*, 1980.

[2] Z. Zhang, "Microsoft Kinect Sensor and its Effect," *IEEE Multimedia*, vol. 19, no. 2, pp. 4–10, 2012.

[3] M. Baum, *Simultaneous Tracking and Shape Estimation of Extended Objects.* Phd thesis, Karlsruhe Institute of Technology (KIT), 2013.

[4] W. Koch, *Tracking and Sensor Data Fusion.* Springer-Verlag Berlin Heidelberg, 2014.

[5] S. Loncaric, "A Survey of Shape Analysis Techniques," *Pattern Recognition*, vol. 31, no. 8, pp. 983–1001, 1998.

[6] Y. Cui, S. Schuon, S. Thrun, D. Stricker, and C. Theobalt, "Algorithms for 3D Shape Scanning with a Depth Camera," *IEEE Transactions on Pattern Analysis and Machine Intelligence*, vol. 35, no. 5, pp. 1039–1050, 2013.

[7] L. Cruz, D. Lucio, and L. Velho, "Kinect and RGBD Images: Challenges and Applications," *Proceedings: 25th SIBGRAPI - Conference on Graphics, Patterns and Images Tutorials, SIBGRAPI-T 2012*, pp. 36–49, 2012.

[8] B. Kehoe, A. Matsukawa, S. Candido, J. Kuffner, and K. Goldberg, "Cloud-based Robot Grasping with the Google Object Recognition Engine," in *Proceedings - IEEE International Conference on Robotics and Automation*, (Karlsruhe, Germany), pp. 4263–4270, 2013.

[9] F. Moosmann and C. Stiller, "Joint Self-localization and Tracking of Generic Objects in 3D Range Data," in *Proceedings - IEEE International Conference on Robotics and Automation*, (Karlsruhe, Germany), pp. 1146–1152, 2013.

[10] L. Potter, J. Araullo, and L. Carter, "The Leap Motion Controller: A View on Sign Language," in *Proceedings of the 25th Australian Computer-Human Interaction Conference: Augmentation, Application, Innovation, Collaboration*, (Adelaide, Australia), pp. 175–178, 2013.

[11] S. Beck, A. Kunert, A. Kulik, and B. Froehlich, "Immersive Group-to-group Telepresence," *IEEE Transactions on Visualization and Computer Graphics*, vol. 19, pp. 616–625, apr 2013.

[12] F. Bosché, "Automated Recognition of 3D CAD Model Objects in Laser Scans and Calculation of as-built Dimensions for Dimensional Compliance Control in Construction," *Advanced Engineering Informatics*, vol. 24, no. 1, pp. 107–118, 2010.

[13] P. Tang, D. Huber, B. Akinci, R. Lipman, and A. Lytle, "Automatic Reconstruction of as-built Building Information Models from Laser-scanned Point Clouds: A Review of Related Techniques," *Automation in Construction*, vol. 19, no. 7, pp. 829–843, 2010.

[14] A. Fernández-Baena, A. Susín, and X. Lligadas, "Biomechanical Validation of Upper-body and Lower-body Joint Movements of Kinect Motion Capture Data for Rehabilitation Treatments," in *Proceedings of the 2012 4th International Conference on Intelligent Networking and Collaborative Systems, INCoS 2012*, (Bucharest, Romania), pp. 656–661, 2012.

[15] K. Khoshelham, "Accuracy Analysis of Kinect Depth Data," in *ISPRS - International Archives of the Photogrammetry, Remote Sensing and Spatial Information Sciences*, vol. XXXVIII-5/, pp. 133–138, 2012.

[16] M. Bloesch and D. Rodriguez, "Kinect v2 for Mobile Robot Navigation : Evaluation and Modeling," in *International Conference on Advanced Robotics (ICAR)*, (Lisbon, Portugal), 2014.

[17] P. J. Besl and N. D. McKay, "A Method for Registration of 3-D Shapes," *IEEE Transactions on Pattern Analysis and Machine Intelligence*, vol. 14, pp. 239–256, feb 1992.

[18] T. Okatani and K. Deguchi, "On Bias Correction for Geometric Parameter Estimation in Computer Vision," in *2009 IEEE Computer Society Conference on Computer Vision and Pattern Recognition Workshops, CVPR Workshops 2009*, pp. 959–966, 2009.

[19] A. Kasper, Z. Xue, and R. Dillmann, "The KIT Object Models Database: An Object Model Database for Object Recognition, Localization and Manipulation in Service Robotics," *The International Journal of Robotics Research*, vol. 31, pp. 927–934, may 2012.

[20] M. Kass, A. Witkin, and D. Terzopoulos, "Snakes: Active Contour Models," *International Journal of Computer Vision*, vol. 1, no. 4, pp. 321–331, 1988.

[21] A. Elfes, "Using Occupancy Grids for Mobile Robot Perception and Navigation," *Computer*, vol. 22, no. 6, pp. 46–57, 1989.

[22] L. Linsen, "Point Cloud Representation," tech. rep., Karlsruhe, 2001.

[23] C. Choi and H. I. Christensen, "RGB-D Object Tracking: A Particle Filter Approach on GPU," in *IEEE International Conference on Intelligent Robots and Systems*, (Tokyo, Japan), pp. 1084–1091, 2013.

[24] S. Seitz and C. Dyer, "Photorealistic Scene Reconstruction by Voxel Coloring," *Proc. of Computer Vision and Pattern Recognition*, vol. 35, no. 2, pp. 1067–1073, 1997.

[25] S. Thrun, "Learning Occupancy Grid Maps with Forward Sensor Models," *Autonomous Robots*, vol. 15, no. 2, pp. 111–127, 2003.

[26] R. a. Newcombe, S. Izadi, O. Hilliges, D. Molyneaux, D. Kim, A. J. Davison, P. Kohli, J. Shotton, S. Hodges, and A. Fitzgibbon, "KinectFusion: Real-time Dense Surface Mapping and Tracking," in *2011 10th IEEE International Symposium on Mixed and Augmented Reality, ISMAR 2011*, (Basel, Switzerland), pp. 127–136, Ieee, oct 2011.

[27] T. Whelan, M. Kaess, and M. Fallon, "Kintinuous: Spatially Eextended KinectFusion," in *RSS Workshop on RGB-D: Advanced Reasoning with Depth Cameras*, (Sydney, Australia), p. 7, 2012.

[28] P. Henry, M. Krainin, E. Herbst, X. Ren, and D. Fox, "RGB-D Mapping: Using Kinect-style Depth Cameras for Dense 3D Modeling of Indoor Environments," *The International Journal of Robotics Research*, vol. 31, no. 5, pp. 647–663, 2012.

[29] L. Kobbelt and M. Botsch, "A Survey of Point-based Techniques in Computer Graphics," *Computers and Graphics (Pergamon)*, vol. 28, pp. 801–814, dec 2004.

[30] R. B. Rusu and S. Cousins, "3D is here: Point Cloud Library (PCL)," in *Proceedings - IEEE International Conference on Robotics and Automation*, (Shanghai, China), 2011.

[31] J. C. Carr, R. K. Beatson, J. B. Cherrie, T. J. Mitchell, W. R. Fright, B. C. McCallum, and T. R. Evans, "Reconstruction and Representation of 3D Objects with Radial Basis Functions," in *Proceedings of the 28th Annual Conference on Computer Graphics and Interactive Techniques*, no. August, (Los Angeles, California, USA), pp. 67–76, 2001.

[32] R. Fabio, "From Point Cloud to Surface: The Modeling and Visualization Problem," *International Archives of Photogrammetry, Remote Sensing and Spatial Information Sciences*, vol. 34, no. 5, 2003.

[33] Y. Cui, S. Schuon, D. Chan, S. Thrun, and C. Theobalt, "3D Shape Scanning with a Time-of-flight Camera," in *Proceedings of the IEEE Computer Society Conference on Computer Vision and Pattern Recognition*, (San Francisco, California, USA), pp. 1173–1180, jun 2010.

[34] P. Jenke, M. Wand, M. Bokeloh, A. Schilling, and W. Straßer, "Bayesian Point Cloud Reconstruction," in *Computer Graphics Forum*, vol. 25, (Vienna, Austria), pp. 379–388, sep 2006.

[35] B. Oehler, J. Stueckler, J. Welle, D. Schulz, and S. Behnke, "Efficient Multi-resolution Plane Segmentation of 3D Point Clouds," in *Lecture Notes in Computer Science (including subseries Lecture Notes in Artificial Intelligence and Lecture Notes in Bioinformatics)*, vol. 7102 LNAI, (Aachen, Germany), pp. 145–156, 2011.

[36] R. B. Rusu, N. Blodow, Z. C. Marton, and M. Beetz, "Aligning Point Cloud Views Using Persistent Feature Histograms," in *2008 IEEE/RSJ International Conference on Intelligent Robots and Systems, IROS*, (St. Louis, USA), pp. 3384–3391, 2008.

[37] Z. Xie, S. Xu, and X. Li, "A High-accuracy Method for Fine Registration of Overlapping Point Clouds," *Image and Vision Computing*, vol. 28, pp. 563–570, apr 2010.

[38] C. Erdogan, M. Paluri, and F. Dellaert, "Planar Segmentation of RGBD Images Using Fast Linear Fitting and Markov Chain Monte Carlo," *Proceedings of the 2012 9th Conference on Computer and Robot Vision, CRV 2012*, pp. 32–39, 2012.

[39] S. W. Kwon, F. Bosche, C. Kim, C. T. Haas, and K. a. Liapi, "Fitting Range Data to Primitives for Rapid Local 3D Modeling Using Sparse Range Point Clouds," *Automation in Construction*, vol. 13, no. 1, pp. 67–81, 2004.

[40] S. J. Ahn, W. Rauh, H. S. Cho, and H. J. Warnecke, "Orthogonal Distance Fitting of Implicit Curves and Surfaces," *IEEE Transactions on Pattern Analysis and Machine Intelligence*, vol. 24, no. 5, pp. 620–638, 2002.

[41] R. Barker, "LSGE: The Least Squares Geometric Elements library," 2002.

[42] B. Leibe, N. Cornelis, K. Cornelis, and L. V. Gool, "Dynamic 3D Scene Analysis from a Moving Vehicle," in *2007 IEEE Conference on Computer Vision and Pattern Recognition*, (Minneapolis, Minnesota), pp. 1–8, 2007.

[43] C. Wu, S. Agarwal, B. Curless, and S. M. Seitz, "Schematic Surface Reconstruction," in *Proceedings of the IEEE Computer Society Conference on Computer Vision and Pattern Recognition*, (Providence, USA), pp. 1498–1505, 2012.

[44] R. Schnabel, R. Wahl, and R. Klein, "Efficient RANSAC for Point-cloud Shape Detection," *Computer Graphics Forum*, vol. 26, pp. 214–226, jun 2007.

[45] D. Comaniciu and P. Meer, "Mean Shift: A Robust Approach Toward Feature Space Analysis," *IEEE Transactions on Pattern Analysis and Machine Intelligence*, vol. 24, pp. 603–619, may 2002.

[46] Z. H. E. Chen, "Bayesian Filtering : From Kalman Filters to Particle Filters , and Beyond," *Statistics*, vol. 182, no. 1, pp. 1–69, 2003.

[47] X. R. Li and V. P. Jilkov, "Survey of Maneuvering Target Tracking. Part I: Dynamic Models," *IEEE Transactions on Aerospace and Electronic Systems*, vol. 39, pp. 1333–1364, oct 2003.

[48] H. a. P. Blom and Y. Bar-Shalom, "Interacting Multiple Model Algorithm for Systems with Markovian Switching Coefficients.," *IEEE Transactions on Automatic Control*, vol. 33, pp. 780–783, aug 1988.

[49] Y. Bar-Shalom, "Multitarget-multisensor tracking: advanced applications," *Norwood, MA, Artech House, 1990, 391 p.*, vol. 1, 1990.

[50] R. P. S. Mahler, "Multitarget Bayes Filtering via First-Order Multitarget Moments," *IEEE Transactions on Aerospace and Electronic Systems*, vol. 39, pp. 1152–1178, oct 2003.

[51] P. Meißner, S. R. Schmidt-Rohr, M. Lösch, R. Jäkel, and R. Dillmann, "Robust Localization of Furniture Parts by Integrating Depth and Intensity Data Suitable for Range Sensors with Varying Image Quality," in *IEEE 15th International Conference on Advanced Robotics: New Boundaries for Robotics, ICAR 2011*, (Tallinn, Estonia), pp. 48–54, jun 2011.

[52] R. B. Rusu, Z. C. Marton, N. Blodow, M. Dolha, and M. Beetz, "Towards 3D Point Cloud based Object Maps for Household Environments," *Robotics and Autonomous Systems*, vol. 56, no. 11, pp. 927–941, 2008.

[53] L. Spinello, K. Arras, R. Triebel, and R. Siegwart, "A Layered Approach to People Detection in 3D Range Data.," in *Aaai*, (Atlanta, Georgia, USA), pp. 1625–1630, 2010.

[54] J. Shotton, A. Fitzgibbon, M. Cook, T. Sharp, M. Finocchio, R. Moore, A. Kipman, and A. Blake, "Real-time Human Pose Recognition in Parts from Single Depth Images," in *IEEE Conf. on Computer Vision and Pattern Recognition (CVPR)*, (Colorado Springs, USA), 2011.

[55] D. Droeschel and S. Behnke, "3D Body Pose Estimation using an Adaptive Person Model for Articulated ICP," in *4th International Conference on Intelligent Robotics and Applications (ICIRIA)*, no. December, (Aachen, Germany), 2011.

[56] C. S. C. Shen, A. V. D. Hengel, A. Dick, and M. J. Brooks, "2D Articulated Tracking with Dynamic Bayesian Networks," in *The Fourth International Conference onComputer and Information Technology, 2004.*, (Wuhan, China), 2004.

[57] L. Raskin, E. Rivlin, and M. Rudzsky, "Using Gaussian Process Annealing Particle Filter for 3D Human Tracking," *Eurasip Journal on Advances in Signal Processing*, vol. 2008, 2008.

[58] I. Oikonomidis, N. Kyriazis, and A. a. Argyros, "Efficient Model-based 3D Tracking of Hand Articulations using Kinect," in *22nd British Machine Vision Conference*, (Dundee, United Kingdom), pp. 1–11, 2011.

[59] M. Montemerlo and S. Thrun, "Simultaneous Localization and Mapping with Unknown Data Association Using FastSLAM," in *2003 IEEE International Conference on Robotics and Automation*, vol. 2, (Taipei, Taiwan), pp. 1985–1991, Ieee, 2003.

[60] F. Steinbruecker, J. Sturm, and D. Cremers, "Real-Time Visual Odometry from Dense RGB-D Images," in *Workshop on Live Dense Reconstruction with Moving Cameras at the Intl. Conf. on Computer Vision (ICCV)*, (Barcelona, Spain), 2011.

[61] H. Du, P. Henry, X. Ren, M. Cheng, D. B. Goldman, S. M. Seitz, D. Fox, I. L. Seattle, and A. Systems, "Interactive 3D Modeling of Indoor Environments with a Consumer Depth Camera," in *UbiComp'11*, UbiComp '11, (Beijing, China), p. 10, 2011.

[62] K. Wyffels and M. Campbell, "Joint Tracking and Non-parametric Shape Estimation of Arbitrary Extended Objects," in *International Conference on Robotics and Automation*, (Seattle, WA, USA), pp. 3360–3367, 2015.

[63] M. Baum and U. D. Hanebeck, "Extended Object Tracking with Random Hypersurface Models," *IEEE Transactions on Aerospace and Electronic Systems*, vol. 50, no. 1, pp. 149–159, 2014.

[64] K. Gilholm and D. Salmond, "Spatial Distribution Model for Tracking Extended Objects," *IEE Proceedings - Radar, Sonar and Navigation*, vol. 152, no. 5, p. 364, 2005.

[65] J. Koch and W. Koch, "Bayesian Approach to Extended Object and Cluster Tracking Using Random Matrices," *IEEE Transactions on Aerospace and Electronic Systems*, vol. 44, pp. 1042–1059, jul 2008.

[66] J. Huang, D. Abendschein, V. G. Dávila-Román, and a. a. Amini, "Spatio-temporal Tracking of Myocardial Deformations with a 4-D B-spline Model from Tagged MRI.," *IEEE transactions on medical imaging*, vol. 18, no. 10, pp. 957–972, 1999.

[67] G. Kurz and U. D. Hanebeck, "Recursive Fusion of Noisy Depth and Position Measurements for Surface Reconstruction," in *Information Fusion (FUSION), 2013 16th International Conference on*, (Istanbul, Turkey), pp. 1958–1965, 2013.

[68] M. Himmelsbach and H. J. Wuensche, "Tracking and Classification of Arbitrary Objects with Bottom-up/Top-down Detection," in *IEEE Intelligent Vehicles Symposium, Proceedings*, (Alcalá de Henares, Spain), pp. 577–582, jun 2012.

[69] M. Wand, P. Jenke, Q. Huang, M. Bokeloh, L. Guibas, and A. Schilling, "Reconstruction of Deforming Geometry from Time-varying Point Clouds," in *Proceedings of the fifth Eurographics symposium on Geometry processing*, (Barcelona, Spain), pp. 49–58, 2007.

[70] M. Werman and D. Keren, "A Bayesian Method for Fitting Parametric and Nonparametric Models to Noisy Data," *IEEE Transactions on Pattern Analysis and Machine Intelligence*, vol. 23, no. 5, pp. 528–534, 2001.

[71] W. H. Wong, "Theory of Partial Likelihood," *The Annals of Statistics*, vol. 14, no. 1, pp. 88–123, 1986.

[72] Z. Griliches and V. Ringstad, "Error-in-the-Variables Bias in Nonlinear Contexts," *Econometrica*, vol. 38, no. 2, pp. 368 – 370, 1970.

[73] V. P. Godambe and M. E. Thompson, "Estimating Equations in the Presence of a Nuisance Parameter," *The Annals of Statistics*, vol. 2, no. 3, pp. 568–571, 1974.

[74] D. Koller and N. Friedman, *Probabilistic Graphical Models: Principles and Techniques.* London, England: MIT press, 2009.

[75] Y. Bar-Shalom, X. R. Li, and T. Kirubarajan, *Estimation with Applications to Tracking and Navigation.* New York, NY, USA: John Wiley & Sons, Inc., 2001.

[76] R. E. Kalman, "A New Approach to Linear Filtering and Prediction Problems," *Transactions of the ASME Journal of Basic Engineering*, vol. 82, pp. 35–45, 1960.

[77] J. Neyman and E. L. Scott, "Consistent Estimates Based on Partially Consistent Observations," *Econometrica*, vol. 16, no. 1, pp. 1–32, 1948.

[78] D. Angelova, L. Mihaylova, N. Petrov, and A. Gning, "A Convolution Particle Filtering Approach for Tracking Elliptical Extended Objects," in *16th International Conference on Information Fusion Istanbul, Turkey*, (Istanbul, Turkey), pp. 1542–1549, 2013.

[79] J. O. Berger, B. Liseo, and R. L. Wolpert, "Integrated Likelihood Methods for Eliminating Nuisance Parameters," *Statistical Science*, vol. 14, pp. 1–22, feb 2007.

[80] M. Feldmann, D. Fränken, and W. Koch, "Tracking of Extended Objects and Group Targets Using Random Matrices," *IEEE Transactions on Signal Processing*, vol. 59, pp. 1409–1420, apr 2011.

[81] K. Granström, C. Lundquist, and U. Orguner, "Tracking Rectangular and Elliptical Extended Targets Using Laser Measurements," in *14th International Conference on Information Fusion*, (Edinburgh, United Kingdom), pp. 1–8, 2011.

[82] N. Petrov, L. Mihaylova, A. Gning, and D. Angelova, "A Sequential Monte Carlo Approach for Extended Object Tracking in the Presence of Clutter," in *Proceedings of the 15th International Conference on Information Fusion (FUSION)*, (Edinburgh, United Kingdom), 2011.

[83] S. A. Murphy and A. W. Van Der Vaart, "On Profile Likelihood," *Journal of the American Statistical Association*, vol. 95, no. 450, pp. 449–465, 2000.

[84] C. Spearman, "The Proof and Measurement of Association Between Two Things," *The American Journal of Psychology*, vol. 15, no. 1, pp. 72–101, 1904.

[85] W. E. Deming, "The Application of Least Squares," *Philosophical Magazine*, vol. 7, pp. 146–158, 1931.

[86] Y. Leedan and P. Meer, "Estimation with Bilinear Constraints in Computer Vision," in *Sixth International Conference on Computer Vision*, no. 1, (Bombay, India), pp. 733–738, 1998.

[87] W. Chojnacki, M. J. Brooks, and A. Vanel, "On the Fitting of Surfaces to Data with Covariances," *IEEE Transactions on Pattern Analysis and Machine Intelligence*, vol. 22, no. 11, pp. 1294–1303, 2000.

[88] B. C. Matei and P. Meer, "Estimation of Nonlinear Errors-in-Variables Models for Computer Vision Applications," *IEEE Transactions on Pattern Analysis and Machine Intelligence*, vol. 28, pp. 1537–1552, oct 2006.

[89] K. Kanatani, "Overviews of Optimization Techniques for Geometric Estimation," *Memoirs of the Faculty of Engineering, Okayama University*, vol. 47, no. January, pp. 1–18, 2013.

[90] Z. Zhang, "Parameter Estimation Techniques: A Tutorial with Application to Conic Fitting," *Image and Vision Computing*, vol. 15, no. 1, pp. 59–76, 1997.

[91] D. R. Cox, "Partial Likelihood," *Biometrika*, vol. 62, no. 2, pp. 269–276, 1975.

[92] S. J. Julier and J. K. Uhlmann, "Unscented Filtering and Nonlinear Estimation," *Proceedings of the IEEE*, vol. 92, pp. 401–422, mar 2004.

[93] J. Steinbring and U. D. Hanebeck, "S2KF: The Smart Sampling Kalman Filter," in *Proceedings of the 16th International Conference on Information Fusion (Fusion 2013)*, (Istanbul, Turkey), pp. 2089–2096, 2013.

[94] B. Efron, "Bootstrap Confidence Intervals for a Class of Parametric Problems," *Biometrika*, vol. 72, no. 1, pp. 45–58, 1985.

[95] R. Goldman, "Curvature Formulas for Implicit Curves and Surfaces," *Computer Aided Geometric Design*, vol. 22, pp. 632–658, oct 2005.

[96] M. Spivak, *A Comprehensive Introduction to Differential Geometry, Volume-I*. Houston, Texas: Publish or Perish Inc., 3 ed., 1979.

[97] J. Steinbring and U. D. Hanebeck, “Progressive Gaussian Filtering Using Explicit Likelihoods,” in *Proceedings of the 17th International Conference on Information Fusion (Fusion 2014)*, (Salamanca, Spain), 2014.

[98] M. Baum and U. D. Hanebeck, “Shape Tracking of Extended Objects and Group Targets with Star-convex RHMs,” in *14th International Conference on Information Fusion*, (Chicago, Illinois, USA), pp. 1–8, 2011.

[99] M. Baum, B. Noack, and U. D. Hanebeck, “Mixture Random Hypersurface Models for Tracking Multiple Extended Objects,” in *Proceedings of the IEEE Conference on Decision and Control*, (Orlando, Florida, USA), pp. 3166–3171, 2011.

[100] K. Granstrom, “An Extended Target Tracking Model with Multiple Random Matrices and Unified Kinematics,” *arXiv*, pp. 1–16, 2014.

[101] B. K. P. Horn, “Extended Gaussian Images.,” *Proceedings of the IEEE*, vol. 72, no. 12, pp. 1671–1686, 1984.

[102] S. Kang and K. Ikeuchi, “Determining 3-D Object Pose Using the Complex Extended Gaussian Image,” in *Proceedings. 1991 IEEE Computer Society Conference on Computer Vision and Pattern Recognition*, vol. i, (Lahaina, Maui, HI), pp. 580–585, 1991.

[103] L. Sun, X. Li, and J. Lan, “Modeling of Extended Objects Based on Support Functions and Extended Gaussian Images for Target Tracking,” *IEEE Transactions on Aerospace and Electronic Systems*, vol. 50, pp. 3021–3035, oct 2014.

[104] A. Poonawala, P. Milanfar, and R. J. Gardner, “Shape Estimation from Support and Diameter Functions,” *Journal of Mathematical Imaging and Vision*, vol. 24, pp. 229–244, jan 2006.

[105] M. Kazhdan, T. Funkhouser, and S. Rusinkiewicz, “Rotation Invariant Spherical Harmonic Representation of 3 D Shape Descriptors,” in *Eurographics Symposium on Geometry Processing*, (Aachen, Germany), 2003.

[106] C. Brechbühler, G. Gerig, and O. Kübler, “Parametrization of Closed Surfaces for 3-D Shape Description,” *Computer Vision and Image Understanding*, vol. 61, no. 2, pp. 154–170, 1995.

[107] A. Rivers, F. Durand, and T. Igarashi, "3D Modeling with Silhouettes," *ACM Transactions on Graphics*, vol. 29, p. 1, jul 2010.

[108] G. Slabaugh and G. Unal, "Active Polyhedron: Surface Evolution Theory Applied to Deformable Meshes," in *Proceedings of the IEEE Computer Society Conference on Computer Vision and Pattern Recognition*, vol. 2, (San Diego, California, USA), pp. 84–91, 2005.

[109] S. Knoop, S. Vacek, and R. Dillmann, "Sensor Fusion for 3D Human Body Tracking with an Articulated 3D Body Model," in *Proceedings 2006 IEEE International Conference on Robotics and Automation*, (Orlando, Florida, USA), pp. 1686–1691, 2006.

[110] L. Zhang, J. Sturm, D. Cremers, and D. Lee, "Real-time Human Motion Tracking Using Multiple Depth Cameras," in *2012 IEEE/RSJ International Conference on Intelligent Robots and Systems*, (Vilamoura, Algarve, Portugal), pp. 2389–2395, Ieee, oct 2012.

[111] O. C. Schrempf, D. Brunn, and U. D. Hanebeck, "Density Approximation Based on Dirac Mixtures with Regard to Nonlinear Estimation and Filtering," in *Proceedings of the 2006 IEEE Conference on Decision and Control (CDC 2006)*, (San Diego, California), 2006.

[112] M. Huber and U. D. Hanebeck, "Gaussian Filter Based on Deterministic Sampling for High Quality Nonlinear Estimation," in *Proceedings of the 17th IFAC World Congress (IFAC 2008)*, vol. 17, (Seoul, Korea), 2008.

[113] T. Okatani and K. Deguchi, "Improving Accuracy of Geometric Parameter Estimation Using Projected Score Method," in *Proceedings of the IEEE International Conference on Computer Vision*, no. Iccv, (Kyoto, Japan), pp. 1733–1740, 2009.

[114] J. Steinbring, "Nonlinear Estimation Toolbox," 2015.

[115] P. Simari, E. Kalogerakis, and K. Singh, "Folding Meshes: Hierarchical Mesh Segmentation Based on Planar Symmetry," in *Proceedings of the fourth Eurographics symposium on Geometry processing*, (Aire-la-Ville, Switzerland), pp. 111–119, 2006.

[116] W. H. Li and L. Kleeman, "Real Time Object Tracking Using Reflectional Symmetry and Motion," in *Proceedings of the 2006 IEEE/RSJ International Conference of Intelligent Robots and Systems (IROS). IEEE*, (Beijing, China), pp. 2798–2803, 2006.

[117] S. Thrun and B. Wegbreit, "Shape from Symmetry," in *Proceedings of the IEEE International Conference on Computer Vision*, vol. II, (Beijing, China), pp. 1824–1833, 2005.

[118] N. J. Mitra, M. Pauly, M. Wand, and D. Ceylan, "Symmetry in 3D Geometry: Extraction and Applications," *Computer Graphics Forum*, vol. 32, no. 6, pp. 1–23, 2013.

[119] D. G. Lowe, "Object Recognition from Local Scale-Invariant Features," in *IEEE International Conference on Computer Vision*, (Kerkyry, Greece), 1999.

[120] T. Riklin-Raviv, N. Kiryati, and N. Sochen, "Segmentation by Level Sets and Symmetry," in *Proceedings of the IEEE Computer Society Conference on Computer Vision and Pattern Recognition*, vol. 1, (New York, NY, USA), pp. 1015–1022, 2006.

[121] A. Tagliasacchi, H. Zhang, and D. Cohen-Or, "Curve skeleton extraction from incomplete point cloud," *ACM Transactions on Graphics*, vol. 28, no. 3, p. 1, 2009.

[122] G. Kurz and I. Gilitschenski, "Recursive Estimation of Orientation Based on the Bingham Distribution," in *Proceedings of the 16th International Conference on Information Fusion (Fusion 2013)*, (Istanbul, Turkey), pp. 1487–1494, 2013.

[123] W. F. Leven and A. D. Lanterman, "Unscented Kalman Filters for Multiple Target Tracking with Symmetric Measurement Equations," *IEEE Transactions on Automatic Control*, vol. 54, pp. 370–375, feb 2009.

[124] M. Baum and U. D. Hanebeck, "The Kernel-SME Filter for Multiple Target Tracking," in *Proceedings of the 16th International Conference on Information Fusion (Fusion 2013)*, (Istanbul, Turkey), 2013.

[125] R. Hartley and A. Zisserman, *Multiple View Geometry in Computer Vision*. Cambridge University Press, second ed., 2004.

[126] J. B. Johnson, "Thermal Agitation of Electricity in Conductors," *Physical Review*, vol. 32, no. 1, pp. 97–109, 1928.

[127] H. M. Kjer and J. Wilm, *Evaluation of Surface Registration Algorithms for PET Motion Correction.* Bachelor thesis, Technical University of Denmark, 2010.

[128] R. P. S. Mahler, "Multitarget Bayes Filtering via First-Order Multitarget Moments," *IEEE Transactions on Aerospace and Electronic Systems*, vol. 39, pp. 1152–1178, oct 2003.

[129] O. Erdinc, P. Willett, and Y. Bar-Shalom, "The Bin-occupancy Filter and its Connection to the PHD Filters," *IEEE Transactions on Signal Processing*, vol. 57, no. 11, pp. 4232–4246, 2009.

[130] M. Deisenroth, M. F. Huber, and U. D. Hanebeck, "Analytic Moment-based Gaussian Process Filtering," in *26th International Conference on Machine Learning (ICML 2009)*, (Montreal, Canada), 2009.

[131] K. Senne, "Stochastic Processes and Filtering Theory," *IEEE Transactions on Automatic Control*, vol. 17, no. 5, pp. 1 – 376, 1972.

[132] N. J. Gordon, D. J. Salmond, and A. F. M. Smith, "Novel Approach to Nonlinear/Non-Gaussian Bayesian State Estimation," *IEE Proceedings F Radar and Signal Processing*, vol. 140, no. 2, p. 107, 1993.

[133] R. Douc and O. Cappe, "Comparison of Resampling Schemes for Particle Filtering," in *ISPA 2005. Proceedings of the 4th International Symposium on Image and Signal Processing and Analysis, 2005.*, (Zagreb, Croatia), pp. 64–69, IEEE, 2005.

[134] U. D. Hanebeck, "PGF 42: Progressive Gaussian Filtering with a Twist," in *Proceedings of the 16th International Conference on Information Fusion (Fusion 2013)*, (Istanbul, Turkey), 2013.

[135] F. Daum, J. Huang, M. Krichman, and T. Kohen, "Seventeen Dubious Methods to Approximate the Gradient for Nonlinear Filters with Particle Flow," in *Signal and Data Processing of Small Targets* (O. E. Drummond and R. D. Teichgraeber, eds.), vol. 7445, pp. 1–9, International Society for Optics and Photonics, aug 2009.

[136] P. Djuric, J. Kotecha, J. Z. J. Zhang, Y. H. Y. Huang, T. Ghirmai, M. Bugallo, and J. Miguez, "Particle Filtering," *IEEE Signal Processing Magazine*, vol. 20, no. 5, pp. 19–38, 2003.

[137] A. Doucet and A. Johansen, "A Tutorial on Particle Filtering and Smoothing: Fifteen Years Later," *Handbook of Nonlinear Filtering*, no. December 2008, pp. 656–704, 2011.

Supervised Student Theses

[138] K. Bouché. *Implementierung eines echtzeitfähigen Trackingsystems basierend auf RGBD-Daten und sternkonvexen RHMs.* Bachelor thesis, Karlsruhe Institute of Technology, 2012.

[139] S. Bullinger. *Telepräsenz mit Virtuellen Beobachtern.* Bachelor thesis, Karlsruhe Institute of Technology, Karlsruhe, 2012.

[140] I. Gabel. *3D-Kugel-Tracking mit Random Hypersurface Models.* Diploma thesis, Karlsruhe Institute of Technology, 2012.

[141] J. P. Gerlach. *Modellierung einer cyberphysischen Telepräsenzumgebung.* Bachelor thesis, Karlsruhe Institute of Technology, 2012.

[142] A. Gorbunov. *Haptische Steuerung eines menschlichen Teleoperators - Telepräsenz am Beispiel einer Blindenführung.* Diploma thesis, Karlsruhe Institute of Technology, 2013.

[143] V. Kaiser. *Projection-Based Gating for Extended Objects.* Bachelor thesis, Karlsruhe Institute of Technology, 2014.

[144] A. Maxein. *Segment. dyn. Cluster in verrauschten Punktwolken.* Minor thesis, Karlsruhe Institute of Technology, 2011.

[145] J. McClelland. *Development of a Human-Computer-Interface for the e-Installation of Marc Lee's "10,000 Moving Cities – Same but Different".* Diploma thesis, Karlsruhe Institute of Technology, 2014.

[146] J. Steinbring. *Deterministic Recursive Bayesian Estimation for Extended Object Tracking.* Diploma thesis, Karlsruhe Institute of Technology, 2012.

[147] P. Weidel. *Sensoreinsatzplanung für Multi-Kinect-Netzwerke.* Minor thesis, Karlsruhe Institute of Technology, 2013.

[148] A. Zea. *Extended Object Modeling and Tracking using Polygons and RHMs.* Diploma thesis, Karlsruhe Institute of Technology, 2012.

Own Publications

[149] M. Baum, F. Faion, and U. D. Hanebeck. Modeling the Target Extent with Multiplicative Noise. In *Proceedings of the 15th International Conference on Information Fusion (Fusion 2012)*, Singapore, July 2012.

[150] M. Baum, F. Faion, and U. D. Hanebeck. Tracking Ground Moving Extended Objects using RGBD Data. In *Proceedings of the 2012 IEEE International Conference on Multisensor Fusion and Integration for Intelligent Systems (MFI 2012)*, Hamburg, Germany, Sept. 2012.

[151] F. Faion, M. Baum, and U. D. Hanebeck. Tracking 3D Shapes in Noisy Point Clouds with Random Hypersurface Models. In *Proceedings of the 15th International Conference on Information Fusion (Fusion 2012)*, Singapore, July 2012.

[152] F. Faion, M. Baum, and U. D. Hanebeck. Silhouette Measurements for Bayesian Object Tracking in Noisy Point Clouds. In *Proceedings of the 16th International Conference on Information Fusion (Fusion 2013)*, Istanbul, Turkey, July 2013.

[153] F. Faion, M. Baum, and U. D. Hanebeck. Depth Sensor Calibration by Means of Tracking an Extended Object. In *Proceedings of the 2015 IEEE International Conference on Multisensor Fusion and Integration for Intelligent Systems (MFI 2015)*, San Diego, California, USA, Sept. 2015.

[154] F. Faion, S. Friedberger, A. Zea, and U. D. Hanebeck. Intelligent Sensor-Scheduling for Multi-Kinect-Tracking. In *Proceedings of the 2012 IEEE/RSJ International Conference on Intelligent Robots and Systems (IROS 2012)*, Vilamoura, Algarve, Portugal, Oct. 2012.

[155] F. Faion, P. Ruoff, A. Zea, and U. D. Hanebeck. Recursive Bayesian Calibration of Depth Sensors with Non-Overlapping Views. In *Proceedings of the 15th International Conference on Information Fusion (Fusion 2012)*, Singapore, July 2012.

[156] F. Faion, A. Zea, M. Baum, and U. D. Hanebeck. Bayesian Estimation of Line Segments. In *Proceedings of the IEEE ISIF Workshop on Sensor Data Fusion: Trends, Solutions, Applications (SDF 2014)*, Bonn, Germany, Oct. 2014.

[157] F. Faion, A. Zea, M. Baum, and U. D. Hanebeck. Partial Likelihood for Unbiased Extended Object Tracking. In *Proceedings of the 18th International Conference on Information Fusion (Fusion 2015)*, Washington D. C., USA, July 2015.

[158] F. Faion, A. Zea, M. Baum, and U. D. Hanebeck. Symmetries in Bayesian Extended Object Tracking. *Journal of Advances in Information Fusion*, June 2015.

[159] F. Faion, A. Zea, and U. D. Hanebeck. Reducing Bias in Bayesian Shape Estimation. In *Proceedings of the 17th International Conference on Information Fusion (Fusion 2014)*, Salamanca, Spain, July 2014.

[160] F. Faion, A. Zea, J. Steinbring, M. Baum, and U. D. Hanebeck. Recursive Bayesian Pose and Shape Estimation of 3D Objects Using Transformed Plane Curves. In *Proceedings of the IEEE ISIF Workshop on Sensor Data Fusion: Trends, Solutions, Applications (SDF 2015)*, Bonn, Germany, Oct. 2015.

[161] G. Kurz, F. Faion, and U. D. Hanebeck. Constrained Object Tracking on Compact One-dimensional Manifolds Based on Directional Statistics. In *Proceedings of the Fourth IEEE GRSS International Conference on Indoor Positioning and Indoor Navigation (IPIN 2013)*, Montbeliard, France, Oct. 2013.

[162] J. Steinbring, M. Baum, A. Zea, F. Faion, and U. D. Hanebeck. A Closed-Form Likelihood for Particle Filters to Track Extended Objects with Star-Convex RHMs. In *Proceedings of the 2015 IEEE International Conference on Multisensor Fusion and Integration for Intelligent Systems (MFI 2015)*, San Diego, California, USA, Sept. 2015.

[163] A. Zea, F. Faion, M. Baum, and U. D. Hanebeck. Level-Set Random Hyper Surface Models for Tracking Non-Convex Extended Objects. In *Proceedings of the 16th International Conference on Information Fusion (Fusion 2013)*, Istanbul, Turkey, July 2013.

[164] A. Zea, F. Faion, M. Baum, and U. D. Hanebeck. Tracking Simplified Shapes Using a Stochastic Boundary. In *Proceedings of the Eighth IEEE Sensor Array and Multichannel Signal Processing Workshop (SAM 2014)*, A Coru na, Spain, June 2014.

[165] A. Zea, F. Faion, and U. D. Hanebeck. Tracking Connected Objects Using Interacting Shape Models. In *Proceedings of the 17th International Conference on Information Fusion (Fusion 2014)*, Salamanca, Spain, July 2014.

[166] A. Zea, F. Faion, and U. D. Hanebeck. Tracking Extended Objects using Extrusion Random Hypersurface Models. In *Proceedings of the IEEE ISIF Workshop on Sensor Data Fusion: Trends, Solutions, Applications (SDF 2014)*, Bonn, Germany, Oct. 2014.

[167] A. Zea, F. Faion, and U. D. Hanebeck. Exploiting Clutter: Negative Information for Enhanced Extended Object Tracking. In *Proceedings of the 18th International Conference on Information Fusion (Fusion 2015)*, Washington D. C., USA, July 2015.

[168] A. Zea, F. Faion, and U. D. Hanebeck. Shape Tracking using Partial Information Models. In *Proceedings of the 2015 IEEE International Conference on Multisensor Fusion and Integration for Intelligent Systems (MFI 2015)*, San Diego, California, USA, Sept. 2015.

Karlsruhe Series on Intelligent Sensor-Actuator-Systems

Edited by Prof. Dr.-Ing. Uwe D. Hanebeck // ISSN 1867-3813

Band 1 **Oliver Schrempf**
Stochastische Behandlung von Unsicherheiten in kaskadierten dynamischen Systemen. 2008
ISBN 978-3-86644-287-0

Band 2 **Florian Weißel**
Stochastische modell-prädiktive Regelung nichtlinearer Systeme. 2009
ISBN 978-3-86644-348-8

Band 3 **Patrick Rößler**
Telepräsente Bewegung und haptische Interaktion in ausgedehnten entfernten Umgebungen. 2009
ISBN 978-3-86644-346-4

Band 4 **Kathrin Roberts**
Modellbasierte Herzbewegungsschätzung für robotergestützte Interventionen. 2009
ISBN 978-3-86644-353-2

Band 5 **Felix Sawo**
Nonlinear state and parameter estimation of spatially distributed systems. 2009
ISBN 978-3-86644-370-9

Band 6 **Gregor F. Schwarzenberg**
Untersuchung der Abbildungseigenschaften eines 3D-Ultraschall-Computertomographen zur Berechnung der 3D-Abbildungsfunktion und Herleitung einer optimierten Sensorgeometrie. 2009
ISBN 978-3-86644-393-8

Karlsruhe Series on Intelligent Sensor-Actuator-Systems

Edited by Prof. Dr.-Ing. Uwe D. Hanebeck // ISSN 1867-3813

Band 7 **Marco Huber**
Probabilistic Framework for Sensor Management. 2009
ISBN 978-3-86644-405-8

Band 8 **Frederik Beutler**
Probabilistische modellbasierte Signalverarbeitung zur instantanen Lageschätzung. 2010
ISBN 978-3-86644-442-3

Band 9 **Marc Peter Deisenroth**
Efficient Reinforcement Learning using Gaussian Processes. 2010
ISBN 978-3-86644-569-7

Band 10 **Evgeniya Ballmann**
Physics-Based Probabilistic Motion Compensation of Elastically Deformable Objects. 2012
ISBN 978-3-86644-862-9

Band 11 **Peter Krauthausen**
Learning Dynamic Systems for Intention Recognition in Human-Robot-Cooperation. 2013
ISBN 978-3-86644-952-7

Band 12 **Antonia Pérez Arias**
Haptic Guidance for Extended Range Telepresence. 2013
ISBN 978-3-7315-0035-3

Band 13 **Marcus Baum**
Simultaneous Tracking and Shape Estimation of Extended Objects. 2013
ISBN 978-3-7315-0078-0

Die Bände sind unter www.ksp.kit.edu als PDF frei verfügbar oder als Druckausgabe bestellbar.

Karlsruhe Series on Intelligent Sensor-Actuator-Systems

Edited by Prof. Dr.-Ing. Uwe D. Hanebeck // ISSN 1867-3813

Band 14	**Benjamin Noack** State Estimation for Distributed Systems with Stochastic and Set-membership Uncertainties. 2014 ISBN 978-3-7315-0124-4
Band 15	**Jörg Fischer** Optimal Sequence-Based Control of Networked Linear Systems. 2014 ISBN 978-3-7315-0305-7
Band 16	**Marc Reinhardt** Linear Estimation in Interconnected Sensor Systems with Information Constraints. 2015 ISBN 978-3-7315-0342-2
Band 17	**Gerhard Kurz** Directional Estimation for Robotic Beating Heart Surgery. 2015 ISBN 978-3-7315-0382-8
Band 18	**Igor Gilitschenski** Deterministic Sampling for Nonlinear Dynamic State Estimation. 2016 ISBN 978-3-7315-0473-3
Band 19	**Florian Faion** Tracking Extended Objects in Noisy Point Clouds with Application in Telepresence Systems. 2016 ISBN 978-3-7315-0517-4

Die Bände sind unter www.ksp.kit.edu als PDF frei verfügbar oder als Druckausgabe bestellbar.